Darlene has invested deeply into my
traveled from Burkina Faso as a 25-year-old to attend a YWAM
international leadership gathering in Lausanne, Switzerland. I
couldn't speak English at the time, but she saw in me something worth believing in – that's part of her gift.

Darlene's teaching on YWAM's Foundational Values
has tremendously shaped my own life and leadership as my
wife and I pioneered YWAM campuses in Togo and Nigeria,
and it has impacted the continent of Africa – especially our
youth and culture. In particular, the value "To Know God"
has transformed the lives of many young militants in Nigeria,
as they have laid down their arms to follow Him and join
our YWAM Discipleship Training Schools. We are now building a University of the Nations campus on 1500 acres of land
that once harbored these militants, to see many more Africans
trained and released into missions.

Paul Dangtoumda
Leader, YWAM Port Harcourt, Nigeria

The YWAM values are like landmarks that show how the Lord
has led us in the past and is guiding us into our future, so
we remain "mission true." I first met Darlene at a Leadership
Training School my wife and I attended in Barbados. Her obedience to follow Jesus and live out of these values created a
space for my calling in YWAM.

Darlene models the importance of always asking the impli-
cational questions "Who are we as a missions movement?" and
"Why do we do what we do?" This book rehearses the answers
to these questions and more, and provides understanding of
the importance of examining and aligning our call with our
beliefs and values.

Today my wife and I lead a University of the Nations
campus in San Jose, Costa Rica, largely as a result of the things
we learned through Darlene's investment into our lives. On
this campus many young people from Latin America and the
nations are saying "YES!" to the Lord, to hearing His voice,
obeying His call and they are committing to never give up!

Giacomo Coghi
Co-founder, University of the Nations
San Jose, Costa Rica

I had the incredible opportunity to "grow up" in the Lord in YWAM. I did my DTS in Lausanne, Switzerland under the Cunninghams' leadership. So much of what I believe and how I lead our community in the Middle East has come from being discipled through their lives in those early days.

Darlene has now given us an incredible gift through this book *Values Matter*. In it you will read the stories that have shaped our mission and been the birthplace for our Foundational Values. These values have come to us from the heart of God and we have the privilege to carry them on from this generation to the next.

This book is a must read for all YWAMers and especially leaders! *Values Matters* conveys the heart of our mission and lights our torch. Let's run with it and light the torches of the generations to come!

Martha M.S.
Living and serving in the Middle East

Values Matter is a must-read book for every DTS student, YWAM staff, YWAM leader, or any individual or family desiring to become involved in missions. Darlene's humility and willingness to be vulnerable, using her own personal stories of God's dealings with her heart to teach YWAM's core beliefs and values have impacted me very deeply, influencing the way I lead and do things. Her personal life and the stories she shares in this book of YWAMers around the world – how they live out the values of YWAM – will impact your life forever.

Leaula Silo Schmidt
Samoan serving in South Asia

To Stan,

DARLENE CUNNINGHAM

Values Matter

Stories of the Beliefs & Values that Shaped Youth With A Mission

Darlene Cunningham

with Dawn Gauslin & Sean Lambert
Discovery Starters by David Joel Hamilton

YWAM Publishing
Seattle, Washington

YWAM Publishing is the publishing ministry of Youth With A Mission (YWAM), an international missionary organization of Christians from many denominations dedicated to presenting Jesus Christ to this generation. To this end, YWAM has focused its efforts in three main areas: (1) training and equipping believers for their part in fulfilling the Great Commission (Matthew 28:19), (2) personal evangelism, and (3) mercy ministry (medical and relief work).

For a free catalog of books and materials, call (425) 771-1153 or (800) 922-2143.
Visit us online at www.ywampublishing.com.

Dedication

To Loren, my partner in life, adventure and ministry.
Without him there would be no story to tell.

To the hundreds of thousands of YWAMers
whose lives have inspired me
and whose obedience has honored God.
Their stories, their wisdom and
their sacrifice has brought great joy
to His heart and to mine
(including my kids Karen, David and Judy).

And to my grandchildren Madison, Kenna
and Liam and their generation
– with the hope that the beliefs,
values and words of the Lord
in this book will guide them.

And to their children – the next waves –
… and the next waves …
… and the next …

Special Thanks

My thanks to three very special friends and co-workers –
this book would not have been written without you! We
share vision and friendship; tacos and laughter!
You are all so very precious to me!

Dawn Gauslin

Your consistent friendship, wisdom and
commitment to communicate
the YWAM values have been a constant inspiration to me.
Thanks for helping me find words to express my heart.

Sean Lambert

You are the one who stepped up and said "It's time for
you to get the values book done – and I am going to help
you do it!" You have been faithful to do exactly that, at so
many levels, and in the most life-giving way possible.

David Joel Hamilton

Our team teaching and sharing life experiences
together throughout the years always bring me
such joy. Your commitment to principle and to
thoroughly research everything according to the
Scripture are foundations I deeply rely on.

Acknowledgments

First and foremost, we acknowledge the mighty hand of God as the explanation for any fruitful ministry that has come through YWAM. We have been fruitful because He has been faithful!

> *"Remain in me, as I also remain in you. No branch can bear fruit by itself; it must remain in the vine. Neither can you bear fruit unless you remain in me" John 15:4.*

We want to thank and bless our broad international, multigenerational YWAM family who have been a part of this amazing story through their sacrifice and commitment. We also thank the wonderful ministry leaders and teachers who have sown into our lives. And we honor the hundreds of thousands of prayer warriors, friends and supporters around the world who have partnered with YWAM and its people. You're a big part of our story!

Early on in the writing process we engaged Scott Tompkins as an editor for this project. Scott is a long-time YWAMer who understands the vision, core beliefs and values of our mission. His contribution has been invaluable and it's hard to imagine how *Values Matter* could have been completed without him.

Special thanks to Marcia Zimmermann for her proofreading skills on the final draft of the book. Thanks to Craig McClurg who designed the cover, to Joseph Avakian for creating the *Belief Tree* artwork, to Judy Robertson for designing the eyeglass illustration and to the late Russ Gauslin for his work, just one week before he went to be with Jesus, checking the accuracy of all scripture references.

We also want to thank YWAM Publishing for their partnership in this book project. We appreciate the visionary and servant leadership of Tom and Terry Bragg and their team of dedicated staff who work endlessly to get godly books into people's hands.

Foreword by Loren Cunningham

Youth With A Mission (YWAM) was founded in 1960, but it really got going in 1963 when I married Darlene. She truly is the co-founder. YWAM would not exist as it is today if it were not for Darlene. She is the talent-spotter, people-developer, team-equipper, community builder and implementer that helped to bring about growth.

In the formative years, God sent us many wonderful men and women of God to teach us about His ways and principles. (He still does so today.) Darlene, who is an excellent teacher in her own right, developed a skilled ability to listen to the teachings, process and summarize them, and pass on the principles to others, teaching them how to do the same.

It was Darlene who helped identify and bring understanding to our Core Beliefs and 18 Foundational Values as a mission. We often refer to this as the *"DNA"* of YWAM – the genetic code that makes YWAM, **YWAM**. She is the flag-bearer and champion for passing on our core beliefs and values.

Values Matters is an amazing resource for both old and new YWAMers alike. I am eager to see this book circulate among our entire mission as a helpful tool to understand the ways God has led us and who we are called to be. Understanding who we are today and how we got here will be key to our future health, multiplication and growth. We want to stay *mission true* to the inheritance God has given us within our DNA.

In the Gospel of John, chapter 15, we are called to abide in Christ, so we may bear fruit – fruit that remains. As we commit afresh to Him, to the vision of waves of young people covering the continents of the world with the Good News, and to our core beliefs and foundational values, I believe we will see an exponential increase in lasting Kingdom fruitfulness in and through YWAM.

Loren Cunningham
Founder, Youth With A Mission

Introduction:
The Power of Story

We all love a good story. But why do stories captivate us? Some stories entertain us, making us laugh or cry. Others challenge and motivate us. Some give us hope, while others produce somber reflection. Some instruct us about true value, while others warn us of dangers that might lie ahead.

Some stories change us, embedding themselves in the center of our being, creating a passionate narrative which molds our worldview, shapes our values and inspires our decision-making. We trust it will be so with the stories of our YWAM beliefs and values that we have captured in this book – and these are only a fraction of the stories we could tell of God's great faithfulness.

Through *Values Matter*, we want to pass on the HIS-story of our cornerstone beliefs and values so that successive generations can tell them to their children and to their children's children, to protect us from drifting from the ways God has led us (Hebrews 2:1). We will relate stories of God's faithfulness to take us through trials and onward to victory. But we also want to be transparent and tell the stories of our failures – how God has dealt with us, and how we responded to Him with a commitment to walk in His ways.

Psalm 78:1-4 captures the heart of why we are writing this book. It declares, "O my people, listen to my instructions. Open your ears to what I am saying, for I will speak to you in a parable. I will teach you hidden lessons from our past – stories we have heard and known, stories our ancestors handed down to us. We will not hide these truths from our children; we will tell the next generation about the glorious deeds of the Lord, about his power and his mighty wonders" (NLT).

God is a Storyteller

Our God is the master communicator. The Bible refers to His communication skills more than any other action He has undertaken – nearly 3,000 times!

When listening to a master in the art of communication we pay attention not only to what is said, but also to how it is said. Approximately 80% of the Bible text is dramatic narrative – it is truth revealed in story form. This is not surprising because the God who inspired the Biblical text also created every human being. And for about 80% of us who are oral learners, the preferred manner of learning is through the art of storying.

Truths, when conveyed through the narrative of a compelling story, impact not only our heads, but also our emotions and our will in a powerful way. For example, the tale of Shadrach, Meshach and Abednego (Daniel 3) becomes transformative because in it, we see ordinary people doing extraordinary things – and we are inspired to do likewise. The story helps the truth land in an integrated way in our heads and hearts so that we can apply it in our own lives.

We want the readers to relate to our beliefs and values in this same way. We trust that these true stories of how God spoke to us and of how real people applied these beliefs and values, will inspire and motivate you. And who better to tell us the stories of YWAM than Darlene Cunningham, the co-founder of our mission? As a spiritual mother, she faithfully passes on these important truths and life lessons to us – her heirs – because throughout her life she has constantly believed in and championed those around her to be all they can be for God.

As you read through these chapters, take these stories to heart. Embrace them. Make the stories your own. Let them inform your mind, touch your emotions and direct your will. Pay attention to how God was at work in the lives of others and join the story.

Listen to God, obey what He says, and never give up!

David Joel Hamilton
University of the Nations
International Vice President for Strategic Innovation

Why the Original Testament?

Throughout this book we will refer to the Hebrew Scriptures (Genesis to Malachi) as the Original Testament, rather than the more traditional term, the Old Testament. We do so because the term "old" connotes something past its prime; something which is perhaps no longer relevant and should be discarded as it has been superseded by the new. But the term "original" speaks of an enduring legacy which presents a solid foundation that should be valued, for upon it the new can be built.

Table of Contents

Chapter One

One Generation to the Next

"I am the fruit of your ministry!" To Loren's and my surprise, a YWAMer seated in the crowd of 3,500 stood up, looked directly at Loren and me, and declared his name and home country. Then he shouted, "I am the fruit of your ministry!" As he sat down, another stood up and did the same thing and then another and another.

As dozens more people gave glory to Jesus, our eyes puddled with tears. It was a lump-in-the-throat, skin-tingling moment of holy joy. We felt such love and appreciation for every individual who had said "yes" to Jesus by joining and supporting this rag-tag movement called Youth With A Mission (YWAM).

These affirmations took place as we celebrated the 50th anniversary of Youth With A Mission at our Kailua Kona campus in Hawaii. It was December, and Loren and I had spent all year traveling to 44 locations in 35 nations, where 50th celebrations drew together more than 30,000 YWAMers and friends. Amazingly, we flew 109 flight segments, and not one flight was canceled or late or hit turbulent weather! Truly, the Lord prepared the way before us in every detail!

We had started the year in New Zealand, and when that first gathering of South Pacific peoples concluded, I thought, *There is no way the next 50th event could be as good.* However, I was wrong. Each gathering was different and reflected the creativity and uniqueness of *that* region of the world.

The theme of our celebrations was "The Flame Goes Forward." We were remembering God's faithfulness to our movement over the **past** 50 years, celebrating His work among us in the **present**, while being infused with faith for all He wanted to do in the **future**. As we traveled from place to place, I realized anew that when we gather as a global family, God speaks to us!

Everywhere we went, we were met with flags of the nations, colorful traditional costumes, multilingual worship, birthday cakes, laughter, drums, maps, torches, children, history timelines, food and dancing – always lots of dancing. This is YWAM! I've never been prouder of our family – or more humbled by all God has done in and through us!

Underscoring every reunion was a spirit of hospitality and an overwhelming expression of gratitude to all who helped to make our ministry possible. We ended each event by focusing on the cross of Christ, celebrating communion, and by signing the Jubilee Covenant, which declared our commitment to carry the flame forward from one generation to the next. I fondly remember people reading the Jubilee Covenant aloud, sometimes in a blending of languages – and of little children lining up to sign their names too.

It was a dizzying and wonderful retracing of YWAM's geography, as we crisscrossed the globe in both urban and remote places – from Argentina to Bangladesh, from the Dominican Republic to Hong Kong, from Sweden to New Zealand, from Uganda to Mongolia, from Canada to Kazakhstan, and all points in between. The sights, sounds, smells, and climate in each location brought back joyful memories of pioneering to Loren and me.

One of my favorite sessions at each place was the reporting time – when locals described their ministries and the fruit of those works. We also loved praying over the "wee-YWAMers" – young children who represent our next generation of world changers.

At each of the 44 gatherings, I honored the sacrifice of all our YWAM staff and volunteers: those who cooked meals for us, picked up teams at the airport, taught in our schools, did maintenance and administration, and welcomed people on our campuses. The list of thanks flowed on and on. We also honored the millions who have supported YWAM and its missionaries in prayer, giving, and friendship.

At our final 50th celebration, the one in Kona, two images stand out in my mind. One was of the 200 staff and students who marched in carrying the flags of their nations. It was such a picture of our international YWAM family and a small foretaste of heaven as pictured in Revelation 7:9, where multitudes from every nation, tribe, people, and language will stand before the Lamb of God in worship. The second was when Loren and I were seated on stage with our children, grandchildren, and my mom, who was 96 at the time. What a vivid picture of our covenantal God working faithfully in four generations of ministers and missionaries!

One morning, soon after that final event, I sat with Loren on our outside deck, sipping coffee and gazing out on the Pacific Ocean. I turned to him and asked,

"What did you see in our 44 global visits that surprised you?"

He seemed momentarily lost in thought, perhaps still in that visionary place where he often goes.

"I was so encouraged to see how healthy the mission is around the world. We have so many dynamic, emerging leaders. And I was thrilled by all the innovations that are speeding up the work God has called us to do."

I paused for a moment, taking a drink of coffee. "Yes, the face-to-face reports we heard were all truly remarkable."

"You know Dar, people have always thought of YWAM as a bunch of short-term workers, but we are so much more now. Thousands of our staff have served the Lord for multiple decades and are still going strong. Our movement is now far bigger than we can count. It's going viral."

"What touched me, Loren, was meeting so many first-generation Christians from historically non-Christian nations that have joined YWAM, and the large number of second and third-generation YWAMers we met. Many kids raised in the mission have chosen to be missionaries themselves."

Loren smiled, "Yes, that blesses me too. I'm also grateful for the new level of unity and partnership among God's people all over the earth."

Throughout that morning, we marveled at the broader movement of past and present YWAMers in what we call the seven spheres of society. These include Family, Economy, Government, Religion, Education, Media and Celebration. Those who have done a YWAM Discipleship Training School carry our DNA into the spheres where they serve, regardless of whether they are still on staff in YWAM – like our son David, who is directing films.

Whenever Loren hears about one of our former students doing great things in the spheres, he gets a twinkle in his eye and says, "Once a YWAMer, always a YWAMer!" We serve a God who works in a diversity of ways through multiple generations.

What is YWAM's Secret?

Often mission leaders, pastors, or business leaders ask me, "What is the reason for YWAM's rapid growth? Organizations don't grow at the rate that you've grown or remain true to their founding beliefs decades later. What's your secret?" The answer:

- We listen to God
- We obey Him
- We persevere

The New Testament book of James encourages all believers to ask God for wisdom (vs. 1:5), to not just hear but do God's will (vs. 1:25), and to persevere when trials come (vs. 1:3).

It sounds all too simple for a complex international, interdenominational mission movement that has impacted millions of people, but it's true. Hearing God's voice, obedience, and perseverance have kept us "mission true." If people don't understand that we believe God speaks and guides us, they will not understand YWAM! We are a missionary movement held together by our shared vision, beliefs, values, and relationships with one another.

This book is about those beliefs and values. I hope everyone who reads it will be inspired to pass them on to the next generation. I know some gifted writers, leaders, and strategists will look at our YWAM Core Beliefs and Foundational Values document and say, "Those are not all *values*." I agree that some could be identified as movement principles, but these are the ways God has led us. They form our organizational DNA – the genetic code that makes us YWAM.

Loren and I are not the leaders of YWAM – God is! He formed this mission as thousands of us followed those simple steps of listening to Him, obeying Him, and persevering. Our young people, now spanning three generations, are the best evidence of what God can do through people in active partnership with the Holy Spirit. We have learned to trust their ability to hear His voice. And as we have championed young people and their gifts and callings, we have seen amazing multiplication. There is no other explanation but God for YWAM's fruitfulness around the world.

Chapter Two

Formative Years

I recently celebrated my birthday (I'm not saying which one! ☺). As is my birthday custom, I began the day by thanking God for my heritage. I am blessed to have solid Christian roots. I was born in Canada and descended from a long line of men and women whose life calling was to share God's Word.

My dad, Ed Scratch, knew God had called him to the ministry too, but as a young man, he wanted no part of that! He trained to be a barber. Just after his graduation, my grandmother called him and said, "Something terrible has happened to your father's eyes. He is totally blind!"

Dad rushed home, deeply concerned over his father's blindness. But granddad's big concern was not about being sightless, but *who* would preach on Sunday at church? He told my dad, "Son, there is no one but you!" So my father spoke in their church that Sunday – probably one of granddad's prepared sermons. Soon after, Dad repented of his unwillingness to accept God's call. He humbled himself, saying: "God, I won't fight Your call any longer! The answer is *yes.*" Within a few days, God touched my granddad's eyes, and he could see again! I am so thankful for God's pursuing love, which enabled the blind eyes of my father's heart to see!

Instead of cutting hair, Dad became a pastor and preached with real anointing. While speaking at a neighboring church one day, he met the sister of the pastor's wife. She was a petite curly-haired blonde who loved God and soon fell in love with Ed. Their marriage created a power-packed team for the Lord.

My mom, Enid Scratch, was born in Wales. Her dad died when she was six, and the family moved to Canada when she was 12. They were church-going people who tried to live by "the Golden Rule." But arriving in British Columbia, they began to attend a storefront church where the people talked about having a "personal relationship" with God. Their faith was infectious. Within a month, my mom and all her family members had radical salvation experiences. Jesus became the center of everything for them.

When you put God first, everything else in life will come into order. I could see from early childhood how God was directing our steps. My parents loved being pastors and cared for the people they served. They never left me out of the team, and not having brothers or sisters probably made that dynamic even closer.

Some people claim to have been "raised in the church," meaning they were taken to church from early childhood. I was literally raised in the basement of one church and the parsonage beside another. I was often put to "bed" on the church floor in the evenings, with my dad's preaching voice lulling me to sleep. It was the norm to have visiting preachers and missionaries stay with us in our home. At mealtimes, we shared testimonies of people coming to know Jesus, of experiencing miracles, and of exotic faraway places where they served.

Growing up with these amazing men and women of God all around me sparked a deep desire to know God as they did. I remember hiding under a church pew one time when the great missionary-statesman to India, Dr. Mark Buntain, was staying with our family. I watched as he paced the center aisle of the empty church, weeping and praying, calling out strange-sounding names of people from his beloved India, asking God to touch them. It deeply marked me that he – and God – loved these people so much!

When I was six years of age, I had an encounter with God and my mom that marked my life. A missionary from Africa was speaking at our church and staying with our family. He had a daughter back in Africa about my age, and like me, she had a record player. Oh, how I loved listening to music on my record player! He said his daughter loved to listen to recorded music too.

One day, Mom said, "Darlene, you have lots of records. Maybe you should think about giving some of yours to this missionary girl in Africa."

I considered her suggestion and decided, *That's a good idea.* I went to my records and pulled out several to send to her – the ones I liked the least. I proudly presented my offering to my mom. She looked through what I had selected and said, "Why not give her *Peter and the Wolf*?"

"Oh no, not *Peter and the Wolf* – that's my favorite!"

"Well, if it's your favorite, don't you think she might enjoy it? Maybe it would be her favorite too."

She wisely did not pressure me – she simply put forward the question. I wrestled with that decision, but when I finally chose to give my best, I felt great joy. That simple act of obedience became a foundation for generosity in my life. God gave His best – and we're to give our best too. I saw that many times, as our family worked together packing barrels of goods to send to overseas missionaries or boxes of goodies to give to prison inmates.

My father's older brother, Clare, also influenced my life for missions – maybe because I believed I was his favorite niece! Uncle Clare was a missionary to China. He told me the most amazing stories about its people and places. I loved it when we would go out to a Chinese restaurant so I could hear him speak Mandarin with the owners and waiters. He also taught me how to eat with chopsticks – none of my friends could do that!

Mom once told me the incredible story of when Uncle Clare first went to China. "He had an undeniable call from God to the Chinese people, but he couldn't speak the language well, despite months of study."

She went on, "One day, when he was visiting a mountain tribe, he was frustrated because he couldn't communicate with them in their language. Just then, an uneducated tribal woman began to speak to Uncle Clare in 'tongues.' She spoke in perfect English, a language she had never learned and had probably never even heard!"

I gasped in surprise! "So what happened?"

"The message that she delivered from God to Uncle Clare was this: God promised to give him the 'gift' of the Chinese language, and from that day onward, Uncle Clare spoke Mandarin fluently – a miracle from God!"

In my childlike mind, I marveled at this amazing God who could instantly empower someone to speak such a strange and difficult language. Uncle Clare's testimony gave me faith to believe that God can do anything!

Our family prayed daily for Uncle Clare. When I was a small child, near the outset of World War II, the Japanese invaded China. They captured Uncle Clare and put him in an internment camp. He had anticipated this might happen and had managed to get his wife and children safely back to

Canada. But he chose to stay in China with these people he loved, to walk with them through this danger and lead even more to know God. After more than two years in the camp, he was on the brink of death by starvation. Then a miracle happened.

This time, Dad told me the story: "One day, your Uncle Clare gathered the little strength he had to take a walk near the wire fence that marked the camp boundary. He prayed, 'God if now is the time You choose to take me home to heaven, I am ready to die for You. But if You will allow me to live, I will continue to share your Good News with the Chinese people.' Just then, a chicken came on the other side of the fence and laid an egg!"

My eyes were as round as saucers, and my chin dropped.

"Clare reached through the fence, grabbed the egg, and ate it – shell and all – to benefit from the calcium. From that day until the day he was released, God sent a chicken every day to lay an egg for him within reach outside the fence! It was his only source of protein. It saved his life!"

This miracle became another foundation stone event in my faith walk. It reminded me: God is never out of answers; He always has a way!

The Japanese released Uncle Clare after three-and-a-half years of internment. He and his family returned to China to continue serving as missionaries. I grew up thinking, *If Uncle Clare was willing to give his life for the Chinese people, they must be the most important people on earth!*

My Missionary Call

My family moved to Olympia, Washington, when I was a child. Growing up, I attended church camp each summer. The camps had lots of fun activities and useful spiritual input. When I was nine years old, I had a distinct encounter with the Lord that marked my "call to missions." In this vision, I saw myself inside a thatch-roof building, sharing the Gospel with hundreds of black-haired Asian children seated on the ground facing me. I knew from that moment I was called to be a missionary – and I presumed that it would be somewhere in Asia.

We moved from Olympia to Akron, Ohio, when I was 13, and then we moved again to Redwood City, California, when I was in high school. After graduation, I went to nursing school. I planned to be a missionary nurse.

At that time, girls typically married at a young age, sometimes right out of high school. I dated a lot of young men, and I had several marriage proposals. But unlike most of my peers, I was not anxious to marry. I think that was because I knew I had a "destiny" in missions, though I am sure I would not have expressed it that way then.

I loved the Lord, and I loved my folks – but I was always a little unconventional and pushing the edges. My dad was a wise man. Even though our denomination was quite strict about social activities that most people thought were "normal," Dad didn't impose rules on me. Instead, he taught me sound Biblical principles by which I could make wise decisions. This was a huge help in my understanding of the nature and character of God. Dad wasn't so concerned about external conformity; he wanted to see heart revelation and internal self-control and governance that would result in right decisions and actions.

Following my graduation, I inquired about working with overseas missionary organizations, but their requirements seemed to make missions inaccessible. I began to rationalize. *I don't have to go overseas to minister. I can do it right here.*

The more I rationalized, the easier it became for me to develop a relationship with a young man who had no passion for the Great Commission. I thought I was in love with him and ready to marry. But I kept this from my parents, who were unhappy with this romance.

Meeting the Man with a Mission

Then Dad called and asked that I go to lunch with Mom and him on Sunday. I thought, *Oh boy…here comes another lecture to try to get me to give up this relationship!* But I didn't want to displease my parents, whom I so loved and respected. So I said, "Yes, I will go."

When I got to church that morning, I realized they had other motives. They wanted to introduce me to a handsome, traveling preacher who was speaking at Dad's church! His name was Loren Cunningham. He shared a [1]vision God had given to him of waves crashing onto the shores of the world. As he watched, the waves became young people, coming from everywhere and going to everywhere with the Gospel, covering every continent. Because of that vision, he had started a movement called Youth With A Mission. His message was: "Young people can be missionaries! They can go NOW." Everything I had said I wanted was offered to me in Loren's appeal.

---

1. See Appendix 3: Legacy Word #1: The Vision of the Waves - (1956).

After the service, I hurried to my car and sped away. *I do NOT want to go out with my folks and that young minister!* But the Lord convicted me. I couldn't live with being rude and inconsiderate toward my parents. So I turned around, parked again, and joined my mom and dad and Loren for lunch, with none of them knowing I had "run away."

The four of us rode together to the restaurant. The meal was full of good conversation, with talk of Youth With A Mission being the center-piece. When we returned to the church, Loren and I walked to our cars and we discovered they were parked side-by-side. Thus began a visit of several hours, standing by our cars in the parking lot.

During that conversation, Loren directed a little "sermonette" at me. After asking questions about my missions call, he said, "Do you know what's wrong with you? You just want to compromise!"

I was offended by his directness – and convicted by the Holy Spirit that he was right!

Why Won't You Say Yes?

That night, following the evening service, Loren and his team of young people went out to a restaurant and we continued our conversations. One of his associates said to me, "Darlene, you're a nurse, and we need nurses in Liberia. You are qualified for this job. Why won't you say yes?"

I replied, "Oh, you wouldn't understand!"

But his directness and persistence brought me to a point of revelation: I had run out of excuses! It exposed the real conflict in my heart: I knew God had called me to be a missionary. Was I going to compromise or obey?

Later that night, I got on my face before God and surrendered to Him the relationship with the young man I thought I would marry. I committed myself afresh to God and said, "Lord, I will obey You. And I will be a single lady missionary all the days of my life if that's Your will." When I gave up my rights and made this commitment, great peace and joy flooded my heart.

Over the next few months, the strangest "coincidences" began to take place. It seemed that Loren was getting an unusual number of invitations to the San Francisco area, where I lived. We began to spend a lot of time together, sharing our passion for Jesus and His call. I applied to serve as a medical missionary with YWAM, so these conversations seemed appropri-ate. I found myself really liking this man, and he seemed to like me too.

Joining YWAM in those days was a different process than it is today. Besides filling out an application, I had to have a face-to-face interview with a panel of pastors and Christian leaders, to determine whether I was "fit to serve" with YWAM.

Loren drove me to the interview, and on the way there, he said, "Darlene, you need to know that I care for you."

I was horrified! *Here I had determined to be a single missionary all my life. I'm on my way to an interview to serve with YWAM – and Loren tells me he cares for me!*

"Don't say that! I'm on my way to my interview! I don't even want to think about that!"

The interview seemed to go well. There were several leaders around the table, and Loren was seated with them. One of them said, "Darlene, you have given excellent answers. But I have one more question. I have known you since your family moved to California, and it seems to me you always had a boyfriend. One of the requirements for serving short-term with YWAM is 'no romantic relationships' so that you can be focused 100 percent on the ministry. Are you currently involved in a relationship with anyone?"

My mind raced: *Am I involved with anyone? Or not?* Loren was sitting right there at the table! But I had made no commitment to him.

I replied, "I am not."

Then my mind stirred again:

Did I just lie? Or did I not? Did I lie? Or did I not?

I was accepted to join YWAM and began to make my plans to go to Africa to serve as a nurse. In the meantime, Loren and I continued to see each other and the relationship grew. One night, after spending the evening together, he drove me home. Standing beside his car, Loren said, "Darlene, I want you to join me in ministry."

I said something like, "Oh, yes, I'm planning to," assuming he was talking about me joining YWAM.

"No, I don't think you're hearing me. I want us to spend our lives together. I want you to be my wife."

Just to tease him, I hesitated and said, "I'll need some time to think about that."

His face fell with disappointment.

After a few seconds, I said, "I've thought about it, and my answer is YES, YES, YES!"

Loren and I were married in June of 1963. When the news of our marriage spread, many exclaimed, "This is the right match." I think what they saw and what they were affirming was our common vision, beliefs, and values in the mission context.

As I think about my godly heritage and Loren's (he also comes from generations of ministers), I am so thankful for all who went before us and imparted their relationship with God. We couldn't have become who we are today, nor could YWAM have become what it is, without our parents, pastors, teachers, intercessors, financial supporters – hundreds of men and women of God who invested in us. Their obedience made our walk of faith and obedience so much easier.

If you are a first-generation believer, you may say, "But I don't have any Christians before me in my family line." How exciting – then the legacy starts with YOU! You can determine, "I will be the new beginning! I will create a godly foundation as an inheritance for my children and my children's children – to be image-bearers of God in missions, ministry, or whatever sphere of life He calls them into."

Chapter Three

The Grand Experiment

I knew from the first time I met Loren he would always be radically obedient to what God called him to do. Yes, **radical**! But **obedient**! After all, everything about the vision for YWAM was outside the 1960s paradigm for missions. It was unheard of to use young people in missions, to do short-term outreaches, to send and receive both internationally and interdenominationally, and to do it all by faith with no salaries.

Early in our relationship, Loren and I planned to meet for dinner at a specific time, and he was late. I waited and waited and waited. Finally, I decided, *That's it! I'm not staying any longer! How inconsiderate!* I jumped in my little black car, jerked it into gear, backed up, and was just about to storm away full speed when, in the rearview mirror, I saw Loren waving and running toward my car. I stopped and opened the window. I'm sure a distinct chill filled the air when I did so.

"Darlene, I'm sorry you had to wait. I intended to be on time, but I was talking to a man about his salvation. That's the most important thing on earth."

Suddenly, I felt ashamed! I recognized this was always going to be Loren's priority. Right then, I chose *not* to be offended. I saw something in Loren's sensitivity to Jesus that was so attractive. His commitment to listening to God's still small voice and his prompt obedience challenged me to be radically obedient to Jesus too!

This vision to take young people and launch them into world evangelism resonated within me. I began to realize that, though Loren was the one declaring the vision, it echoed in my heart, and it was my vision as well. It clearly aligned with the stories I had read in the Bible of God using young people like Samuel, Daniel and Joseph. We weren't really doing anything new at all – we were just following God's examples in Scripture. And it worked because it's His design: God trusts young people.

Maybe I couldn't see the vision of the waves of young people in the same way that Loren did. Still, I could see what they needed to have when they landed on the shores of the nations – food, housing, spiritual and cultural equipping, and so on – all the practical things needed to support the ministry.

The vision began to burn in my bones. I knew in my heart, *We can do this! God is going to call just the right people to this mission who carry His gifts within them! I have this awesome responsibility of helping them to discover and use their God-given gifts for Kingdom purposes! What an honor!*

When planning for our honeymoon trip, Loren laid out a world map on the floor, and he began to talk about God's design in different cultures. "They will do things differently. Have an open heart and an open mind to learn from them." Through his eyes, I received a love and respect for the nations that has grown ever stronger.

Our around-the-world honeymoon took us to Europe, Asia, the South Pacific, and the Caribbean, fulfilling ministry commitments Loren had made prior to our wedding plans. We slept on cots and church floors; we sometimes showered under a garden hose in our bathing suits; we ate whatever our local hosts offered. It wouldn't be the right honeymoon for most couples, but it was the right one for us.

If a newly married couple is called to a lifetime of ministry, the best way for them to get to know one another is to DO ministry together. On our trip, I observed other missionaries, deciding who I wanted to be like and who I did *not* want to be like! The journey confirmed my love for the nations. It further convinced me of God's desire to use youth – even those younger than Loren and me – in missions.

Embarking on The Grand Experiment

Loren's vision of waves of young people going to the nations began to unfold in the mid-1960s when we launched "Summer of Service" (SOS) outreaches in the Caribbean. During the school year we would crisscross the USA, speaking and mobilizing workers. Then, as summer approached, Loren would drive a rumbling yellow school bus across the States, picking up young volunteers and driving them to Florida. There we formed into all-male and all-female outreach teams.

The first summer, 1964, there were 146 from the USA plus 64 Caribbean youth involved with SOS in the Bahamas, Dominican Republic and Turks and Caicos Islands. It was a rugged "boot camp" of faith that produced fruit that remains to this day. Thousands came into relationship with Christ, and scores were healed as we went door-to-door and island-to-island, sharing the Good News of Jesus.

I was a natural people-observer, and I was always "panning for gold" among the participants. I'd ask, "Your application said you were the oldest child in a family of eight. Did you help with the cooking? Yes? Oh, good – you can oversee food services."

"You gave a public testimony once? Okay, you can lead the preaching!"

"You play soccer? Let's have you organize some sports teams!"

Well, it might not have been quite that simple, but you get the idea....

These "kids" proved they could be responsible, and there was no limit to what they could do when tuned into God. Honestly, we were all a bit amazed that God would use *us*.

One of my favorite stories from our first Summer of Service underscores the joy of believing in young people. On the Bahaman island of Exuma, two 17-year-old girls went out to share their faith. As they walked down the lane in the tropical heat, they met a man with a withered arm leaning against a palm tree.

They struck up a conversation, and one of them, Sharon, said, "You know, there was a man in the Bible who had a withered arm just like yours, and Jesus healed him. Do you want us to pray that Jesus will heal your arm?"

"Oh, yes," the man replied.

The two girls closed their eyes as Sharon gently laid her hands on the man and prayed for God to heal his arm. When they opened their eyes – lo and behold – God answered their prayer. The man's arm shot out, totally straight and restored! Sharon was so shocked that she fainted on the spot!

That's our great God – using this unconventional group of young people – because He believed in us! That summer we experienced healings and miracles that showed God's loving care: We had many reports of food and supplies being multiplied and vehicles getting "healed." But the big thing was seeing peoples' lives transformed as we shared the story of Jesus.

God was forming **in** us the foundations of YWAM – as much as He was working **through** us to see the lost come to Christ.

Loren and I referred to this idea that God could use young people in missions as "The Grand Experiment." We were often in impossible situations, utterly dependent on God. And He proved Himself faithful. Through our fruitfulness He also confirmed to skeptics that we HAD heard from God.

God had made it clear to us before that first summer that we were always to extend trust to those we led. We were not to lead by rules and regulations; we were not to be the police nor act as parents (we were only a few years older than most), but we were to be co-workers and friends. We had guidelines for our life together, but the spirit behind the guidelines was always to serve, not to control. How gracious of God to be so specific regarding the culture of trust He wanted to establish in the foundation stones of YWAM.

Summer of Service wasn't a Caribbean vacation. We all worked very hard. Loren and I were near exhaustion after our first outreach, in part because we failed to recruit follow-up help. We became so grateful God called us to work in teams! He gave wisdom so far beyond our years. But as we continued "The Grand Experiment" the next summer and the next, one thing became obvious: To rightly represent God to the people, our participants needed to KNOW HIM better themselves. They needed a solid Biblical foundation of understanding God's character and His ways.

Loren also recognized that we, as leaders, needed to discover keys for growth. One day back in California, as we were driving down the road, he said to me, "Darlene, what's wrong with my leadership?"

"What do you mean? I think you're a good leader!"

He said, "Yeah, but we're only seeing addition, not multiplication. People come with us for a summer, but they don't stay long-term. The vision God gave me was of waves of young people – hundreds, then thousands and tens of thousands – into the millions. We will never see the fulfillment of our vision at this rate – we're still just a trickle."

I agreed, "It seems there are some missing ingredients."

Shortly after that conversation, God called Loren to go to New Zealand. It was the first separation in our four years of marriage, as I stayed back in

California. During that time God began to do "soul surgery" on me, as He exposed areas of pride in my heart and my "flexibility" with the truth.

At the same time God was also working in Loren's life. In New Zealand he met Joy Dawson, a homemaker who had learned to hear the voice of God with remarkable clarity. She had become an intercessor for peoples and nations. Her life of listening to God and obeying Him in detail had a marked impact on Loren.

At the same time I had been reading a book about some women who would go to a church prayer meeting where God would tell them things about strangers to pray for. My response was, "Lord, I want to hear You like that." I was pregnant with our first child, Karen, at the time. I felt the Lord challenge me to declare, "By the time this child is born, I want a new ministry to be born in me – a ministry of hearing God's voice and intercessory prayer."

Loren and I had no idea that God was doing a deep work in the other at the same time. When he returned from New Zealand, God confirmed the word He spoke to each of us separately – YWAM was to start a school in which we could teach people to know God better.

Training – a Multiplier for Missions

Ideas began to tumble out as we discussed creating a school. Loren said, "I think running schools could be the key to what we've been asking God – how to grow YWAM by multiplication. I feel that God is saying training is to be the 'multiplier for missions.'"

As we discussed ideas for training, we determined to invite teachers who were *doing* what they taught, not just teaching theory. We also decided to use a modular approach. Rather than having students take several courses each quarter, modular schools would focus the teaching on one theme at a time.

I added, "Having the students, staff and speakers live and learn together in an integrated environment could have lots of benefits. I can imagine them talking together over meals and praying into the night…."

Soon the direction to start a YWAM training school was confirmed "out of the blue" in several astonishing ways. First, by a scholar and prophet from Canada, Dr. Willard Cantelon, who was meeting with Loren's father and unexpectedly asked to see Loren.

They had breakfast together the next morning, and he said, "Loren, I've been praying for you. God wants you to go to Switzerland and start a school with visiting speakers who *do* what they teach."

With surprise, Loren replied, "Thank you. This is a clear confirmation of what God has spoken to us. We are planning to leave tomorrow on an around-the-world trip that includes Switzerland!"

Dr. Cantelon asked, "Do you have contacts there?"

"No – we don't know a soul in Switzerland," Loren admitted.

Dr. Cantelon smiled. "I do. He owns a hotel with an empty annex next door. Let me contact him to make an introduction."

That contact later enabled us to rent classroom space for our school.

Shortly after meeting Dr. Cantelon, Loren was invited to teach at an event where Duncan Campbell, a distinguished Bible teacher, was also scheduled to speak. We called him "Brother" as a term of respect as he was much older. We were all housed in the same guest facility.

One evening, Brother Duncan walked out of his room at the same time as Loren and I. He said, "God spoke to me, Loren. He told me I'm to come to teach in your school. Do you have a school?"

Loren replied in faith, "Yes – next year in Switzerland."

"Good, I will look forward to it."

We had already printed brochures in faith to start the school on February 1, 1969. We called that very day to our Pasadena office and said "Mail the brochures!" We had 1,800 on our mailing list.

The next thing we knew, we were flying back to Europe to start our first School of Evangelism (SOE). Its primary focus would be to help people come **to know God and make Him known**.

Chapter Four

Where Did YWAM's Beliefs and Values Come From?

The Purpose Statement as YWAM's Worldview

Before we look at each of YWAM's 18 Foundational Values, please understand that each is rooted in our worldview and our core beliefs. Our first official document was the "YWAM Statement of Purpose" written in the early 1960s. It was intentionally not called a belief statement because, had we done so, we would have been viewed as a church denomination and would not have been able to pioneer a truly interdenominational movement. In Europe at that time, having a statement of belief or a statement of faith was the definition of a denomination. But there was more wisdom in that initial decision than we realized at the time.

We now see that what we were led to write as our "YWAM Statement of Purpose" is, in fact, a declaration of our Biblical Christian worldview which is foundational to everything else. It lays out the underlying truths which support all that we aspire to think, say and do. It lays out the reality of who God is and what He has done. It also reminds us of who we are and what God calls us to do. It affirms the Biblical foundation of truth and upholds our responsibility to walk with God in extending His Kingdom on earth.

Here is that two-paragraph declaration:

YWAM's Statement of Purpose

Youth With A Mission (YWAM) is an international movement of Christians from many denominations dedicated to presenting Jesus personally to this and future generations, to mobilizing as many as possible to help in this task, and to the training and equipping of believers for their part in fulfilling the Great Commission. As citizens of God's Kingdom, we are called to love, worship, and obey our Lord, to love and serve His body, the Church, and to love all peoples everywhere, which includes presenting the whole Gospel for the whole person throughout the whole world.

We of Youth With A Mission believe in God – Father, Son and Holy Spirit – and that the Bible is God's inspired and authoritative Word, revealing that Jesus Christ is God's Son; fully God and fully human; that people are created in God's image; that He created us to have eternal life through Jesus Christ; that although all people have sinned and come short of God's glory, God has made salvation possible through the incarnation, life, death, resurrection and ascension of Jesus Christ; that repentance, faith, love and obedience are fitting responses to God's initiative of grace toward us through the active ministry of the Holy Spirit; that God desires all people to be saved and to come to the knowledge of the truth; and that the Holy Spirit's power is demonstrated in and through us for the accomplishment of Christ's last commandments, *"Go into all the world and preach the Good News to everyone"* (Mark 16:15 NLT) and *"Go and make disciples of all the nations…"* (Matthew 28:19 NLT).

When YWAM turned 25 in 1985, I was sharing stories of how God had led us. That got me to thinking, "What do we value as YWAM?" My ponderings were fueled by questions like, *Why doesn't YWAM have an international headquarters? Why does it insist on working in teams?* And always the BIG one: *Why doesn't YWAM pay salaries?*

I wrote a letter to YWAM staff worldwide, identifying some of our foundational values. Later that year, for the first time, I taught on those values at a Leadership Training School (LTS) in Kona. One young man came to me and pleaded, "Darlene, this teaching is so helpful. You need to write down the values and explain. Those of us who came to YWAM more recently don't know what you are referring to when you say, 'Remember when God spoke to us' about this or that."

The Spirit of God continued to stir my spirit with these thoughts: *How can we be sure the next generation of YWAMers, and the next and the next... will know the stories of our roots and share our spiritual DNA? And how can we keep from drifting away from our original call?*

When I first spoke at the LTS, I identified five foundational values – the ones considered so radical when we began:

- YWAM is called to be visionary
- YWAM is called to champion young people
- YWAM is called to be international and interdenominational
- YWAM is called to depend on God for finances
- YWAM is called to work in teams

Identifying these values and sharing the stories of how they came about seemed to strike a chord with people. YWAM Foundational Values became a "buzz" of discussion worldwide. Floyd McClung, who was our International Director at that time, taught these five values at a Leadership Training School in Amsterdam the next year. And from his own experiences as a senior YWAM leader, he added a few more. Several other leaders began to teach on foundational values and added more.

I then compiled the dozen values we had identified and presented them to the next LTS I led in Kona. There were many long-time international YWAM leaders in that school. We asked them if they had a "yea and amen" in their spirits to the values we had identified. They did – and they added a few more.

These beliefs and values were such a part of our core that it was quite a challenging process to extract and distill them. But we knew we had to do this if we were going to pass them on. We could no longer just hope people would "catch" the values by association. We had to intentionally identify and impart the values to the next generations!

In February of 1989, several LTS staff met in my living room to word-smith, affirm and pray over the "YWAM Foundational Values" document. We sent it on as a proposal to our International Council, which approved it as an official YWAM document. It has been reviewed, polished and edited a few times since then – each time, with a new "official" document being released and posted on ywam.org so the whole mission is working from the same document.

Always Begin with Beliefs

With the development of our foundational values firmly settled, I was sure we were ready for the future. But the Lord soon showed me we weren't as prepared as I thought. Most of our first YWAM staff were from the United States, Europe, Australia and New Zealand. Though we desired to be more international and non-Western, that was the reality then. Those early YWAMers typically had in their cultural, family and church roots a basic Judeo-Christian foundation.

Belief Tree

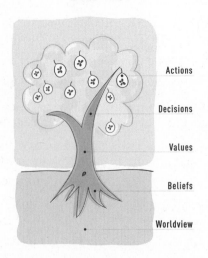

As YWAM grew to include first generation Christians from Hindu, Buddhist, Muslim and other backgrounds, we realized we could no longer presume our students shared a Judeo-Christian worldview. We also recognized that many in Western society had shifted toward secular humanism, setting the individual as the reference point for truth. They said: "Whatever you believe to be true, is true for you."

Darrow Miller, co-founder of Disciple Nations Alliance, brought a key, connecting piece. He came to speak on Biblical Christian worldview at a Leadership Training School I was overseeing in Pune, India.

His teaching included an illustration he called [2]The Belief Tree, which resonated with my spirit. As I studied the Bible with this in mind, it was amazing to realize how many times it uses agricultural examples to make a point. With his permission, I borrowed this illustration and adapted it for YWAM. It has revolutionized my understanding because everything we teach and model "hangs" on beliefs of some kind. The Belief Tree

---

2. A more detailed explanation of The Belief Tree teaching is included in Appendix 2 and on YWAMvalues.com.

illustration gives us vocabulary and a process both for individual and corporate decision-making.

We begin with the soil representing the environmental **worldview** that influences people – it may be Buddhist, Hindu, Animist, Muslim, secular humanism, etc. The roots represent the basic **beliefs**. For YWAM, we are rooted in a Biblical Christian worldview. The trunk of the tree represents our **values**, which grow out of our beliefs. The branches represent the **decisions** we make – either individually or corporately – based on our values and beliefs. And the fruit represents the **actions** that result from our beliefs, values and decisions.

For there to be integrity and a seamless flow between our beliefs and our actions, there should be no disconnect in what we say we believe and the resulting values, decisions and actions. The fruit of our lives and ministries carry the genetic code to pass those beliefs and values on to the next generation. Of course, at the core of every seed must be the original DNA of Jesus! We are called to be like Him – we are His image bearers.

In the development of our "YWAM Foundational Values," I came to realize that we had not been identifying and verbalizing the underlying "roots" – the Biblical *beliefs* that must undergird them! Because these beliefs were so resident in me and most first- generation YWAMers, I had assumed they were there in everyone. But from Darrow's teaching, I came to understand we must teach beliefs before values, as they are the roots from which life-giving fruit comes! Knowing God for who He truly is, is the basis and core of our beliefs.

In YWAM, we must make no policies that cannot be connected back to our beliefs and values. Otherwise they become lifeless rules or religious rituals. The same is true for our personal decisions. We should encourage others to ask us, "Why do you do what you do?" We should be able to explain our rationale and the Biblical principles that have guided us. If we can't do that, then their questions will prod us on to seek more revelation or re-alignment

The following are some of our core beliefs that undergird our foundational values. We embrace many additional core beliefs based in Scripture that address the nature and character of God, the nature of man, the consistency of truth, the consequences of our decisions, etc. Most of these beliefs are not unique to YWAM, but are shared by all Christians everywhere.

YWAM's Core Beliefs

Youth With A Mission (YWAM) affirms the Bible as the inspired and authoritative Word of God and the absolute reference point for every aspect of life and ministry. Based upon God's Word, who He is, and His initiative of salvation, through the atoning work of Jesus (His death, burial and resurrection), the following responses are strongly emphasized in YWAM:

- **Worship**: We are called to **praise and worship God alone** (Exo 20:2-3; Deu 6:4-5; 2Ki 17:35-39; 1Ch 16:28-30; Neh 8:2-10; Mar 12:29-30; Rom 15:5-13; Jud 24-25; Rev 5:6-14; Rev 19:5-8).

- **Holiness**: We are called to **lead holy and righteous lives** that exemplify the nature and character of God (Lev 19:1-2; Psa 51:7-11; Jer 18:1-11; Eze 20:10-12; Zec 13:9; Luk 1:68-75; Eph 4:21-32; Tit 2:11-14; 1Pe 2:9,21-25; 1Jo 3:1-3).

- **Witness**: We are called to **share the Gospel of Jesus Christ** with those who do not know Him (Psa 78:1-7; Isa 40:3-11; Mic 4:1-2; Hab 2:14; Luk 24:44-48; Act 3:12-26; Act 10:39-43; 1Co 9:19-23; 2Co 2:12-17; 1Pe 3:15-18).

- **Prayer**: We are called to **engage in intercessory prayer** for the people and causes on God's heart, including standing against evil in every form (Gen 18:20-33; Exo 32:1-16; Jdg 3:9,15; 1Ki 8:22-61; Eze 22:30-31; Eze 33:1-11; Mat 6:5-15; Mat 9:36-38; Eph 3:1421; 2Th 3:1-5).

- **Fellowship:** We are called to **commit to the Church** in both its local nurturing expression and its mobile multiplying expression (2Ch 29:20-30; Psa 22:25-28; Psa 122:1-4; Joe 2:1517; Mat 18:19-20; Act 2:44-47; Act 4:32-35; 1Co 14:26-40; Eph 2:11-18; Heb 10:23-25).

- **Service:** We are called to **contribute toward God's Kingdom purposes** in every sphere of life (Deu 15:7-11; Deu 24:17-22; Psa 112:4-9; Pro 11:10-11; Zec 7:8-10; Mat 5:14-16; 2Th 3:13; Tit 3:4-8; Heb 13:15-16; Jam 2:14-26).

Grouping the Foundational Values

The 18 "YWAM Foundational Values" help define our uniqueness as a mission. In the chapters that follow, we will explore each one, explaining how God spoke to us to embrace it as a foundational value, and looking at how we can apply it today. Always remember these values flow out of and are the expression of our Biblical Christian worldview and our core beliefs.

A few years ago, when many businesses were beginning to identify and communicate their "core values," members of YWAM's Global Leadership Team set out to distill our foundational values list into five core values. After days of wrestling with the document, the consensus was that each value had come to us through specific words of the Lord, and we were not to change them! The only adjustment made at that time was to move some belief statements into our "Core Beliefs" statements, to underline their significance.

Since then, God has helped us to see more clearly how they connect and fit together. One of our leaders, Sean Lambert, was on a plane to London and felt he received some insights regarding how the values could be arranged into four groupings. This book is laid out in those four groupings, with all 18 values fully embraced. This is not a required way to teach the values, but some may find it helpful in understanding the values and how they can be passed on to others. The four groupings are:

- We Want to Know God
- We Are Visionary
- We Value People
- We Are a Global Missions Movement

We now include the "Statement of Purpose" and "Core Beliefs" with the "YWAM Foundational Values" document.[3] The beliefs and values statements are not just good ideas. With each one, there are ten supporting Scriptures: five from the Original Testament and five from the New Testament, without any repetition.

---

3. The official "Statement of Purpose, Core Beliefs and Foundational Values of YWAM" document is included in Appendix 1. This document is also available at ywam.org and at YWAMValues.com.

One Scripture we often quote to one another as we discuss the nature and character of God is Psalm 103:7. "He made known His ways to Moses, His deeds to the people of Israel." My hope for YWAM's future generations is that we would be a people who would move beyond just knowing about God – His deeds – and be a people who are eager to discover His ways – WHO God is, and WHY He does what He does! We want to KNOW GOD.

I. We Want to Know God

VALUES:

Know God (#1)
Hear God's Voice (#3)
Practice Worship and Intercessory Prayer (#4)
Have a Biblical Christian Worldview (#9)

The YWAM story is defined by a relentless passion to know God, His nature, character and ways. All our ministry fruitfulness flows from that foundational commitment. There is no one like God. He is holy, set apart and beautiful. God is the initiator of relationship with us, and the ultimate communicator in matters great and small. Our passion to know Him more deeply produces in us responses of worship, of desire for personal holiness, of sharing God's burdens through intercessory prayer for people and nations. The Holy Bible is our textbook and reference point for understanding God and every aspect of life and ministry. We encourage everyone to actively hear from God, obey and persevere.

Chapter Five

Know God
(Value 1)

YWAM is committed to know God, His nature, His character and His ways as revealed in the Bible, the inspired and authoritative Word of God. We seek to reflect who He is in every aspect of our lives and ministry. The automatic overflow of knowing and enjoying fellowship with God is a desire to share Him with others.

2Ki 19:19; Job 42:5; Psa 46:10; Psa 103:7-13; Jer 9:23-24;
Hos 6:3; Joh 17:3; Eph 1:16-17; Php 3:7-11; 1Jo 2:4-6)

As I looked out our bedroom window at "the Chalet" in Lausanne, Switzerland, it was snowing outside – that first light snow which makes the world look magical. I walked downstairs and into the classroom with baby Karen on my hip. As I entered, I saw awe, wonder and devotion on the faces of the students. Our guest speaker was describing the attributes of our wonderful God – who He is and the way He works. It was captivating. You could almost see the students breaking free from narrow, preconceived ideas and falling in love with Him, as fresh revelation dawned.

At lunchtime, conversations revolved around their new awareness: "I never thought of God like this before – that His love is so unconditional, so broad, so deep … so, so personal." I remember another student exclaiming, "Now I'm beginning to understand why prayer is so important. God has chosen to share with us His heart for people and situations around the world, and when we pray in agreement with His will, it changes things! It makes me want to pray more!"

The more deeply we gazed upon God, the more we wanted our lives to reflect Him. Repentance was not driven by judgment or legalism. As we saw His holiness, it was natural to want to be like Him – pure and white like the fresh snow falling outside.

Our Greatest Need: To Know God

This was our first School of Evangelism (SOE) in Lausanne – the missions training school Loren and I had dreamed of for so long. We knew this rich reservoir of "Knowing God" would overflow into our "Making Him Known." God had promised us that training would be the "multiplier for missions" we were longing to see.

That first 14-month school – the forerunner of many – began with a Summer of Service outreach (July, August); three to four months of language study (September, October, November, December); three months of classroom training (January, February, March); a three-month Middle East Field Trip studying the words of Jesus on location by the Sea of Galilee, etc. (April, May, June); and ending with a second Summer of Service outreach (July, August). It included many of the innovative God-inspired elements that still characterize YWAM's University of the Nations (UofN) today. It was modular in structure, with each study module building upon another, like Lego™ blocks. Visiting speakers came directly from their fields of expertise to teach in the classroom, not only to impart knowledge, but to impart faith. We endeavored not to learn theory, but to apply in practice everything that was taught. And it all took place in a community environment where teachers, staff and students lived and learned together.

All around Europe, the hippie movement was embracing a life of sex, drugs and revolution. Young people were shouting "God is dead." Communism was rising, an ideology which claimed God wasn't just dead; He never existed. We were embarking on such an opposite path – discovering that God was very much alive and wanting to connect with us individually.

The Lord brought gifted men and women of God as our speakers – people who truly knew Him and brought an impartation of faith for whatever subject they taught. They included:

Duncan Campbell, who came to speak in our SOE, just as he had promised. He had been a first-hand witness and the anointed leader of the Hebrides Revival in the mid-20th century, which transformed the Scottish islands. The Spirit of God came upon its population with such power and conviction that people lay repenting in the heather. With his thick Scottish accent he declared, "God is a God of relationship who woos us with love and conviction to know Him and be like Him." He imparted faith for revival to happen again in our day – through us!

Campbell McAlpine, an Englishman who led us into a love for the Word of God and a lifestyle of Bible meditation. Through these disciplines, we discovered new depths of understanding the ways of God.

Corrie ten Boom, from Holland, taught us the power of forgiveness. In forgiving the Nazis who took the lives of her beloved father and sister and millions of others during World War II, she showed there are no boundaries to God's love, and there is no one so vile that God will not forgive.

Brother Andrew, also from the Netherlands, challenged us that knowing God propels us to make Him known, even at the peril of our own lives, by going into "closed countries" with His Good News. We soon found our YWAM teams doing just that!

Gordon Olson and **Harry Conn** led us to marvel at the nature and character of God. He is infinite and eternal, all powerful, all wise and all knowing. Yet He chooses to exhibit to us character qualities of love, kindness, justice, mercy, grace and faithfulness.

Joy Dawson, the New Zealand housewife who became a global advocate and teacher on intercessory prayer, urged us to walk in the fear of the Lord and taught us principles for hearing His voice.

Dr. Francis Schaeffer, who founded L'Abri, just 45 minutes across the mountains from us in Switzerland, centered the foundations for our beliefs.

With young, post-Christian radicals shouting, "There are no absolutes," Dr. Schaeffer's teaching gave us pillars of truth that anchored our beliefs and values – and gave us answers for their questions, such as the time Loren was speaking at a university on "How to prove there is a God." A hippie-looking youth turned to me and mocked, "Wow, what an illusion! I'm an atheist. I don't believe there is a God!"

I responded, "Really? Tell me about the God you *don't* believe in. What is he like?"

He replied, "Oh, he's awful. And he's angry. He doesn't care about people – he just wants to send everybody to hell."

"Oh – I agree with you then. I don't believe in *that* god either!" and I began to describe the characteristics of our good, loving and wonderful Father God. He had never heard the truth about God's character before!

Dr. Schaeffer underscored this great truth: God is not only infinite, but personal, having an intellect, will and emotions. He created us (human-kind), though we are finite, in His image as personal beings. This means that we are capable of communication and relationship with God. He created us to KNOW HIM!! Yet it will take our whole lifetimes plus all of eternity to understand not even one-zillionth of one percent of who our great God is! But we will learn more of Him always and forever.

We are forever grateful to God for bringing these outstanding men and women from various nations and church backgrounds to confirm the foundations God was laying for our missions training. With this diversity of input on a broad range of topics, Loren's leadership role was crucial (as is the role of every school leader to this day). He was the "weaver" of the content, underscoring the Biblical principles and continually highlighting the character and nature of God. The SOE teaching later served as the core curriculum for developing YWAM's Discipleship Training School (DTS).

Lynn Green, a student in one of those early SOEs, who went on to pioneer YWAM in the United Kingdom said it this way, "The quest to know God is at the heart of YWAM, thus we have the freedom to obey His commands and directions. Though we are a missionary agency, with our eyes firmly fixed on reaching the whole world, that is not our deepest motivation. If it were, we would be in constant danger of being over-driven … We seek to multiply an environment in which each person is encouraged and provoked to seek a constantly growing relationship with God. From that intimacy with God, we know He will lead us, individually, as teams, and as an entire movement to demonstrate and proclaim the knowledge of Him to people everywhere."

Sometimes as we meditated on the holiness of God, He would bring waves of conviction of sin upon our SOE staff and students. We responded with deep repentance. These times didn't come with a sense of God's judgment or wrath. They revealed to us His lovingkindness. He cared so much that He would not leave us to continue in sin that would have destroyed us. Repentance led to a restoration of joy and freedom.

Just as God had promised, training became our "multiplier," and YWAM began experiencing phenomenal growth with centers and training schools springing up all over Europe, Africa, the Middle East, Asia and beyond. He also was beginning to call people to missions "long term."

As we focused on knowing God, the automatic overflow became the desire to make Him known. Many times, as we would lay a map of the world out on the floor during a prayer time, God called people to pioneer new works in new nations – Germany, England, the Netherlands, Denmark, Afghanistan, Pakistan, Ivory Coast ... It was so exciting to see God give these young leaders direction to go and pioneer in the nations. I believe each was a direct result of our emphasis on knowing God.

Chapter Six

Hear God's Voice
(Value 3)

YWAM is committed to creating with God through listening to Him, praying His prayers and obeying His commands in matters great and small. We are dependent upon hearing His voice as individuals, together in team contexts and in larger gatherings, as an integral part of our process for decision making.

(1Sa 3:7-10; 2Ch 15:2-4; Psa 25:14; Isa 6:8; Amo 3:7; Luk 9:35; Joh 10:1-5; Joh 16:13-15; Heb 3:7-8,15; Rev 2:7,11,17,27; Rev. 3:6,13,22)

"Bullets whizzed above our heads as we crawled military-style through the thick underbrush. We could hear the cries of the people on the bus we had just exited, and we knew they were being killed."

I was amazed and aghast, as my friend Paul from Burkina Faso relayed his story to me. I asked, "How did you escape from the bus?"

"My friend John and I had traveled from Togo to Port Harcourt, Nigeria, to visit the city where we felt God was calling us to start a YWAM training center. After assessing things there, we caught a bus back to Togo. Then we saw a bus with a flat tire in front of us. Our bus driver pulled over to help.

"Suddenly I heard the Holy Spirit tell me, 'Paul, get off this bus NOW.' I turned to John and told him what I heard. He said, 'If you're leaving, I'm coming with you!'"

Paul explained, "We were in the back of the bus and people weren't happy as we pushed our way through the aisle to get out. They protested, 'Our driver will help the other bus and we can go on. You'll waste our time if you get off.'

"But I said to John, 'It's more important to listen to God's voice, not people!' We jumped down from the bus and observed a Volvo approaching. The car stopped and turned off its headlights. The doors swung open and men began to climb out – carrying automatic weapons!

"'Do you see what I see?' John whispered.

"'Yes, they are going to rob all the people on our bus.' We simultaneously jumped into the bush and started crawling for our lives. When the robbers heard movement in the bush, they began shooting, but because we were crawling, no bullets touched us."

"Thank the Lord!" I exclaimed, "What happened next?"

"Then Satan started speaking into my mind to put fear in my heart, *Paul, do you really want to come back to this place where you may lose your life? It's dangerous. Surely you could go somewhere else to serve God.*

"Then suddenly I heard the gentle voice of the Holy Spirit say, *Paul, don't be afraid. I am with you. I will protect you. I will guide you until the mission I have for you will come to pass.* Darlene, I realized that Satan will not easily allow you to take the place he has claimed – you have to fight for it!"

As I listened to Paul's story, I recognized he was preaching my message: Listen to the voice of God; obey, and don't quit! This is a life or death example of the necessity of hearing and obeying God's voice, but the same principles apply in our everyday lives.

Is That Really You, God?

When Loren and I were working with John and Elizabeth Sherrill and Janice Rogers (Loren's sister) on his first book, the Sherrills wanted to find the main "storyline" of YWAM. For three intense days they listened as we told stories of how YWAM began and how it functions today. They then went away and prayed regarding a theme for the book. The title reflects their conclusion: *Is That Really You, God?* Ours is the story of people seeking to hear God's voice, to do what He instructs, and to stand firm in faith.

God is an amazing communicator. The most common phrases in the Bible are "God said" or "the Lord said." They are used 1,500 times in the Original Testament alone. But He speaks in different ways: through an audible voice, through dreams and visions, through angels, through that still small voice in our hearts, through the words of a godly friend or teacher, through new revelation into the Scriptures. God can speak any way He chooses to – He even spoke through a donkey once! He is looking for listening hearts. For me, God often speaks through a gentle nudge in my spirit, or a whisper into my mind. Sometimes God's voice sounds like my dad's voice – especially if He is correcting me! ☺ And sometimes when I'm asking Him a question, I hear nothing at all. That is the biggest test, when I need to hang on to what I know of His character.

Joy Dawson: Hearing God's Voice in Detail

I had heard many wonderful stories about Joy Dawson from Loren's 1967 trip to New Zealand, so when I met her, I was eager to learn from her. I was encouraged to discover she wasn't a pale, super religious-looking person who appeared to have spent her life cloistered in a prayer closet. She had a bubbly personality and wore a cute sundress. I had never met someone who heard God's voice with such amazing accuracy. She knew details about people she had never met and places she had never been that only God could have revealed to her. I wanted that kind of relationship with God and so did the young people we were leading.

Loren and I learned from our parents how to hear from God, but I was challenged by Joy's life to go deeper and be more specific. I did my own experiments to see if God would speak to me in detail like He did to her.

Whenever Loren and I were sharing about YWAM in a meeting, I would ask the Lord, "Who should I talk to afterward?" He would point out specific people, and sometimes give me a "word of knowledge" for them: *This person is going to be a key missions leader … that person has a call from God to be a teacher, and they are fighting it … you're to challenge this person to pray about going to West Africa.* As I gave God opportunity, expecting Him to speak to me, He would do so. I thought, *Wow! This is amazing! It really does work!!*

This is a practice I endeavor to do to this day – leaning in to hear His still small voice regarding who to pray for or encourage.

God Speaks in Matters Great and Small

The amazing thing about God's voice is that He speaks "great and mighty things" that astound scholars and impact nations (Jeremiah 33:3) and stories so simple that a child can understand.

At one of our early prayer meetings, Reona Peterson-Joly heard "the word of the Lord" to go to Albania. At the time, it was ruled by a communist dictator who declared Albania to be the "first totally atheistic nation on earth."

Night after night, I prayed with Reona and others in preparation for this dangerous mission. One night, she saw in a vision the face of a cleaning woman she felt she would meet there. In 1973, when she and her friend Evey managed to get into Albania, a woman came into her room and brought a tray of food. Reona realized it was the woman God had shown her in the vision!

When the woman returned later in the day with more food, she sat down on the bed, took both of Reona's hands in hers and looked deeply into her eyes. God spoke to Reona in the moment, and she said slowly in English: "Marx, Lenin – No! Jesus – Yes!" Tears came into the woman's eyes and she leaned over and embraced Reona. In her limited English she said, "Me Christian too!"

Later that afternoon, Reona and Evey were arrested, interrogated and put in prison for their "Christian activities." Evidently the authorities had discovered some Gospel literature the pair had placed at various places since they arrived in Albania. They were told they would be shot at dawn by a firing squad for their "crimes." Instead, they were miraculously released. Though they had no money or vehicle, numerous people – possibly angels – helped them get back to Switzerland. You can read the full story in Reona's book *Tomorrow You Die*.

God speaks, whether in death-defying circumstances like those above, or in daily events. One day, I was frustrated because I couldn't find my car keys. My young daughter Karen said, "Mommy, they are under the newspaper." Sure enough, that's where they were! I asked, "How did you know that?" and she said, "I asked Father God and He told me where the keys were." And then she added, "Aren't you glad you have me?"

I love that God is so personal and speaks to us about matters both great and small.

Hearing God – the Key for Making Decisions

I wonder how much time we waste fussing over things God could show us, if we only would take the time to ask. Dependence on hearing God's voice has had a huge impact on how we, in YWAM, make corporate decisions. It is a major explanation for our sustained fruitfulness and growth over many decades. Beware of having more management meetings than prayer meetings! In our staff and leadership meetings, we must take the time to seek God together for His wisdom in making decisions.

Proverbs 16:9 says, "In his heart a man plans his course, but the Lord determines his steps." Planning in and of itself is not wrong, but we must remain open to God to give us fresh creative revelation. James 1:5 says, "If any of you lacks wisdom, you should ask God, who gives generously to all without finding fault, and it will be given to you." What a wonderful privilege and gift to us that we can freely ask God for wisdom when we need it.

We held our first Leadership Training Seminar in Kona in 1976, before we had the campus property. We had been meeting and holding our schools in an old tomato shed above town. Right before the seminar was to begin, the county authorities stepped in and said, "You're supposed to be growing tomatoes here – not people!" They barred us from using the tomato shed as a classroom. With this dilemma and the 150 participants' imminent arrival, I asked Loren:

"Are you sure you and the other leaders heard from God about holding this event?"

"Yes," he replied. "We asked God together, and there was clear confirmation by the group."

"Are you sure of the dates?"

"Yes."

"Are you positive that it was to be *this* year?" I persisted.

Loren assured me, "Yes. God said it is to happen this year."

"Well, then it will happen." And it did. At the last minute, God provided an auditorium for our classroom with a kitchen nearby. And as for housing, we prayed, and He spoke into our hearts and minds locations to check out and provision was there. The principles are: hearing the Word of the Lord gives us faith, faith leads to action, and perseverance brings fulfillment of the vision!

Sean Lambert, leader of YWAM San Diego/Baja, reported to me a wonderful story of God at work in a meeting of their 18-member board of directors. They were considering whether they should obtain short-term accident insurance for each of the participants they hosted to help build Homes of

Hope. Since they hosted thousands of volunteers every year, this was a decision that would significantly impact the budget.

Several board members felt the price for each participant was already high, so they did not want to add trip insurance fees. Other board members believed it was prudent to obtain this new insurance. The discussion continued back and forth with no progress. Finally one board member, a Christian businessman, turned to Sean and said, "In situations like these, don't you YWAMers ask God what to do?"

Sean, suddenly convicted, hung his head, knowing the board member was right. The board had spent lots of time discussing the pros and cons of the decision, which was good, but they had not sought God for His counsel. In faith, Sean invited all the board members to bow their heads and together ask God to give them wisdom.

Almost immediately God spoke into Sean's mind the words, "the Good Samaritan story." As he reflected on the parable from Luke 10, he realized it was about someone who was hurt on a trip. A good Samaritan arrived to help transport the wounded person to where he could get medical care. The Samaritan also promised extra financial provision if there was any additional need. At the end of the story, Jesus declared, "This is what it means to love your neighbor."

Sean, inspired by the parable's clear link to the insurance discussion, stopped the prayer time and reported everything God had dropped into his mind about being ready to care for injured people. The once divided board, now inspired with God's fresh revelation and wisdom, voted unanimously to obtain the accident insurance. The entire prayer time, reporting and decision-making process took less than 10 minutes. God can speak to us in detail about anything – even insurance.

These days, travel is less and less safe and we need to be wise, with no presumption about where we go, when we go, and what we do and don't do. Some years ago, my friend Maria was leading a performing arts team based out of Hong Kong. The ministry, called *Windows*, sought to always ask God for His guidance in creating their dance routines, music and drama presentations – but also on when and where they would minister.

One morning while on an outreach in Paris, the team prayed for the city. They were planning to perform that day at five locations. But, to their surprise, God spoke to them like He did to the Apostle Paul's team in Acts 16:6: "Don't go out today. Stay where you are and pray for the city." They were disappointed to stay home, but they obeyed His voice. That evening, they received a phone call from the U.S. Embassy, as the uncle of one of the students worked there. He was so concerned about the team because all five locations they planned to visit that day had been bombed by terrorists!

Maria's team was safe, because they listened and obeyed Jesus! We are not always delivered from the situation like Maria's team, but God promises to be with us and guide us through even the most difficult times, if we will listen to Him.

Divine guidance and hearing God's voice is one of the most thrilling aspects of our walk with Him. Christianity is not a methodology or a blueprint – it's based on two-way communication with the Creator of the universe. Now that's exciting!

Revelation and Reason

One thing Loren does when God speaks to him (revelation), is to take the word God has given and scroll through the Bible in his mind to see how it aligns with other verses on that subject (reason). He "scrolls" from Genesis to Revelation, looking for relevant Biblical stories and principles regarding the fresh insight God has imparted. As he goes through this process, he will pause and ponder over a section, considering what it says about God's principles and ways. Later, when he shares with others what God has spoken, it includes a wonderful mix of new insights and sound Biblical reasoning.

Whenever we receive what we feel is an impression from the Lord, we should always ask ourselves, "Is this scriptural and does it align with God's character and ways?" God's voice will NEVER contradict what He has already revealed about Himself in the Bible, nor will He speak something contrary to His nature and character. Spiritually mature believers embrace both revelation and reason.

I also want to include a sincere warning to not casually claim "God said ..." if it's just our own idea or opinion. We do not want to misrepresent Him to others! If we discover we have not heard correctly, we should go back and share this with any individuals or groups who were affected by what we attached to God's name.

Hearing God's voice is such an important subject and I believe it's vital to share the teaching that is included in the original YWAM story, *Is That Really You, God?*

Twelve Points to Remember: Hearing the Voice of God[4]

If you know the Lord, you have already heard His voice – it is that inner leading that brought you to Him in the first place. Jesus always checked with His Father (John 8:26-29), and so should we. Hearing the voice of the heavenly Father is a basic right of every child of God. In this book we have tried to describe a few of many ways of fine-tuning this experience. The discoveries are never just theory. They come out of our own adventures:

1. Don't make guidance complicated. It's hard *not* to hear God if you really want to please and obey Him! If you stay humble, He promises to guide you (Prov. 16:9).

    Here are three simple steps that have helped us to hear God's voice:

    • *Submit* to His lordship. Ask Him to help you silence your own thoughts and desires and the opinions of others that may be filling your mind (2 Cor. 10:5). Even though you have been given a good mind to use, right now you want to hear the thoughts of the Lord, who has the best mind (Prov. 3:5-6).

    • *Resist* the enemy, in case he is trying to deceive you at this moment. Use the authority that Jesus Christ has given you to silence the voice of the enemy (James 4:7; Eph. 6:10-20).

    • *Expect* an answer. After asking the question that is on your mind, wait for Him to answer. Expect your loving heavenly Father to speak to you. He will (John 10:27; Ps. 69:13; Exod. 33:11).

2. Allow God to speak to you in the way He chooses. Don't try to dictate to Him concerning the guidance methods you prefer. He is Lord – you are His servant (1 Sam. 3:9). Listen with a yielded heart; there is a direct link between yieldedness and hearing.

    God may choose to speak to you through His *Word*: This could come in your daily reading, or He could guide you to a particular verse (Ps. 119:105); through an *audible voice* (Exod. 3:4); through *dreams* (Matt. 2) and *visions* (Isa. 6:1, Rev 1:12-17. But

---

4. *Is That Really You, God?* © 1984 by Loren Cunningham. Second edition 2001, updated 2010, pp. 200-203.

probably the most common of all means is through the quiet *inner voice* (Isa. 30:21).

3. Confess any unforgiven sin. A clean heart is necessary if you want to hear God (Ps. 66:18).

4. Use the Axhead Principle – a term coined from the story in 2 Kings 6. If you seem to have lost your way, go back to the last time you knew the sharp, cutting-edge of God's voice. Then obey. The key question is *Have you obeyed the last thing God told you to do?*

5. Get your own leading. God will use others to confirm your guidance, but you should also hear from Him directly. It can be dangerous to rely on others to get the word of the Lord for you (1 Kings 13).

6. Don't talk about your guidance until God gives you permission to do so. Sometimes this happens immediately; at other times, there is a delay. The main purpose of waiting is to avoid four pitfalls of guidance: (a) *pride*, because God has spoken something to you; (b) *presumption*, by speaking before you have full understanding; (c) missing God's *timing and method*; (d) bringing *confusion* to others; they too need prepared hearts (Luke 9:36; Eccles. 3:7; Mark 5:19).

7. Use the Wise Men Principle. Just as the Three Wise Men individually followed the star and, in doing so, were all led to the same Christ, so God will often use two or more spiritually sensitive people to *confirm* what He is telling you (2 Cor. 13:1).

8. Beware of counterfeits. Have you ever heard of a counterfeit dollar bill? Yes, of course. But have you ever heard of a counterfeit paper bag? No. The reason is that only things of value are worth counterfeiting.

   Satan has a counterfeit for everything of God that is possible for him to copy (Acts 8:9-11; Exod. 7:22). Counterfeit guidance comes, for example, through Ouija boards, séances, fortune-telling, and astrology (Lev. 20:6; 19:26; 2 Kings 21:6). The guidance of the Holy Spirit leads you closer to Jesus and into true freedom. Satan's guidance leads you away from God into bondage.

   One key test for true guidance: Does your leading follow principles of the Bible? The Holy Spirit never contradicts the Word of God.

9. Opposition of man is sometimes guidance from God (Acts 21:10-14). In our own story, we recognized much later that what seemed like blockage from our denomination was, in fact, God leading us into a broader scope of ministry. The important lesson here, again, is *yieldedness* to the Lord (Dan. 6:6-23; Acts 4:18-21). Rebellion is never of God, but sometimes He asks you to step away from your elders in a way that is not rebellion but part of His plan. Trust that He will show your heart the difference.

10. Every follower of Jesus has a unique ministry (1 Cor. 12: 1 Pet. 4:10-11: Rom. 12; Eph. 4). The more you seek to hear God's voice in detail, the more effective you will be in your own calling. Guidance is not a game – it is serious business where we learn *what* God wants us to do in ministry and *how* He wants us to do it. The will of God is doing and saying the right thing in the right place, with the right people, at the right time, and in the right sequence, under the right leadership, using the right method, with the right attitude of heart.

11. Practice hearing God's voice and it becomes easier. It's like picking up the phone and recognizing the voice of your best friend – you know his voice because you have heard it so much. Compare young Samuel with the older man Samuel (1 Sam. 3:4-7; 8:7-10; 12:11-18).

12. Relationship is the most important reason for hearing the voice of the Lord. God is not only infinite but also personal. If you don't have communication, you don't have a personal relationship with Him. True guidance … is getting closer to the Guide. We grow to know the Lord better as He speaks to us, and as we listen to Him and obey, we make His heart glad (Exod. 33:11; Matt. 7:24-27).

Once we HAVE heard from God, we need to obey Him in detail! God desires instant, joyful, whole obedience. Partial obedience or delayed obedience is disobedience.

No Self Autopsies

God wants to speak to us more than we want to hear what He has to say. If you don't hear clearly right away, don't worry – just wait in faith.

Recently I was talking with a young woman, just setting out on her YWAM experience. She wanted so much to do what was right, but kept second-guessing herself thinking, *Did I do this or that wrong and that's why I can't hear?* I recounted to her what Loren once said to me, "Quit trying to be the Holy Spirit. It's His job to convict you, not yours!"

Because I'm so analytical, I can second-guess my thoughts and actions too. My response should always be "Lord, You know I want to please You. And at this point You know I'm not hearing clearly, so that must mean I don't have to know the answer yet. I thank You for wisdom and trust Your guidance will come at the right time."

Believing God to Speak to Others

We must honor and respect the word of the Lord in others, even when it's not what we want to hear. I had a big life-lesson regarding this principle once. Our ministry accountant was a much-loved and talented woman who worked with us for years. One day she asked to meet with me and, to my surprise, she said, "I feel it's time for me to go. I don't believe God wants me to continue to serve as the YWAM accountant."

I thought *Oh, no!* and I used all my personal influence to persuade her to stay. It worked, and she stayed – but she became very critical and negative. I later had to repent, because I had not respected the fact that she was truly hearing from God when she came to me. She had lost her grace for the job she was carrying, and I had manipulated her into staying! If we say we believe God can speak to everyone, then we need to honor their ability to hear from Him.

I once tried to answer questions from a businessman who could not figure out how YWAM operates. I explained that we do have some management processes in place, but we organize ourselves behind what God speaks to us, not the other way around. We are not fruitful because we are organized, we are fruitful because we hear from God and then obey. We are not smart enough to have envisioned the values that formed YWAM. God is the brilliant one!

Chapter Seven

Practice Worship
and Intercessory Prayer
(Value 4)

YWAM is dedicated to worship God and engage in intercessory prayer
as integral aspects of daily life. We also recognize the intent of Satan to
destroy the work of God and we rely upon God's empowering presence,
the Holy Spirit, to overcome his strategies in the lives of individuals
and in the affairs of nations.

(1Sa 7:5; 2Ch 7:14; Psa 84:1-8; Psa 95:6-7; Psa 100:1-5; Mar 11:24-
25; Act 1:14; Eph 6:13-20; 1Th 5:16-19; 1Ti 2:1-4)

Worship, intercessory prayer and spiritual warfare are closely interwoven practices. You may ask, "Why are they included in the YWAM Foundational Values? Aren't these aspects of faith that every Christian should practice?" Yes, they are, but God has underscored each one in unique ways throughout YWAM's history.

The Power of Worship

Jesus confirmed that the first and greatest commandment is to "Love the Lord your God with all your heart and with all your soul and with all your mind and with all your strength" (Mark 12:30). Worship is the expression of that love through devotion, songs, service, art, dancing, kneeling and other acts.

Worship is a huge part of our development as a mission! It is not a "tacked-on" activity. King David wrote in Psalm 34, "I will extol the Lord at all times: his praise will always be on my lips." That is how it should always be with us. Worship is a lifestyle. It bubbles up continuously in the heart of YWAMers – in the wee hours of the night, in morning prayers, in our daily work and in expressions relevant to our generation or culture. The more we learn of the nature and character of God, the more we are drawn into worship, individually and corporately. YWAM has many 24-7 prayer rooms around the world, as well as whole ministries devoted to worship and intercessory prayer.

In the early 1980s, we launched a ministry called FEET (Far East Evangelism Teams) in Hong Kong. The name was based on Romans 10:14-15: "How can they hear without someone preaching to them…. How beautiful are the feet of those who bring good news." Though the ministry focus was on evangelism (tens of thousands of people came to the Lord just within its first five years), FEET was born out of worship and waiting on God. They devoted the first six weeks of outreach preparation to worship and receiving an impartation from God, before they ever formed teams or talked about where they would go to minister.

They would get so caught up in worshiping the Lord that sometimes they missed meals or continued in worship until after midnight. Some days were spent in adoring God for the beauty of His holiness; other days, in thanking Him for His faithfulness; and other days, in expressing love for His father heart. They sang their hearts out, and God filled them afresh with Holy Spirit power. For the next three decades and beyond, these five-month FEET outreaches flowed like waves across Asia and other continents.

We see in Revelation 7:9 that fellowship with Him, expressed through worship, is God's desire for all people and nations. Worship is not just music, but music often helps to give expression to our hearts. Every generation and every culture may have a different expression of worship. We celebrate this in YWAM, as a youth-centered, global missions movement. The multi-national, multi-lingual, multi-dimensional worship we experience together is a foretaste of heaven!

In the early days of YWAM Lausanne, God inspired new songs of worship through Linda McGowan-Panci and others. What we learned about God's nature and character began to emerge in new music. Many of Linda's songs were compiled into a songbook which became the best-selling French publication of its time (200,000 copies published). It spread throughout French-speaking countries and is still used today in French churches.

Later, when we moved to Kona, Hawaii, God used a couple from New Zealand, David and Dale Garratt, to inspire and lead us in worship. They called their ministry "Scripture in Song" because their worship songs were composed of pure Bible passages. We literally sang the Psalms, and that's how I memorized many of them. Often today, a scripture will pop into my head in response to a question I'm asking the Lord. It's because those songs planted the words in my heart and brain. Music is such a wonderful way to retain Scripture!

In 1982, we were faced with the threat of losing the Kona property God had directed us to buy. Worshippers led us in prayer and spiritual warfare to contend for the land where the University of the Nations now stands. David and Dale recorded an album on the campus, *Call to War*, that became our rallying cry.

The Glory of the Nations in Worship

One of the greatest gifts we have in YWAM is the diversity of cultural worship expressions. During the YWAM 50th anniversary events, Loren and I experienced such joy as we participated in a myriad of unique cultural expressions of worship to Jesus.

God has planted in each nation sounds and colors and celebration that He longs to have released to bring glory to Him. These cultural expressions, when in alignment with the Word of God, allow people to express their love for Jesus from the core of their being. From the yoiking of the Scandinavian Sami, to the haka of the Polynesian Maori, to the arias of Italian opera, to the hip-hop of young Latinos, to the drums of the Africans, to the fan dances of Korea, and the Hallelujah Chorus of Handel's *Messiah*. When the aim is to bring glory to Jesus, the joy is contagious. The celebrations of different cultures help all of us to worship God more freely!

Work Should Be Worship

Have you ever thought about worshiping God through the practical work you do? Francis Schaeffer, Darrow Miller and others taught us that the Biblical Christian view of work is that God created us to enjoy our vocation.

The root word for work and worship in Hebrew is the same – *Avodah*. God didn't invent work as punishment for human beings' sin; He gave mankind the sacred vocation of tending the garden and all the animals before sin even entered the world.

Work was always a part of God's good plan for humanity. It was meant to be life-giving, to bring glory to God, and to bring us personal fulfillment. The evil one wants to rob us of the joy of work by diminishing the value of the gifts God has put in us and the sacredness of our vocational call. He is the one who says "Oh, what you have to offer is not important – it's not really spiritual."

The reality is that when we freely give to God our time and abilities, our labor and efforts, it is an offering back to God, a reflection of the beauty of His creation. God is glorified by our vocational work and through it, *Avodah* (worship) happens!

Intercessory Prayer

When Joy Dawson taught YWAMers to hear God's voice, it was not simply for personal guidance. She introduced the dimension of listening to God in intercessory prayer. Through intercession, God shares with us the burdens, griefs and joys of His own heart! Jesus Himself was and is an intercessor. Hebrews 5:7 says, "During the days of Jesus' life on earth, he offered up prayers and petitions with fervent cries and tears … and he was heard because of his reverent submission."

Joy taught us God is searching for those who are willing to sacrifice their time to pray God-directed prayers for people and nations. So much of the world's suffering is because of sin on both an individual and global level. The Lord is not indifferent to this suffering, but He gave us free will to choose good or evil. He intervenes when His people humble themselves and seek to do His will. Through intercessory prayer, He invites us to be co-laborers and co-creators with Him. As we, God's image bearers, align ourselves with His will and pray His prayers, we partner with God in transforming people and nations. What a tremendous privilege!

I've often said that every good thing God has ever done through Youth With A Mission was born in prayer. As I look back, I realize it was our corporate intercessory prayer times that gave our people ownership in the YWAM vision and inspired them to take on new endeavors for God. Everybody contributed to discerning what the word of the Lord was. It wasn't just "announced." Intercessory prayer profoundly promoted unity and produced tremendous Kingdom fruitfulness.

When we hear the voice of God *together*, it gives us confidence "this indeed is God," and it increases our faith. The visions we took on didn't come out of planning sessions; no one voted on them. New things were born, new YWAM locations were launched, new kinds of evangelism were created – everything came out of corporate intercessory prayer. Seeking God and hearing together gave us more strength than just confirming an individual leader's sense of what God was saying. The corporate word of God was not only a unifier but created the forward motion of YWAM.

Following one of our intercessory prayer times in Switzerland in the early days, Loren read a letter from Dr. J. Christie Wilson, a tentmaker missionary who spent 23 years in Afghanistan. Dr. Wilson was pleading for YWAM to send a team to his beloved Afghans. Loren encouraged each of us to seek God on our own that night, without talking to anyone else, and ask if we were to say "yes" to the invitation. The next morning when Loren asked if anyone felt led to go, Lynn Green, who was 21 at the time, was the only one who "heard the call." (Lynn is now a senior international leader in YWAM.) Loren had a meeting with Lynn and asked,

"Are you sure you're to go to Afghanistan? Do you know that you could be executed for sharing the Gospel there?"

"Yes, I'm sure I'm to go!"

"Do you know where it is?"

"No."

Loren produced a map and showed him. "How do you plan to get there?"

"I don't know – maybe I will hitch-hike?"

Later that year Lynn *did* go to Afghanistan in YWAM Lausanne's old VW van together with Jim and Janice Rogers, Loren's sister and brother-in-law, and a small team.

They were arrested at the border. The 6,000 Gospels of John printed in the local language they had hidden in their van were discovered, and they were held under house arrest for hours while a panel of 12 judges/elders (all of whom were Muslim imams) read the literature as "evidence." They later released the YWAM team. But when they asked, "What about the literature?" their judges said, "Give it to the people." So they did. YWAM has had fruitful ministry in Afghanistan from that day until today, through every war and government transition.

In our mission's early years, international news from more remote areas was sketchy at best. Few people had traveled to Muslim, Buddhist and Hindu nations. So God planted the world in our hearts through intercessory prayer. One time He led us every night for three solid weeks to pray for China. These meetings came together spontaneously night after night. God gave us specific cities and things to pray for, and later in newspaper and magazine articles, we learned about specific answers to the very things we had prayed.

This type of prayer is still happening daily around the YWAM world today. We seek to live a lifestyle tuned in to hear God's voice about matters great and small. Intercessory prayer is His primary way of launching us out. As we pray, see the need, and hear the ache in God's heart for people to know Him, our natural faith response has been, "Here am I, send me."

Standing against the Enemy

Our work in missions is about bringing the light of Jesus into dark places. When we help individuals, communities and nations to find forgiveness and freedom in Him, it arouses the enemy of our souls.

Just as God is real, the Bible teaches us that Satan and his evil cohorts are real. In Ephesians 6:10-18, the Apostle Paul exhorts us to be strong in the Lord and alert to the schemes of the devil. In verse 12 he says, "…Our struggle is not against flesh and blood, but against … spiritual forces of evil." He challenges us to stand firm, in the full armor of God. In Daniel chapter 10, God heard and sent an answer to Daniel's prayer right away, but the evil one delayed the answer. After a 21-day battle, the answer finally got to Daniel. In John 10:10, Jesus said Satan's nature is to kill, steal and destroy. He is a thief who wants to rob our joy and derail our relationships with God and others.

YWAM recognizes we are in a spiritual battle for individuals and nations. Dean Sherman, one of our leading teachers on this theme, says the key to victory is to "be impressed with God, not the enemy!" As 1 John 4:4b says, " … the one who is in you [the Holy Spirit] is greater than he who is in the world."

We can discern the enemy's tactics by seeking God's counsel in challenging times. I love the story of King Jehoshaphat in 2 Chronicles 20. A vast army was coming to attack the people of Judah. What is the king's response? He stands before the Lord with all the people in prayer and intercession, and they listen for instructions from God for how to win the battle.

Then Jahaziel, a prophet, passed on God's instructions. He said, "Do not be afraid … for the battle is not yours but God's … stand firm and see the deliverance the Lord will give you." The next day they sent out worshipers. As they marched toward the battle, they declared aloud who God was, singing of His enduring love. As they worshiped, the Lord sent an ambush and defeated the invaders – without King Jehoshaphat's army ever having to raise their swords!

We overcome the evil one and win our battles by standing firm in God. It's vital that we take time to hear His instructions, stand firm in our faith and declare the greatness and power of God, not the power of the enemy.

In Nigeria, a militant who had killed many people ran toward Alex, one of our young leaders, with a knife, intending to kill him. Sensing it was a spiritual attack, Alex stood his ground and rebuked Satan in Jesus' name. The attacker fell to his knees at Alex's feet and asked, "How can I be saved?"

It's important that we don't give the enemy a "foothold" through carelessness or sin. I remember the story of a pastor's wife and her daughter, who were gossiping about another pastor who had failed morally. A terrible feeling of darkness came over them. Then they recognized they had been glorifying the enemy. They repented and the darkness lifted.

I will not waste the time or ink telling more of Satan's stories. He tried to thwart the ministry of Jesus, but he couldn't. He can't stop the witness of anyone fully submitted to God. James 4:7 exhorts us to submit ourselves to God, resist the devil, and he will flee from us! And 2 Thessalonians 3:3 reminds us that the Lord is faithful, and He will strengthen us and protect us from the evil one.

Because the spiritual realm is unseen, at times younger or immature believers may claim Satan is at work more than he really is. If one of our outreach teams runs out of gas in their van, it may be that they simply forgot to put enough gas in it, not that Satan is out to get them. Godly discernment (a mark of spiritual maturity) is a key to effective spiritual warfare and accurate intercessory prayer. Just as we recognize foreign accents when people speak, as we grow in discernment, we should more easily recognize when the evil one is at work.

Worship gives God the glory for Who He is; intercession allows us to partner with Him and what He wants to do; and spiritual warfare brings defeat to the enemy's counterattacks. God has called us in YWAM, as one of our Foundational Values, to take the offense and engage in all three.

Chapter Eight

Have a Biblical Christian Worldview
(Value 9)

YWAM is called to a Biblical Christian worldview. We believe that the Bible – the textbook for all of life – makes a clear division between good and evil; right and wrong. The practical dimensions of life are no less spiritual than the ministry expressions. Everything done in obedience to God is spiritual. We seek to honor God with all that we do, equipping and mobilizing men and women of God to take roles of service and influence in every arena of society.

(Deu 8:1-3; Deu 32:45-47; 2Ki 22:8; Psa 19:7-11; Luk 8:21; Joh 8:31-32; Php 4:8-9; 2Ti 3:16-17; Heb 4:12-13; Jam 4:17)

It was hot and humid, and the taxi I was riding in seemed to be hitting every pothole in the rutted Cambodian road. I was exhausted, hoping to get a little sleep, but even the thought of sleep was knocked out of my head as we bounced along for seven hours. I had just finished teaching at the first Discipleship Training School at our new campus in Battambang, and I had agreed to go to Phnom Penh to speak to our staff there. *What was I thinking?*

As I laid my weary head back on the taxi's rear seat one more time, I began to ponder the question Jesus posed to His disciples in Mark 8: "Who do you say that I am?"

To my surprise, the Holy Spirit began to "download" a message to me in a way I had never experienced. Instantly, I was energized and wide awake. I grabbed my yellow legal pad and began to write word-for-word the message God was giving me. It was an added miracle that later, I could read what I had written, given all the jolts in the road! I call the message "Who Is Jesus to You?" Below is a small portion of the message that shows how practical He was. The complete message can be found at YWAMValues.com.

Jesus was practical:

- He was a carpenter: He knew how to build and fix things.
- He was a chef: He prepared breakfast for His team.
- He was a caterer: He provided and served fish and bread for 5,000 people.
- He was an event organizer: He planned a love feast.
- He was a creative problem solver: He resolved a beverage problem at a wedding.
- He was an expert on fishing: He knew just where to fish for maximum results.

Do we think of Jesus as being anything less than Spirit-led and obedient to the Father? He said in John 14:31, "I do exactly what my Father has commanded me." And yet He did these practical things, as directed by His father.

I sometimes throw out this thought-provoking question to unsuspecting audiences: "Which one is more spiritual – raising the dead or washing the dishes?" Nearly always, someone blurts out, "raising the dead!" Then he or she backtracks on their response. Honestly, that is the automatic inward response of most everyone. We believe it is more "spiritual" to do something supernatural, when the simple answer is that it's more pleasing to God to do whatever He asks. So it can be far more spiritual and pleasing to God to do the dishes, if that is what the Father asks of us.

The Bible does not call some aspects of daily life "spiritual" and the other parts "non-spiritual." God honored the skillful craftsman, artist and musician (Exodus 34-35, 1 Chronicles 15), not just the preacher or prophet.

Still, this non-Biblical, dualistic thinking about some jobs being sacred and others being secular is rampant throughout the body of Christ. I believe it brings great sadness to Jesus. He knows how He has made each one of us – what gifts He placed within us. They are designed to bring purpose to us and pleasure to Him when we use them. Jesus was Spirit-natural. God wants us to be the same whether we're washing the dishes or raising the dead!

Missionary Plumbers … Secretaries … Scientists … Mechanics

Back when I was overseeing operations in Kona, we had a wonderful plumber from Scotland volunteering on the campus. Mr. Dougall was a joyful and servant-hearted man. One day as I was passing by while he was hard at work, I paused to say "Thank you so much for giving your plumbing skills to help us. We so need the gift you have to offer!" He replied in his thick Scottish brogue, "Oh no, Mrs. Cunningham – it is I who should be thankin' you! I had no idea that I could be a missionary plumber!"

You don't have to be a preacher to be a missionary – accountants, secretaries, administrators, mechanics, gardeners, artists, linguists, web designers, and scientists can ALL be missionaries if they do their ministry unto the glory of God.

Consider the life of John Calvin, one of the leaders of the Reformation, who initiated education for all classes of society. He wanted everyone to be able to read and write, and he taught that all work was holy. One day Loren and I had a conversation about Calvin and this division between "sacred and secular" thinking.

I said, "Loren, I can't believe that this non-Biblical trend is so pervasive within the Church."

He agreed with my observation and said, "That's why we need to have a Biblical Christian worldview. Guided by the Bible and the Holy Spirit, *every*thing we do can be done for the glory of God. *Every*thing can be sanctified and sacred."

Within the Bible are instructions for health, family, finances, agriculture, education, government, and so much more.

In the 1980s, a former executive with IBM taught in our Leadership Training Schools on organization, financial management, and leadership styles. He and I were supposed to lead a management seminar together in Hong Kong. But he ran into passport problems and couldn't come, so I was left to teach the seminar on my own! I had read books by various management gurus, but I had never taught a whole week on these topics. Panic set in as I left for Hong Kong: "God, what am I going to do?" All the books I had read were based on Western business models, and I was headed to Asia.

God's response to my panic? "Relax, Darlene. Anything that works and is successful leadership or management is based in Biblical principles! Just ask Me to show you the principles." Then I realized that I had already been managing more than 500 staff in operations, just trying to listen to Jesus. The Holy Spirit began to show me the scriptural basis for what I was doing. I discovered so many management principles in God's word: Jethro's advice to his son-in-law Moses in Exodus 18 about how to organize the judicial system; Jesus' example of breaking His followers into groups of 3, 12 and 120 for different roles, and so on. My favorite example is Nehemiah's motivational leadership plan for rebuilding the walls of Jerusalem. God gave me fresh new teaching each day for the seminar, all based on Bible examples!

Foundations of our Worldview

You may ask, "How did a Biblical Christian worldview become one of our YWAM Foundational Values?" Dr. Francis Schaeffer, who was the first person we heard teach specifically on the importance of having a Biblical Christian worldview, had a tremendous impact on YWAM and many other ministries.

His classic book, *How Should We Then Live?*, underscored the importance of understanding what we believe and why, as he sounded the alarm about the rising wave of humanistic thinking in Western culture. He wrote, "People have presuppositions, and they will live more consistently on the basis of those presuppositions than even they themselves may realize …. Most people catch their presuppositions from their family and surrounding society, the way a child catches the measles. But people with understanding realize that their presuppositions should be chosen after a careful consideration of which worldview is true."

His conclusion, of course, was that the Biblical Christian worldview is true – that God created humanity in His image, which is the basis for all human dignity.

In our first SOE in Switzerland, Schaeffer identified the Four Basic Premises of Christianity that are included in my teaching on The Belief Tree:

1. God is infinite and personal
2. Men and women are finite and personal, created in God's image
3. Truth is constant and knowable
4. Choices are significant and have consequences

These form the cornerstones of a Biblical Christian worldview. They are the "taproot" of our beliefs. They stand as absolutes in the midst of swirling worldviews based in Buddhism, Hinduism, Islam, animism, communism and secular humanism, which puts what man thinks and does in the position of god.

When each person "does what is right in his or her own eyes" a lawless spirit pervades. That spirit is at work throughout the world, trying to undermine the Biblical "absolutes" that God established for our welfare. They are moral standards of right and wrong, good and evil recognized for centuries.

Biblical absolutes include "You shall not murder; you shall not commit adultery; you shall not steal; you shall not give false testimony against your neighbor; you shall not covet…." (Exodus 20:13-17). The telling of truth does not have exceptions. Even the laws of the land uphold this as an absolute. We can't be people who change the "truth" as circumstances change (situational ethics). "True truth," as Dr. Schaeffer called it, is not relative; it is an absolute and remains unchangeable.

Discipling Nations

The second half of Value 9 says "*We seek to honor God with all that we do, equipping and mobilizing men and women of God to take roles of service and influence in every arena of society.*"

Jesus commanded us to disciple nations, not just do what has come to be called "religious work," like starting a church or ministry. To do this, we need understanding of what Schaeffer called the "Lordship of Christ over all of life." This does not mean we dominate people and cultures or force them to convert. Rather, Christians should influence society toward a Biblical Christian worldview by how we live.

Jesus said we are to be the salt of the earth, seasoning society. He said we are to be the light of the world (Matthew 5:13-14). The last thing Jesus said before He ascended into heaven was to "go and make disciples of all nations, baptizing them in the name of the Father and of the Son and of the

Holy Spirit, and teaching them to obey everything I have commanded you" (Matthew 28:18-20).

How do we "disciple nations?" One way is by influencing the areas that shape a nation. One excellent example of a nation discipler is William Carey, the British missionary to India in the 19th century who is called "the father of modern missions."

Yes, he did the "religious" work of a missionary, preaching the Gospel and translating and printing the Bible in 44 Indian languages and dialects. He believed God wanted every individual to have access to the Bible, no matter their social status or economic position.

Carey also produced textbooks, dictionaries, and classical literature, which served primary school children, college-level students and the general public. He opened the first primary school in all of India, educating boys and girls of all castes. At that time the poor people of lower castes or females were not allowed to be educated. He founded Serampore College to train indigenous ministers and teach arts and sciences. This college became the first degree-granting institution in all of Asia.

Carey was also a horticulturist and a botanist. He invented the Indian savings bank, and he introduced the steam engine to India. He was truly "a man for all seasons." His influence in areas of social reform resulted in the banning of infant sacrifices and widow burning, a turning point in Indian culture.

Vishal Mangalwadi, a friend of YWAM and world renown teacher of Biblical Christian worldview, says of Carey, "… he saw India not as a foreign country to be exploited, but as his heavenly Father's land to be loved and saved …. He believed in understanding and controlling nature instead of fearing, appeasing or worshipping it; in developing one's intellect instead of killing it as mysticism taught. He emphasized enjoying literature and culture instead of shunning [them] ….

"By the time Carey died, he had spent 41 years in India without a furlough. His mission could count only some 700 converts in a nation of millions, but he had laid an impressive foundation of Bible translations, education and social reform."[5]

My friend Christine Colby, who is the Director of University of the Nations' Center for Community Development, teaches around the globe on

---

5. *Christianity Today* (Nov. 7, 2016 edition).

Biblical Christian worldview. She believes it is the first foundation needed for community development – addressing the erroneous beliefs and values that have shaped people's thinking. For example, those with a "live for today" worldview cut down trees that could feed and house them in the future. Those who believe their land is cursed by evil spirits won't plant crops. Those who believe it is "God's will" for them to be poor won't take initiative to rise out of poverty.

Christine says, "To have a Biblical Christian worldview is to have God's perspective on His world and our lives. We all come from different cultures. Even when we become believers, we don't instantly have God's view – we still carry our own cultural views. God encourages us in the Bible to meditate on His Word day and night to change our way of thinking. He instructs us to do this because He knows that we need to have our worldview transformed to align with His."

Romans 12:2 says, "Do not conform any longer to the pattern of this world, but be transformed by the renewing of your mind. Then you will be able to test and approve what God's will is – his good, pleasing and perfect will."

Seven Spheres that Influence Society

One of God's defining words to YWAM – The Seven Spheres of Influence[6] – came through Loren while we were on vacation in the Rocky Mountains of Colorado. He had been asking God for understanding on how to see a nation discipled, and God spoke to him about "seven classrooms." They were seven influential spheres of society that shape the worldview of a culture. This was a breakthrough insight. He realized that if Christians would teach and live God's principles and practices in each of these seven arenas, we could see the transformation of our communities and nations.

The first morning of our holiday, a park ranger delivered a message to our door that had been received at the ranger's station seven miles away. Bill and Vonette Bright, the founders of Campus Crusade for Christ (Cru), were in Colorado too and wanted to meet with us. We accepted the invitation with great excitement, as Loren was eager to share with Dr. Bright his new revelation. Loren tucked into his jacket pocket a page from his yellow legal

---

6. Appendix 3: Legacy Word #2: The Seven Spheres of Influence

pad, on which he had written the things God had showed him about the seven spheres.

Loren and I walked in the front door and had not even sat down, when Dr. Bright produced a paper of his own and began to show Loren the seven areas God had shown *him* of how to influence society and see nations transformed – the same seven areas! We were thrilled. When Loren pulled out his own yellow paper from his jacket pocket, it confirmed what God had shown them both and their excitement grew. Within a month, I heard Dr. Schaeffer on the radio, sharing about the same areas of influence that God had revealed to him.

In 1978, when we launched YWAM's University of the Nations together with Dr. Howard Malmstadt, we structured the colleges of the university around these seven "classrooms" or seven spheres, because our goal is to train missionaries to become nation transformers. The seven spheres include the areas of Family, Economy, Government, Religion, Education, Media and Celebration. These spheres exist within every society on earth – whether rural or urban, whether primitive or complex. They are to each society what the basic biological systems are to the human body – a crucial part of God's plan, which bring life when they are functioning according to God's design.

YWAM the Movement, Working in the Spheres

In YWAM we have come to understand that Christians will never disciple nations and transform society by becoming separationists. Rather, Jesus calls us to influence society by living godly lives amid a godless society, seeking the Lord for ways to impart His principles into business, government, education, etc. Hundreds of thousands of people who have attended our schools or worked with YWAM for a season have been called by God into the spheres. This is not a lesser calling – it is a missions calling! They can be missionary lawyers, educators, journalists, athletes, hairdressers, mechanics, carpenters, etc. Those who have taken the Biblical principles they learned in YWAM and are applying them in the spheres are part of "YWAM, the movement." We celebrate them!

II. We Are Visionary

VALUES

Be Visionary (#5)
Champion Young People (#6)
Make God Known (#2)
Do First, Then Teach (#12)
Exhibit Servant Leadership (#11)

YWAM began with a vision of waves of young people flooding across the world, with each wave going farther than the one before it. We equip and champion youth, releasing them to fulfill their God-given destiny. We aim to be creative and relevant, continually pioneering, doing new things in new ways. We make God known, proclaiming the Good News of Christ to everyone, everywhere. We serve the poor and needy. And we will make disciples until the knowledge of the glory of God covers the whole earth. We recognize true spiritual authority flows from living what we believe before teaching it to others. We look to Christ as our example for servant leadership and as servant leaders we uplift, support, protect and care for those we lead.

Chapter Nine

Be Visionary
(Value 5)

YWAM is called to be visionary, continually receiving, nurturing and releasing fresh vision from God. We support the pioneering of new ministries and methods, always willing to be radical in order to be relevant to every generation, people group, and sphere of society. We believe that the apostolic call of YWAM requires the integration of spiritual eldership, freedom in the Spirit and relationship, centered on the Word of God.

(Num 12:6; 1Sa 12:16; Pro 29:18; Eze 1:1; Hab 2:23; Mar 1:35-39; Luk 9:1-6; Act 16:9-10; Act 26:19; 2Pe 3:9-13)

Recently, I was pondering some of the unique ways God has equipped YWAM to be a visionary pioneer movement. He has called us to continually be receiving, nurturing and releasing fresh vision from God. Thoughts began to cascade from my mind faster than I could write them down:

We carry 200+ different passports.

We are young and old, but mostly young.

We come in all sizes and shapes and every wonderful shade of skin color that God ever created.

We speak hundreds of different languages.

We love flags and maps.

We prove daily that all nations and generations can work well together.

We love going to the most remote places on earth with the Good News – from Stone Age tribes to urban high-rise dwellers.

We minister to children and elderly; rich and poor.

We are convinced that every talent can be used for the glory of God: rap, hip-hop, ballet; painting, photography, drawing, sculpture, etc.

We have remarkable worship bands and composers who constantly write new songs. We play classical music too.

We dig wells and build homes.

We do eye surgeries, play sports, make films, use Internet technology and deliver babies for the glory of God.

We plant churches in unchurched places.

We feed the poor and the needy – especially refugees and homeless – but we can put on a five-star meal when needed.

We respond to injustice not just because of human need, but because it breaks God's heart. And we help write laws to right those wrongs.

We minister to the sick and the well; the imprisoned and the free.

We create micro-businesses and train former prostitutes, militants and street kids with marketable skills.

We build bridges of communication between rebels and governments, and help warring ethnic tribes to resolve their conflicts.

We have a passion for ice cream, peanut butter and cheap air tickets.

We pay our YWAM school tuition in dollars, rupees, kroner, bhat, won, shillings, rubles, rand, pesos, dinar, yen, euros, lira, yuan, pounds ... and in rice, beans, papayas, goats and chickens.

We have homes all over the world on ships, in castles, hotels, barns, tents ... even in jails.

We can pack fast.

We can wear the same clothes for a very long time, but we clean up well.

We can sleep anywhere – hammocks, floors, airport benches, and when standing in long lines.

We can eat anything and have seen more food miracles than we can recount.

We travel by air, boat, train; in cars, buses and trucks; on the backs of horses, donkeys and camels. And we're also experts in the science of pushing vans.

We tolerate mice, rats, cockroaches, fleas and mosquitoes, but are terrified of dogs when going door-to-door.

Oh, yes, and we preach … on university campuses, in red light districts, on boats, planes and trains.

We love to teach about the character of God and how His world works.

We know that God is good, He speaks, and He will always be faithful to fulfill His promises.

We love God, His Word, and His world.

All these characteristics equip us to be the apostolic, visionary tribe that God has called YWAM to be.

Innovative Disrupters

Being visionary is in the original DNA of YWAM. From our outset, we have been doing never-done-before initiatives. As a result, we are always going to be a bit disruptive to people who are maintainers.

Dean Sherman, one of our pioneers, once said, "Because we are visionary, YWAM will never have enough. We'll never have enough land, money, facilities, equipment, resources or people. If we ever have enough, it will be a sad day, because it will mean we have ceased to have new vision, so we have died."

Those joining YWAM must accept this inevitability: Where there is new vision and innovation, there will always be some bedlam. It's not that we value being disorganized, it's that we value fresh vision more than having everything neat and tidy. We value growth, effectiveness and fruitfulness. We truly need and desire for people to come with the skills to help make things run more efficiently – but they must be people who embrace young people and are flexible enough to live with some disorder. It's like the Holy Spirit hovering over the formless waters at the time of creation. When God spoke, creativity and order emerged.

When Loren and I returned to Lausanne in the 90s to help rebuild there, we seemed to face one crisis after another. One day, I overheard a girl in the stairway talking on the phone. She said, "You know how it is when the Cunninghams are in charge. It's so chaotic! But you can feel the presence and the blessing of God here!" It would have been inappropriate for me to interrupt and tell her how much I agreed with her – both about "the Cunninghams" and about the Spirit of God in the place! I'll choose chaos – as long as God is working in the midst of it.

Missionary Nerds

Whenever I'm speaking to a new intake of DTS students, I like to pull in a few YWAM staff who are not seen as traditional missionaries to shake up the students' view of missions. I want to help them see YWAM's visionary side and show them that whatever gifts and skills they possess can be used for God. I'll often introduce Jill and Chong Ho, two of my favorite YWAM innovators.

One time in Kona I opened the interview with, "Jill, tell us about your growing up years."

She responded, "Well, I was an unusual child. I loved the nations. Other girls had posters of puppies and princesses on their bedroom walls. I had world maps."

Jill went on to earn a university degree in geography and began working in the field of cartography.

"How did you end up in YWAM?" I queried.

"I heard about an opportunity with YWAM's 4K Mapping Project that would allow me to make maps as a missionary. I was surprised and pleased that I could merge my two passions. In that role, I've now made hundreds of huge floor maps for YWAM, churches and mission workers to use for prayer, strategizing and targeting the neediest peoples and places on earth.

"The largest was one I designed for a gathering in Hong Kong. That map was 85 by 170 feet (26 by 52 meters), which enabled more than 2,000 internationals, including many Mainland Chinese, to walk and pray on the nations of the world. It was so exciting to see the Chinese worship and pray on one of my maps."

Jill's "nerdiness" has helped shape how global missions is done!

Then I called on Chong Ho, who was born in Korea, but came to America as a child. He studied Computer Science and founded a prosperous software company before joining YWAM. When he arrived in Kona, we were desperate to find someone who could write software to support a global records system for the University of the Nations. There had never been a truly global university before ours.

I asked him, "What happened when you sat down to try to design this program?"

"I asked the Holy Spirit for revelation, and then the most extraordinary thing happened. Over a three-week span of time, it was like having a warp-speed download of how to do it, and I typed in code almost non-stop, until my fingers were weary to the bone."

Every time Chong Ho describes this encounter with the Holy Spirit's creative power, it reminds me of how George Frideric Handel composed the music for *The Messiah* within a two-week period in 1741. Handel had been asked to write music to Scripture passages. He felt weak and inadequate. He had suffered a stroke, his eyes were bad, and he had other ailments. But under the Holy Spirit's anointing, he wrote *The Messiah*.

Chong Ho's visionary work created something new, radical and relevant for our global university. He said, "In 2003 we were finally able to compile information hand-gathered over the previous 25+ years and merge it into one, globally accessible records system. Usually, when someone writes a new computer program, it has to go through many weeks of testing to find and fix all the glitches. But as we rolled out the global records system that God had 'downloaded' to me, there were no glitches. That's impossible! But God does the impossible!"

Chong Ho's next story had all of the DTS students on the edges of their seats:

"We took an IT team right to the frontlines in one war-torn country in the Middle East. We were able to use a handheld WiFi generator to allow refugees – and the fighters on the frontlines – to download the Bible and videos like *The Jesus Film* in their native language. We also took a solar power projector, screen, and microphone system. It was amazing in this volatile setting to be able to show *The Jesus Film* to crowds of up to 1,000 at a time outdoors. Many people came to the Lord there."

As Chong Ho was telling his IT adventure stories, a young man sitting in the second row caught my attention. He was bouncing in his chair, exclaiming, "I'm an IT nerd! I didn't know I could be a missionary nerd!" After DTS, that young man took the UofN Foundations of Information Technology course and joined Chong Ho's team!

I heard of a young woman from Australia who was an animal behaviorist who came to YWAM thinking she would need to lay aside her career and expertise to become a "real missionary." She thought, "How could God possibly use my skills in missions?"

She served in Rwanda, where land mines left from former wars were maiming people. She cried out to God, "I wish I could do something to help." He said, "You can!" Listening to His voice, she developed a technology to train lab mice to detect land mines! Many lives were saved because of this animal behaviorist visionary, doing new things in new ways.

In YWAM, we want to be continually receiving, nurturing and releasing fresh vision from God. If you try to limit people to serving only your vision, you may kill it. But if you are generous, like God is generous, encouraging people to go serve wherever He calls them, He will draw more and more people to you. If you're truly visionary, you will want to help build up others, not just build up your own ministry or location.

What if Jesus Returns When You're in the Movie Theater?

When I was growing up, the Church became quite isolationist. Leaders projected a feeling that they "didn't want to be tainted by the world." So they did just what Satan hoped for – the Church abdicated their roles of influence in key areas of society – the entertainment industry, government, education, business, science, etc.

In my denomination it was considered "against our religion" to watch movies. I heard people say, "What would happen if Jesus returned and you were at the cinema? He wouldn't enter an unholy place, so you'd be left behind." It was all quite scary, and I remember thinking, "Wow, something evil must be happening in those places!"

My mom and dad were not so "narrow" in their thinking but, out of respect for them and their role as pastors, I refrained from going to the cinema. Then one night as a teenager, I ventured out with a couple of friends to see a movie called *The High and the Mighty*. I wanted to discern for myself what was so "unholy" about motion pictures. The movie was wonderful! It was about people on an airplane that was about to crash, and it highlighted the things each individual realized they needed to make right in their lives as they faced imminent death. At the end I walked out of the theater wondering, *what was so unholy about that?*

Christians in my generation somehow got the idea that sharing the Gospel could only be done in church or at revival meetings. In their desire to be "holy," they had isolated themselves from the world. How very opposite to the model of Jesus, who dined with prostitutes, tax collectors and sinners!

I'm not saying it's fine for Christians to watch any and every movie that is produced! Some movies today *are* truly evil. We must be discerning. But to be relevant to every generation, we can redeem for God's purposes the communication tools of that generation. Movies can be made that illustrate

Biblical principles of love, forgiveness, the value of every human being and so much more!

In my church as a child, if the banker committed his life to Christ, the church tried to get him to quit his job and bring his skills to work for the denomination. How different it is when people with such skills get the broader understanding of how they can influence their arena of society to bring about positive change. Yes, it's good to be "salt and light," doing Bible studies at lunchtime at the bank to lead people to Jesus and help them grow in their personal faith. But let's also consider the opportunity to help create banking policies based on Biblical principles that are just and fair to help those in need. The banker can work to bring transformation within the sphere – God's will on earth as it is in heaven.

How Does the Process of Releasing New Vision Work?

You may ask, "How can you trust inexperienced young people to be pioneers and do new things?" We trust them because God does. The essential qualification is understanding who God is and, based on His character and His Word, stepping out in faith. Like the Belief Tree shows, values grow out of beliefs, enabling people to make principle-based decisions. With those foundations there is no problem trusting the youngest among us to go cross-generational and international.

When past generations of Christians saw sinful men making motion pictures, I wish they could have seen with eyes of vision that this communication tool (and many others) could be redeemed to create powerful platforms for presenting the Good News to younger generations. Instead legalism set in and no one seemed to ask, "How could this medium be used for Kingdom purposes?" They closed their minds and rejected it, losing a powerful tool of influence.

Our first YWAMers wore white shirts and skinny ties in the 1960s. Back then that form of dress communicated respect. If our young men wore that today, they would look culturally irrelevant. We need to hold to our beliefs and values, but package our message in relevant ways.

Elements Needed for Apostolic Growth

The last part of this value says, *"We believe that the apostolic call of YWAM requires the integration of spiritual eldership, freedom in the Spirit and relationship, centered on the Word of God."*

Loren has an excellent message on [7]Spiritual Eldership that explains how this works in practice. In it, he shares the Elements for Apostolic (Visionary) Growth that should thrive among us as a mission and provide moorings for our future development. These elements must always function under the Lordship of Jesus:

Freedom in the Spirit – Every individual, from the youngest to the oldest, has the freedom in the Spirit to hear and obey the word of the Lord. But this is not done in a vacuum or independently.

Spiritual Eldership – New vision that will have a broad impact should be shared with recognized elders. These individuals are not necessarily older in age (Timothy, a youth, was an elder and appointed other elders). But they are people who have a breadth and depth of experience and spiritual maturity, and they fulfill the leadership criteria outlined in 1 Timothy 3 and Titus 1.

Every leader should be open to receive, value and nurture new vision. As a servant leader, they have a responsibility to take to God in prayer any word that is brought to them by an individual, and to test it according to the Scriptures. This trust is sacred, and they should receive this new, baby vision like a grandparent would receive a grandchild. God's heart is broken when new vision is stomped on by leadership. He says, "It would be better for you if a millstone were hung around your neck..." Luke 17:2 (NRSV).

Relationship – Our freedom in the Spirit and eldership roles are to operate through an open flow of communication, honoring and respecting one another, recognizing that the Holy Spirit resides in each one of us.

Being visionary is one of the things I love most about our tribe. Just as the ocean waves thrust onto the shores, recede, and then thrust forward again, so every new generation of YWAMers crashes forward with fresh vision and new ways of doing things. God wants us to be radical in order to be relevant to every generation, people group and sphere of society. This is YWAM's never-ending visionary, apostolic call … wave upon wave upon wave.

---

7. The full "Spiritual Eldership" document can be found at YWAMValues.com and ywam.org.

Chapter Ten

Champion Young People
(Value 6)

*YWAM is called to champion youth. We believe God has gifted
and called young people to spearhead vision and ministry. We are
committed to value, trust, train, support, make space and release them.
They are not only the Church of the future; they are the Church of
today. We commit to follow where they lead, in the will of God.*

(1Sa 17:32-50; Ecc 4:13-14; Ecc 12:1-7; Jer 1:5-10; Dan 1:17-20;
Joe 2:28; Joh 6:9; Act 16:1-5; 1Ti 4:12-16; 1Jo 2:12-14)

After I spoke at an event in Rio de Janiero, a stocky young Brazilian with black wavy hair and a contagious smile approached me.

He said, "Darlene, I'm Ricardo. I'm one of your waves!"

English wasn't his first language, and amidst the crowd noise, I didn't quite catch what he said. He saw the puzzled look on my face, so he said it again, "You know – I am one of your waves. Loren saw waves. I am one of them!"

Ricardo then poured out his story. "I was a street kid with no family, living under a bridge in a Rio slum. Some YWAMers found me. They brought me into their children's home, and I met Jesus there! They educated me, and then I did a Discipleship Training School and some other YWAM schools. And now I'm teaching others how to know Jesus and how to become part of the waves."

Ricardo was indeed one of the waves, and he was making more waves. As these young Brazilians hit the shores, transformation was coming to the society around them.

YWAM is a movement designed by God to value, trust, train, support, make space and release young people. Youth are full of energy and adventure; they are willing to try new things; they have not developed cynical "it can't be done" attitudes. They tend to be fearless. They are full of zeal and eager to discover who they are as followers of Jesus. There is a trust within them that, since God created them with their gifts and talents, He will guide them to where their aptitude can be best used. I love young people!

We believe God speaks to young people. We train and encourage them, and then we follow them. This isn't just our own good idea, it's a "God idea." We see throughout Scripture that God trusts young people to reveal and accomplish His plans: David was a teenager when God used him to slay Goliath and rescue his nation. Samuel was just a boy when he heard and responded to God's voice. Shadrach, Meshach and Abednego were teenagers when they were thrown into Nebuchadnezzar's fiery furnace for their commitment to worship God alone. Mary was just a young girl when the Lord entrusted her with the most precious responsibility in the world – bearing and raising the Son of God! Many of the early disciples were youths, and Paul promoted and commended Timothy to spiritual leadership when he was a still a young person.

"Young Man, Has God Called You to be a Missionary?"

Shortly after Loren and I were married, we met a middle-aged missionary named Sy Huckerbee in Kingston, Jamaica. He had heard that my maiden name was Scratch and he asked, "Do you know Alf Scratch?" I replied, "Yes, that's my grandfather." I was quite surprised to hear Granddad's name in a place so far away, from a person I'd never met before. My granddad had been a Pentecostal preacher in Canada in the early 1900s.

Pastor Huckerbee said, "Darlene, when I was a 19-years-old, I felt God call me to be a missionary in Central America. I knew it was God, and I knew I was to go right away. So I went to the mission board of our denomination, of which your grandfather was a member."

Despite the urgency he felt from the Lord, the board declined to send him until he attended Bible college and fulfilled several other requirements that would take years to accomplish. I knew all too well this story of closed doors or endless "hoops" to jump through to get to the mission field.

He continued, "I left that board room disappointed and discouraged – I was so sure I had heard from the Lord. As I slowly walked down a long hallway, I heard heavy footsteps behind me. I turned around and there was your granddad. He said, 'Young man, has God called you to be a missionary? And do you know for sure that He is wanting you to go *now*?'

"I responded with a firm, 'Yes!'"

"'Then get down on your knees. I will pray for you and send you out!' Right then and there, your granddad commissioned me as a missionary to Central America! After years of pioneering churches there, the Lord led me to Jamaica."

The seeds for God's plan to use young people in missions are not only clear throughout Scripture, but they were evident in both Loren's and my family backgrounds. If my granddad had lived to see the start of Youth With A Mission, I know he would have been totally supportive of our vision to use young people. Granddad had already "bucked the system" to open the door for young people to get into missions!

We are YOUTH With A Mission

When Loren was called to start this movement, he knew the focus must always be upfront, proclaimed in the name: "YOUTH with a mission." This means we are forever associated with the frailties and strengths of youth. Even today, some warn us that we can't trust youth to be missionaries because they lack theological training and their immaturity will lead to cross-cultural and moral failures. Yes, our young people have made some mistakes, but through the first sixty years of the mission their zeal for God, their willingness to listen, obey and go to difficult places have brought God's transforming love to millions of lives.

Starting with our earliest outreaches in the 60s, we had such a conviction that YWAM was not to be led through rules; rather, that when young people were given understanding of God's principles, they would choose to do right. We were not to treat them like children. We were young at that time ourselves, and God was trusting us! We were to do likewise, and trust these young people to be responsible, nurturing them and helping launch them into missions. We knew the leadership gifts God had placed within

Loren and me were to be used as tools to release others for whatever God wanted *them* to accomplish!

I believe that during those first summers, our foundational value of championing youth was confirmed. Our call to believe in young people is why God brought YWAM into existence.

DTS Is the Doorway to YWAM

We knew young people didn't need a theology degree to be able to go out and tell people about Jesus, but they did need teaching from God's Word about His nature and character, particularly how to hear and obey His voice. God began shaping that training process and many of our foundational values in our first School of Evangelism in Switzerland. The key curriculum elements of that school were later combined into a shorter version we called the Discipleship Training School (DTS).

Over the years, many pastors and leaders have asked me, "How has a mission of YWAM's size, complexity and breadth remained true to its beliefs and values all these years?" My answer is "the DTS." This is the doorway that every staff member of YWAM must come through, and the entry course for every University of the Nations student.

By [8]2020, DTSs were being offered every year around the world in more than 95 languages, graduating 10,000 students per year globally. A half million (mostly young) people have completed a DTS somewhere in the world since 1974, and we have graduated students from 182 countries! Truth be told, many people meet Jesus as Savior during their DTS, and He forever changes the course of their lives.

One of my young co-workers coined the phrase: "The University of the Nations is a wave machine for missions." That is totally true but I would add to that imagery the DTS – with youth leading youth – as the ride-of-a-lifetime wave maker! I love DTS because it embodies all that this value talks about. It is one of our best demonstrations of believing in youth, pouring into them, and seeing multiplication of young workers. It is our most effective "wave maker."

I love this description from the International DTS Centre team about the DTS experience: "Within the 'live-learn' environment of the DTS, students

---

8. Statistics provided by the International DTS Centre and do not include the hundreds of students who attended YWAM Schools of Evangelism from 1969-1974, prior to the establishment of Discipleship Training Schools.

find a rich journey of exploring God's character and nature and they discover His intention for creation, including us, His precious image bearers. They grow in Christian formation as they understand the impact of how Jesus lived His life on earth, including redemption, sin and the cross. The Holy Spirit brings greater revelation of what it means to be a part of God's family as His children and the Church. And as the participants are embraced into fellowship of the Trinity, they learn more and more how to do life with God as Jesus showed us."

Every DTS includes an outreach, which for many is their first step in responding to Jesus' Great Commission to "go into all the world." DTS outreach teams have been serving in the world 24 hours a day, seven days a week for more than four decades. The breadth of ministry these outreach teams participate in range from coming alongside local churches as they serve their communities, to serving in far-off countries in orphanages, refugee camps, tribal villages, hospitals, prisons, schools and soup kitchens. This is just a small taste of the diverse ministry in which these teams participate, as they extend the kingdom of heaven into all spheres of society, as their loving response to a loving God.

With the Discipleship Training School carrying the key elements to keep us true to our vision, beliefs and values, it is one of our cornerstones. I say to our DTS leaders and staff, "YOU are the most important people in this mission because you are the initial ones who model and pass on our beliefs and values. As the DTS goes, so goes the mission …."

(DTS curriculum, training resources and staff development documents can be found at http://ywamdtsreframe.com and http://ywamdtscentre.org)

Youth Calling, Discipling and Releasing Youth

Because God called us to be YOUTH with a mission, there is an increased anointing when we fulfill what is written in this value: when we trust, train, support, make space and release young people.

Often I teach large groups of young DTS leaders and staff. As I look into their eyes, I think, *You are the reason this mission works!!* They are my heroes. They take what they have learned, go on outreach and then return to lead others. They love the DTS adventure because that's where they discovered God could use them!

Most find their way to a DTS by word-of-mouth, friends telling friends about what they have learned and experienced. But every year all around the world, other short-term programs attract students into DTS: youth camps, summer outreaches, YWAM teams evangelizing on high school and university campuses. There are waves of many sizes and shapes that feed into the DTS wave maker.

You may ask, "How can young people lead with so little experience?" One of our Foundational Values is "Do first; then teach." But they *have* done it; and now they are teaching it. They have been taught the DTS curriculum; they have encountered God in new ways themselves; and they have done on-the-field evangelism. They can become mentors to their peers with understanding of the most relevant issues faced by their generation. They relate much more closely to them – their joys, their lifestyle, and their struggles – than someone three times their age.

Our young leaders welcome older generations to walk alongside them, helping to develop their leadership skills, giving input, and encouraging them. We have the right combination of wisdom, input and oversight. But because we are *YOUTH* with a mission, we are committed to letting young people lead and spearhead new initiatives. As I look around the YWAM world today, I see that most of our well-established ministries and newer, fruitful ministries were started by young people. It is the anointing of God upon youth that qualifies them, not their vast experience.

I have observed that if a YWAM location fails to "value, trust, train, support, make space and release" youth, young people are not attracted to that place.

Don't misunderstand me – every campus needs older people who have experience in legal and financial matters, real estate, insurance, administration and a myriad of areas that require specific knowledge and skills that youth have had no time or life experience to gain. For example, we can't run a university with 18-year-olds! But they must be the *right* older, more mature people – those who are committed to training and releasing youth, not filling the space themselves.

That's why the Crossroads Discipleship Training School was created – to attract older people with life skills who are committed to pass on their knowledge to youth. Older folks can be invaluable coaches and developers, but they can also be dream-killers if they don't invest in youth!

My friend Phillip is a wonderful example of a "life coach." He is a highly skilled tradesman who came to work with us in campus construction. He is a great blessing with our construction projects, but his heart is to build people. He runs a trades track in some DTSs, discipling young men and women in various trade skills. He is dearly loved, and he is raising up an army of builders – both those who build buildings and those who build people.

We are YOUTH With A Mission. And as I'm getting older, I say it louder every year! As Loren and I travel the world, we have discovered that the locations with the greatest fruitfulness are the ones where youth are given leadership. The places pulsing with life are multi-generational, but with youth as the largest demographic. They are also international both in constituency and in outreach.

I often say, "If YWAM ever gets old and boring, I'm getting out." To which Loren always responds, "And I'm coming with you!"

Chapter Eleven

Make God Known
(Value 2)

YWAM is called to make God known throughout the whole world, and into every arena of society through evangelism, training and mercy ministries. We believe that salvation of souls should result in transformation of societies thus obeying Jesus' command to make disciples of all nations.

(1Ch 16:24-27; Psa 68:11; Psa 71:15-16; Psa 145:4-7; Mat 28:18-20; Mar 16:15; Act 1:8; Act 13:1-4a; Rom 10:8-15; Rom 15:18-21)

YWAMers may be the most creative people in the world when it comes to finding ways to tell people about Jesus. Yes, we do traditional proclamation and event evangelism, but we also do very untraditional outreaches to cowboys, fashion models, biker gangs, war refugees, university students, sex workers, filmmakers, surfers, rappers, teachers and tango dancers.

We take seriously the Lord's call to "Go into **all** the world and preach the gospel to **every** creature" (Mark 16:15 NKJV). That means every nation, every culture, every arena of society **where we are not** gets to hear the Good News that forgiveness of sin and eternal life are available through a relationship with Jesus Christ. I am honored to be associated with so many younger and older believers who have boldly taken up that call to "Make God Known" in the difficult places. One of those places is Nigeria.

In 2009, Loren and I flew across West Africa and into the oil boomtown of Port Harcourt. We were greeted by smiles and singing, but the drive from the airport to the YWAM center highlighted the contrasts of this beautiful land. Nigeria's great palm forests, oceans and rivers were being fouled by corruption related to its great oil reserves. Its roads had potholes the size of buses.

When the traffic became impassable, guards armed with machine guns jumped out of the police car leading our caravan and ran forward through the stopped cars until they found the non-moving vehicles and "motivated" their drivers to move. Despite its oil wealth, locals told us that the countryside received only two to three hours of electricity per month, and no one knew when it would go on or off. The running water was equally sporadic. All of this was the result of corruption, injustice and greed.

The armed escorts were along not only to move the traffic, but to guard us from militant gangs, who had begun kidnapping and killing foreigners to get attention for their cause. They were enraged by the injustices taking place in Nigeria. God was weeping over them too.

Once we were settled at the YWAM campus, we heard the story of how the government had called a live TV meeting with church leaders, oil executives and others to discuss the militant problem. The oil executives offered large amounts of money to various influential church leaders to "motivate" them to back the government against the insurgency. Our YWAM leader, Paul, who was in attendance felt from the Lord that he was not to accept the money. He knew it would come with strings of control attached. So he refused the money and left the meeting.

That night three militants came to Paul's house. They had watched the TV program and they asked, "What are you about? Why didn't you take the bribe from the oil company?" Paul explained that his motivation was not money, but God's love, and his desire was for the militants to know Jesus. Like Nicodemus, who came by the cloak of darkness, those three militants were impacted by the love of God and they were "born again" that night.

They knew they could trust Paul, so they invited him to come to their camp where they were hiding because of government death threats. Paul became a peacemaker and the go-between, and went to the government, telling them, "If you will promise not to shoot them, the militants will lay down their arms." The government agreed. The militants surrendered their arms, and thousands were moved to a "rehabilitation camp."

Paul told us that filthy conditions in the camp sparked new resentment and violence. Learning of this situation, some Port Harcourt DTS students prayed and felt the Lord wanted all the male students to go live and serve in the camp. Paul tried to talk them out of it, but they persisted, and after prayer the Holy Spirit convinced him to let them go. When they arrived, they began cleaning toilets. The militants were aghast. "Why are you doing that?" The students said it was because Jesus loved them and was concerned for their needs. As a result, many of the militants turned their hearts to the Lord. This opened the door for the next DTS outreach team to run a "Transformation Course" in the camp.

When Loren and I arrived in Port Harcourt, a large number of former militants were attending a DTS. They were rough and raw – one student asked if he could go dig up a gun he had hidden and sell it to pay his DTS fees.

When we met the former militants' DTS on the campus, the air was hot and humid, as bodies packed the hall. We were thrilled as we heard their powerful testimonies of how God saved them out of lives filled with murder, rape, robbery, looting, cultic activities and demonic possession. Many wept for joy at the forgiveness and cleansing they had received in Christ.

We were frozen in our seats as one young Nigerian came to the microphone and said, "I used to kidnap white foreigners…" His eyes shifted to Loren and me "…like you!" He paused for effect, then went on, "And I have NOT been 'rehabilitated.'" It was chilling! But then he broke into a beautiful smile and said, "But I HAVE been transformed by Jesus!" The crowd roared with shouts and applause.

By 2020, more than 35,000 militants had laid down their arms. Of those, more than 3,000 had made Jesus the Lord of their lives and attended a DTS, and were endeavoring to bring God's transforming power to their nation.

What is evangelism? It is proclaiming or communicating the Good News of Jesus Christ to everyone everywhere. John 17:3 says "Now this is eternal life: that they know you, the only true God, and Jesus Christ, whom you have sent." As we embrace God's call to communicate Good News to everyone everywhere, it means we are relevant in the language and the culture of the hearer. Our communication needs to be creative, adaptive and relational. YWAM is called to **all** the places where God is yet to be made known. So that **every** person may one day pray as Jesus did in Matthew 6:10, "Your kingdom come, your will be done on earth as it is in heaven."

We encourage evangelism as a lifestyle, taking whatever opportunities we have to build friendships, serve and share the Good News of Christ. God's call to YWAM is also to be strategic with the Gospel, targeting and praying into **places where we are not**.

I led a Leadership Training School (LTS) in Worcester, South Africa, that drew 124 of our leaders and potential leaders from all over Africa, as well as far-flung places like Bangladesh, Brazil, Fiji and Korea.

Though we were thrilled with the diversity of nations and peoples in the school, we were not satisfied to sit back on our accomplishments. The challenge God gave us was to focus *not* on where YWAM teams and centers already existed, but on where we were *not*. On the day that LTS ended in 1998, we had 53 operating locations throughout Africa. My friend David Hamilton did a follow-up census, and within two years, the number had more than doubled to 108 locations. Most of those new pioneering initiatives were launched from the South African LTS, and many of them have since spawned new locations and ministries as well.

Within the mission, our call to make God known is expressed in three main thrusts: Evangelism, Training and Mercy Ministries.

Evangelism

Evangelism is the heartbeat of YWAM. It's the main thing we do all day, every day, all around the world. We communicate the Good News of salvation through Jesus Christ on the streets, door-to-door, on university and high school campuses, in stadiums, through creative music, with street dramas, showing *The Jesus Film*, making podcasts, sharing testimonies in churches, jails, red-light districts or doing kids camps. We share Jesus while grooming the dog, teaching English as a second language, fixing motorcycles, giving haircuts, watching whales, doing photography. We share our faith, our testimonies, our experiences with God in all of life. We make God known – it's who we are; it's what we do.

I heard of a young YWAMer who was just driving down the street one day and felt the Lord say, "Turn around and go back to those kids." He had to ask, "What kids, Lord?" He replied, "The ones waiting on the street corner for their school bus." He hadn't noticed them. He turned around, parked, got out of his car, approached the kids, began sharing his faith, and a ministry of "bus stop Bible studies" was born. The kids were bored and eager to listen – and now others are doing bus stop Bible studies all over town. Many young people have met Jesus while they were just hanging out, waiting for their school bus!

Mercy Ministries

Yes, effective evangelism involves proclaiming and communicating God's love to others, but it also includes demonstrating the love of God through acts of mercy. In Matthew 25:31-46, Jesus tells a parable instructing us to show mercy and kindness to those in need. Everywhere you turn, there is human need. If we do not reach out with God's love to help meet not only people's spiritual poverty, but their physical and emotional needs, then we are not rightly reflecting the love of God, who is concerned with every dimension of a person's life.[9]

YWAM's call to mercy ministries began when our very first volunteers, Dallas and Larry, helped build a road to a leper colony in Liberia. That call was reconfirmed and expanded worldwide in 1979 and 1980, when Cambodian, Vietnamese and Laotian refugees began pouring into temporary camps in Thailand due to instability in the region. The Cambodians were fleeing from the Khmer Rouge, who sought to remake Cambodian society and slaughtered over two million peaceful Khmer in the process.

When the images and stories of these refugees began to surface in the media, YWAMers around the world responded. At first, they were the "boots on the ground," assisting the Red Cross and the UN High Commission for Refugees. But when those agencies left, YWAM remained in several camps, digging latrines, providing medical care, doing feeding programs, setting up a soap factory, post office and preschools. In one camp they even formed a "YWAM bank" because the black-market money exchange was so corrupt. Their practical expression of God's love had a huge impact and, as best we can estimate, within the first five weeks of the crisis at Khao-I-Dang Camp alone, more than 20,000 refugees met Jesus.

From those days until now, YWAMers have responded to refugee crises all around the globe, whenever people are displaced by wars, governments, discrimination or natural catastrophes. We are involved in many other ministries of mercy as well. They are reaching out to those trapped in the sex trade, building homes for the homeless, running health clinics in needy places, doing

---

9. See Appendix 3: Legacy Word #3: The Christian Magna Carta.

food and clothing distribution, running pregnancy centers, doing midwifery, creating advocacy films and tools to combat injustice, creating safe havens to receive child soldiers, starting ministries for AIDS orphans, and so much more.

YWAM Ships also continue to grow in numbers and effectiveness, ministering to isolated islands and in crisis situations, and along coastlands and upriver locations that cannot be reached any other way. Their staff and volunteers are making God known through a blend of evangelism, training, and medical ministries.

Training

God's promise to us that training would be a multiplier for missions has proven true. In every school, we emphasize God's love for the nations. His desire, as expressed in 1 Timothy 2:4, is "for all people to be saved and come to a knowledge of the truth." Many times, as we lay a map of the world out on the floor during a prayer time, God sovereignly calls people to pioneer new works in new places. I believe the direct overflow of our seeking to know God more will always result in a desire to make Him known.

Our training programs have introduced our students to new ways to share their faith, have given them new skills, and have helped them see how to use the gifts God has given them to serve people, whether in a frontier missions setting or in the marketplace.

A Triple-braided Cord Is Not Quickly Broken

God didn't call YWAM to only one kind of expression. He called us to embrace all three – Evangelism, Training and Mercy Ministries – even though each individual or campus may have more emphasis on one area than another. It's not evangelism *or* training *or* mercy ministries. It is evangelism *and* training *and* mercy ministries. So those doing mercy ministries can't say, "Oh, we're not called to evangelism or training." And those doing evangelism can't say, "No, we don't do training – we only do evangelism." And those called primarily to mercy ministries can't say, "Oh, we just minister to human need. We don't do evangelism or training." Our true call and fruitfulness as a mission is in blending the three elements of evangelism, training and mercy ministries together.

Evangelists without training or a compassion for the poor give an incomplete picture of the God who created us and loves us and wants to restore us back into relationship with Himself. Training centers that don't send out students and staff to share their faith risk giving them only head knowledge. And mercy ministries that don't proclaim Jesus are in danger of becoming simply humanitarian causes without saving, transformative power.

Ecclesiastes 4:12b says, "A cord of three strands is not quickly broken." There is power, unity, diversity and blended strength in ministering through all three strands woven together. YWAM is most healthy as a mission and the most representative of who and what God has called us to be when all three expressions are functioning together.

One of my most fulfilling experiences is when I walk into a conference hall filled with young people, where there is a huge, colorful 4K world map on the floor. The term 4K[10] refers to the 4,000+ Omega Zones that quantify the world's most unreached areas. We engage in many intercessory prayer walks on the map. We can easily identify where YWAM is doing evangelism, training and mercy ministry, and we can also easily see where we are not. Often our prayer participants place Post-it notes on Omega Zones where God is speaking to them about adopting new people groups or engaging with the spheres of society in that location.

The Transformation of Nations

The salvation of individual souls is not the only end goal of evangelism. That is the Mark 16:15 Great Commission goal of proclamation. But the Matthew 28:18b-20 Great Commission goal includes discipling nations, "All authority in heaven and on earth has been given to me. Therefore go and make disciples of all nations, baptizing them in the name of the Father and of the Son and of the Holy Spirit, and teaching them to obey everything I have commanded you. And surely I am with you always, to the very end of the age."

How are we to see nations discipled and transformed? By living and teaching the principles of God's word within all of the spheres that influence society. That's not just the sphere of Religion/the Church, but also in the arena of the Family, Economy, Government, Education, Media/Communication and Celebration.[11]

---

10. For more information, go to 4kworldmap.com.

11. See Appendix 3: Legacy Word #2: The Seven Spheres of Influence.

Discipleship is a multi-generational costly process. If we look at the model of Jesus, He spent three years teaching and modeling the ways of God for His twelve disciples. We need to be willing to invest months and years of teaching and modeling into people we lead to Christ. One of the great challenges of the Church today is that many of those who receive Jesus as Savior at a church or evangelism event sometimes don't understand how to apply Biblical principles in their daily lives.

Investing in even one person can sometimes have a powerful impact on a nation. A Cambodian man named Dara is one such example. His parents escaped the horrors of the Khmer Rouge "Killing Fields" and were living in the Thailand refugee camps mentioned above. Dara was born there, and he remembers as a young boy meeting people from other countries who came to help. They played games with him and other children. And they gave them food, clothing, and education. Dara says, "All these things were done by YWAMers. I don't know why they loved us so much. They lived with us, taught us, helped us."

A few years later, Dara's mother returned to Cambodia with him and his younger brother. She couldn't find work and became quite ill. Every day Dara sorted through the trash on the streets, trying to recycle anything usable to buy food for his family. His destitute mother decided that the best thing for her boys would be to place them in an orphanage. But they were all full. Then she heard of another possibility and took them there. She asked if they would receive her two sons. They answered, "No, we won't take your sons. But we will take *you* and your sons. We don't want to separate your family." She later learned that it was a YWAM ministry!

Dara's mom was able to learn a trade there, and he and his brother were able to go to school. Dara met Jesus there, and later completed a DTS and several other University of the Nations' courses. He now has a UofN degree in Christian Ministries.

Dara married a wonderful woman named Ngim, who was also saved from the streets, and they have a lovely family. She went on to direct a youth center ministry, and Dara became the Director of Training at UofN Battambang. He also has a beautiful voice and recorded some of the first Cambodian Christian worship music. Their lives are the fruit of YWAM mercy ministries, evangelism and training, and they have become nation disciplers in several arenas of Cambodian society.

Whenever Dara shares his story with those ministering to refugees, he says, "Don't look at them as children at risk – look at them as future leaders who will bring God's transformation to their nations."

The Future of Making God Known

There are endless creative ways to make God known. Currently, we are only scratching the surface. We are proclaiming Him in great cities and remote mountain villages, in urban concrete jungles and Amazon rainforests, to all generations and people groups. Whenever and wherever we can, we are working to communicate the Good News of Christ in **all** the world and to make disciples of **all** nations.

Psalm 71:17-18 says, "Since my youth, O God, you have taught me, and to this day I declare your marvelous deeds. Even when I am old and gray, do not forsake me, O God, till I declare your power to the next generation, your might to all who are to come."

Who can compare to our wonderful God and His marvelous deeds among the nations? May we never stop taking new initiatives to know God and to make Him known!

Chapter Twelve

Do First, Then Teach
(Value 12)

YWAM is committed to doing first, then teaching. We believe that firsthand experience gives authority to our words. Godly character and a call from God are more important than an individual's gifts, abilities and expertise.

(Deu 4:5-8; Ezr 7:10; Psa 51:12-13; Psa 119:17-18; Pro 1:1-4; Mat 7:28-29; Act 1:1-2; Col 3:1217; 2Ti 4:1-5; 2Pe 1:5-10)

When Loren and I set up the first School of Evangelism in Switzerland, we had a clear word from the Lord: we were not to invite anyone to teach in the school unless they had a passion for God themselves, and they were *doing* what they were talking about. That was the foundation.

This was not a foreign idea to us, because both sets of our parents modeled to us that ministry was their life and life was ministry. The work of God was never a job. They were doers of the Word, day, night and weekends – with great joy and faith because it was their life calling.

As Loren and I began to travel around the world to start YWAM, we often stayed in the homes of pastors and missionaries, drinking tea at the kitchen table until the wee hours of the morning, sharing testimonies of God's goodness. We wanted to have "authentic" people like these teach in our schools, people who were doing what they taught.

We carefully observed Christian leaders and teachers, watching for those with godly character who were walking in faith, full of joy over God's call. When we found people like this who taught subjects we needed, we invited them to teach in our schools. The doing part meant they were up-to-date on what they taught and had authority.

Impartation through Living Curriculum

We thrived on learning from men and women of God who taught us from the Word and from their life experiences. We called this our "Living Curriculum."

Brother Andrew would tell stories of God's faithfulness as he smuggled Bibles behind the Iron Curtain into communist countries. He imparted a gift of faith into the students, and soon they were walking in that same radical, almost reckless, faith. Whenever our students went into a closed nation, they practiced the things he taught them. He didn't just tell them *how* to do it, he imparted faith to accomplish the task.

The same was true of Corrie ten Boom, who imparted a spirit of forgiveness because she had, in fact, walked through the painful process of forgiving those who had killed her father and sister in a Nazi concentration camp. This teaching provoked our students to ask God to search their own hearts for any areas of unforgiveness, and grant forgiveness to those who had hurt or offended them.

When Joy Dawson came to teach on the principles for effective intercession, her examples were often fresh from time spent with the Lord that very morning. There was an in-the-moment impartation into the students. As they practiced and applied what she was teaching, a new wave of students became intercessors.

This faith-in-action impartation has become "living curriculum" within all of our YWAM schools today and into the future. I can't teach about hospitality unless I'm hospitable; I can't teach about depending on God for finances unless I'm living a lifestyle of dependence on Him; I can't teach about hearing God's voice unless I am listening and obeying Him.

Application Must Follow Education

If we don't apply what we have heard, then it just becomes stagnant head knowledge. Jesus warns us about those who hear without doing in

Matthew 7:24-27, "Therefore everyone who hears these words of mine and puts them into practice is like a wise man who built his house on the rock …. But everyone who hears these words of mine and does not put them into practice is like a foolish man who built his house on sand. The rain came down, the streams rose, and the winds blew and beat against that house, and it fell with a great crash." This mandate is also based on the solemn warning of James 1:22, "Do not merely listen to the word, and so deceive yourselves. Do what it says."

In the 1980s, a master educator named Dr. Ted Ward spoke at some of our training sessions. What he taught was wonderful confirmation of the way God had led us to design our schools from the outset. Dr. Ward was pleased to discover that within YWAM/University of the Nations training, there was freedom to maximize formal, non-formal and informal learning opportunities. One thing he highlighted as optimal for learning was a concept called "close coupling," where teaching and doing are integrated. Rather than having years of academic study before students put things into practice, he challenged us to sandwich internships and application closely together: learn, apply, learn, apply. He said this always results in greater retention.

And he encouraged us that even our DTSs, which usually have three months of lectures and two months of outreach, can be designed to have greater "close coupling" so students learn about God's heart for the poor and needy in the morning, and minister to refugees and street people in the evening. Others can hear teaching on how to minister to children during the week, then do an outreach to local children on the weekend.

Starting with our early schools, we also used the outreaches as an evaluation tool. If the things we taught in the classroom didn't work well on outreach, then we realized we hadn't done a good enough job of teaching. The outreach, proving the truth and effectiveness of what we were learning, was as important as the teaching.

Loren and I, as school leaders, stayed with the students because the outreach was a continuation of their learning process. We went together to communist, Catholic, Protestant, Coptic Orthodox, Moslem and Jewish nations, experiencing the world in microcosm. If the things we were teaching didn't work in those worlds, then we needed to find out why and correct them.

Now many mainstream universities offer apprenticeships/internships where people learn by doing. They do so because enthusiasm and retention goes way up. God designed YWAM's University of the Nations to operate this way from the outset, so we don't have a lot of structure to deconstruct to be able to "flex" with this approach to learning.

Connectedness – Weaving the Threads Together

This "living curriculum" impartation and application can be likened to weaving together threads in a fabric for strength and beauty and durability. These threads are the foundations for everything we do in training. The design is the work of our gracious God.

Our school staff must work with the Master Weaver to observe where there are weaknesses in the fabric, where a different color needs to be intertwined, or when application is needed to reinforce the learning. The Holy Spirit brings synthesis so that everything becomes clear and practical.

Competency and Character

We believe both character and competence are essential in those who teach. We sometimes have people from other universities or walks of life who talk about joining YWAM. Though we may need their expertise within our staff, when we mention that we pay no salaries and require them to enter through the DTS doorway so they can absorb our beliefs and values, the excitement sometimes wanes.

From time-to-time we also meet gifted non-Christian teachers who see the good works that YWAM does and are willing to teach in our schools. When our need is great and their abilities are such a "perfect" match, it's a temptation to compromise our values and invite them. Especially at the DTS level, we need to invite only those speakers who have a deep love for God and a Biblical Christian worldview.

As we choose speakers for our schools, we should ask the ruthlessly honest question: "Does this person practice what they preach?" Do they only teach ancient stories, or do they walk in current revelation? And are they "living letters" – men and women of God who have the integrity to be "known and read by all men" (2 Corinthians 3:2)?

We are so grateful and so indebted to the thousands of highly qualified teachers who are men and women of God, who have shared their wisdom and experience with us throughout the years. Many have imparted knowledge, competency and zeal, which have produced much spiritual fruit.

When Loren or I speak at a church or conference, we typically are asked to do one or two sessions a day, of maybe 30-60 minutes. Not so with YWAM! We work our speakers morning, noon, and night! They may teach two sessions in the morning (often with translation), and then meet with students over lunch. Then, just when he or she is about to take an afternoon nap, there's a knock on the door asking a question or seeking their counsel. They may teach an evening workshop too. It's amazing that they keep coming back! But there is something about the hunger in our students that energizes them. I think there is a great sense of fulfillment, knowing they are planting in fertile ground.

When I think about this needed combination of competency, character and zeal, the first person who comes to my mind is Dr. Howard Malmstadt, the co-founder and Founding Provost of the University of the Nations. Though this man had scholastic competency in myriad of fields – he was a "giant" in the realm of science and a master educator – he had godly character and humility to match. Wikipedia says Dr. Malmstadt is "widely considered the father of modern electronic and computerized instrumentation in chemistry." And though he wrote ten internationally used textbooks, more than 150 scientific articles, and mentored many PhD candidates, he entered YWAM through the DTS doorway. He spent most of his mealtimes at campus lunch tables, talking one-on-one with students who didn't even know they were in the presence of greatness because Howard was just like that – humble and unassuming.

The great poet Edgar Guest wrote, "I would rather *see* a sermon any day than *hear* one." Learning from Howard was the "living curriculum" of that experience, and may it be so with every one of us who teach. If we want to impact the next generation of young people for God and world missions, we must be men and women of godly character who are authentic and available. And we must be doers and models of what we teach, imparting faith alongside knowledge.

Our founding scripture for YWAM's University of the Nations, which also should be a life goal for us individually, is 2 Peter 1:5-10 "... make every effort to add to your faith goodness; and to goodness, knowledge; and to knowledge, self-control; and to self-control, perseverance; and to perseverance, godliness; and to godliness, mutual affection; and to mutual affection, love. For if you possess these qualities in increasing measure, they will keep you from being ineffective and unproductive in your knowledge of our Lord Jesus Christ. But whoever does not have them is nearsighted and blind, forgetting that they have been cleansed from their past sins. Therefore, my brothers and sisters, make every effort to confirm your calling and election. For if you do these things, you will never stumble and you will receive a rich welcome into the eternal kingdom of our Lord and Savior Jesus Christ."

Chapter Thirteen

Exhibit Servant Leadership
(Value 11)

YWAM is called to servant leadership as a lifestyle, rather than a leadership hierarchy. A servant leader is one who honors the gifts and callings of those under his/her care and guards their rights and privileges. Just as Jesus served His disciples, we stress the importance of those with leadership responsibilities serving those whom they lead.

(Deu 10:12-13; Psa 84:10; Isa 42:1-4; Mic 6:8; Mar 10:42-45; Joh 13:3-17; Rom 16:1-2; Gal 5:13-14; Php 2:3-11; 1Pe 4:10-11)

God taught me the value of servant leadership in a dramatic way during my first year of marriage. Loren had ministered in many places, so when we set out on an around-the-world honeymoon, everyone seemed eager to see who he had married.

I was so excited to engage in this life of missions, and I went to our first stop with great anticipation. After some initial niceties, people began to ask questions like "Where did you go to Bible college?"

"Oh, I didn't go to Bible college. I'm a nurse."

They looked back at me a bit surprised.

Loren was from a musical family and had been the leader of a traveling singing group, so the next question was, "Oh, do you sing with Loren?"

"No. I don't sing. I just make a joyful noise."

"Oh, surely you must sing alto?"

"Believe me, if I could find alto, I would sing it!"

I thought our next stop would be better. But it wasn't. In the next few places, I was put through all the same questions, and I didn't seem to be measuring up to any of their expectations.

Some would say, "Oh, you must play the piano for Loren!"

"No, my mother tried to teach me, but if you haven't got the talent, you just don't have it!"

"Oh, what a shame," some whispered.

Others said, "Oh, you must type Loren's newsletters!"

"No. I'm the only person you know whose typing is harder to read than their handwriting!"

Then there was another problem. Loren had never travelled with a wife, so he didn't realize there were unspoken "rules" about clothing, hair, etc. I'm not talking about culturally appropriate dress based on location, but about "lady missionary expectations" from fellow missionaries! Somehow my hems were wrong, my sleeves were wrong, and worst of all, my hair was too short. Since having long hair seemed important to everyone if I was to be a "real" missionary lady, I bought a hairpiece that made my hair look long.

At our next stop an elderly woman said to me, "Oh, it is so good to see that Loren married such a nice Christian girl with such long hair!" I had finally pleased someone! Then she asked, "How long is your hair?"

"Oh, it's so long, I can sit on it!" What I said was true. I could take off the hairpiece and sit on it. I was fed up with all the questions and blurted out, "I can even stand on it!" Her eyes got really big! "And I can throw it across the room!" Honestly, that's the only time I lost my self-control over these interrogations and had a sassy mouth!

This criticism of not looking right, not sounding right, and not meeting expectations had become a great concern to me. One night, I laid down on the floor to cry out to God. "Father, You did a miracle to give my Uncle Clare the gift of the Chinese language. Please give me the gift of music so I can be the wife and ministry partner to Loren that everyone expects I should be."

Just then, Loren walked into the room.

"Darlene, what are you doing on the floor?"

"I'm praying. I don't know if you have noticed, but I'm about to ruin your ministry! I don't have any of the gifts that people expect me to have to be your wife and ministry partner!"

He looked shocked. Then he paused and said, "Darlene, you have lots of areas of gifting. I could designate a leadership role for you in our ministry, but I'm not going to do that. This is between you and God."

He walked out of the room, and I thought, *He's the meanest man I ever met!*" But he was right – this was between me and God.

As I lay there asking the Lord for the gift of music, He began to convict me. I realized I didn't want the gift of music to bring glory to Him – I just wanted people to like me! I didn't want these abilities for *His* glory; I wanted them for *my* glory! There wasn't an ounce of servant leadership in my motivation, just a lot of self-pity. I was deeply repentant.

Then God spoke to me in as close to an audible voice as I have ever heard: "Darlene, I gave you the gifts that you have. The ones you do NOT have are part of My design!"

Next, He directed me to 1 Samuel 25, the story of Abigail. When David asked her to be his wife, her response was, "Here is your maidservant, a servant to wash the feet of the servants of my lord" (vs. 41 NKJV). She didn't ask to serve the king; she volunteered to serve those who washed his feet! Then the Lord whispered to me, "I was a foot washer, and I want you to be a foot washer too."

There's no competition or pride in that title: "Reverend Foot Washer" or "Foot Washer PhD."

I reflected on the Last Supper, when Jesus took off His outer clothing, wrapped a towel around His waist and washed His disciples' feet. "'Do you understand what I have done for you?' he asked them. 'You call me Teacher and Lord, and rightly so, for that is what I am. Now that I, your Lord and Teacher, have washed your feet, you also should wash one another's feet. I have set you an example …. Now that you know these things, you will be blessed if you do them'" (John 13:13-17).

I determined I would be a foot washer. I would be a servant to others. I would do whatever God asked me to do, and I would do the jobs that needed to be done even if nobody else wanted to do them. My identity would be as a servant of the King of kings. A great joy came over me knowing this issue was settled.

When we arrived at the next location, we met our missionary hosts, and the wife seemed nervous. She had a paper in her hands and kept fidgeting with it. Then she said, "Darlene, I hope this is alright. I had no way to contact you before you got here." She unrolled the paper. It was a poster saying, "Darlene Cunningham, Graduate Nurse to Speak." She had scheduled me to share at nursing fellowships in that city. I assured her I would be happy to speak. After all, I had told the Lord I would do *whatever* He asked!

My speaking times to the nurses went so well that on Friday night, the wrap-up event for Loren's evangelistic campaign, they asked me to be the main speaker. I was so nervous. And I was afraid I might be unable to think of enough things to say, so I worked out a back-up plan with Loren. I said, "You come sit on the stage. I'll speak for as long as I can, and then I'll turn and say '… and here's Loren' as though it was always planned for me to go first and then introduce you."

Loren agreed. But the evening went so well, and I had such a flow of God's inspiration upon my message, that I kept going for 45 minutes. There was never any "and here's Loren." He was truly surprised! But God anointed my sharing, and at the end, many people came forward to receive Christ.

From that day until this, I have never lacked for something to do. But I want to do it all for God's glory and His pleasure, not for my own. The example of Abigail's life deeply marked me.

Jesus warned us against the dangers of a transactional and "top-down" leadership model. In Mark 10:42-45, He said: "You know that those who are regarded as rulers of the Gentiles lord it over them, and their high officials exercise authority over them. Not so with you. Instead, whoever wants to become great among you must be your servant, and whoever wants to be first must be slave of all. For even the Son of Man did not come to be served, but to serve, and to give his life as a ransom for many."

Being a servant leader does not necessarily mean the leader has to be the one cooking the food or washing the dishes or cleaning the toilets. Servant leadership is about working for the entire community, whether leading a prayer time, doing long-range planning, calculating finances, doing hospitality, seeking God about important decisions or discipling young leaders.

The crowds asked Jesus to do many things, but He understood His assignment came from His Heavenly Father (John 15:19). Servant leadership is first and foremost about listening to the Master, not the pressures and requests of other people! Jesus only did the things the Father initiated – He did not heal all the sick or meet all the needs! I'm convinced that if the enemy cannot divert us *from* the call of God, he will try to drive us to destruction *within* the call of God, by running ourselves ragged trying to please everyone around us!

A "time-wise" friend once told me: God is not unjust. He does not ask us to do the impossible. There is time within 24 hours a day to do the will of God. So if you are complaining, "I just don't have enough time," take it as a warning. Ask yourself, "What am I doing that is **not** the will of God?" Or "How do I need to readjust my priorities? What responsibilities should I pass on to others?"

What Servant Leadership Is

Servant leadership, at its core, is a willingness to lay down our own human agenda and to take on God's agenda.

Philippians 2:1-8 is a clear call to all believers about servant leadership. It exhorts us to do nothing out of selfish ambition, but in humility value others above ourselves. We are not to look at our own interests, but to the interest of others. We are to take on the mindset of Christ, who being in nature God, laid down His rights and took on the nature of a servant, dying on the cross for us all.

At many of our ministry locations, we have workdays to prepare for special events or the arrival of new students. It has made a deep impression on our students and younger staff to see our senior leaders out sweeping floors, washing windows, pulling weeds and doing other tasks. As leaders, we must never project the attitude that such tasks are "beneath us."

When teaching at a YWAM campus, I often pose the question, "Whose role is the most important – the leader or the cook?" Back when Loren and I were more involved in the daily details of the Kona campus, we could be gone for several weeks and the place kept running well. But let the cook be gone for just one day and see what an uproar would result! Every role done with a true heart to serve is vital and glorifies God.

If people reach for only authority it is not wise to give it to them. If, however, they reach out to accept responsibility, give it to them. And give them the authority required to fulfill the job. True humility is the willingness to be known for who we are, including our weaknesses and strengths.

Serve Not Only the Church But the World

YWAMers are encouraged to be servant leaders in their churches, communities, families and any other doors that open in the world around us.

Our servant-heartedness should be consistent in every circumstance, and we should serve believers and non-believers with equal zeal.

Near the end of the Vietnam War, "Boat People" tried to escape to Hong Kong and other places. Many of these refugees died by drowning. Thousands were robbed, beaten, raped or killed by pirates. Many of those who survived ended up in Jubilee Refugee Camp in Hong Kong.

At the height of Jubilee's population in 1979, over 8,000 refugees lived in a building designed to house 800. In one building, only 9 of 144 toilets were functioning. Old sewers pipes leaked, leaving rooms and cooking areas ankle deep in water and human waste.

That year, YWAM sent a team to Hong Kong to minister to the refugees in Jubilee Camp. Putting their love into action, they went to work cleaning, painting and repairing. The refugees themselves had suffered so much loss that morale was low, and many had lost their will to live. But their curiosity was piqued by these young internationals who were wading through sewage and unclogging toilets for them. Their message to the refugees was "you are important to God and to us." Their practical servanthood opened the doors of people's hearts for them to share the Gospel. Ultimately, many refugees came to find new hope, purpose and eternal destiny in Christ.

Because of the Jubilee Camp work, the government allowed YWAM to rent a sprawling, three-story building on Hong Kong Island for a very good price! Our staff occupied that building for more than 10 years. From there, they spawned Far East Evangelism Teams, ministries to the homeless, to drug users, feeding programs, and started Mother's Choice as an alternative to abortion for distraught young pregnant women.

Some Hong Kong staff started Small World Christian Kindergarten, which continues to operate there. Though they know it is a Christian school, Muslim, Buddhist and even atheist parents send their children to this school because they know they will get "the best education."

Take the Banquet Table to the People

A specific mantle of servant leadership for me has been our Leadership Training Schools. In 1989, after leading several of these schools, I gathered a team of leaders together for prayer and evaluation. By then, 85 percent of our senior leaders had attended an LTS, so our question was, "Lord, what's next?"

God's answer surprised us. We came to realize that all the leadership schools held up to that time had been offered only in English and only in first-world locations. The word of the Lord to us was, "Take the banquet table of leadership training to the people. Take it to the two-thirds world to make it more accessible geographically; make it more affordable; and offer it in the languages of the focus region."

Since 1991, my team and I have been running leadership training events around the globe. Our primary goal has been to equip more next-generation, non-Western leaders.

We've led what we call YWAM DNA Infusion events in Cambodia for South East Asia (offered in Khmer, Burmese, Vietnamese, Chinese and Korean); in South Africa for southern and central Africa (offered in English and French, with worship in Afrikaans, Xhosa and Zulu); South Korea for East Asia (offered in Korean, Mongolian, Mandarin, Japanese and English); in Australia for the Pacific region; in Brazil, Chile and Mexico for the Latin world (offered in Spanish, Portuguese and English); and in Egypt for the Middle East, North Africa and Central Asia (in English and Arabic).

Why am I writing about this in such detail? To make a point. Servant leadership requires that we make the extra effort to be inclusive, to go where the people are, and to open doors for others.

Could there be anything more personally rewarding and more fruitful for Kingdom purposes? I don't think so. I feel like the most blessed person on earth to get to do what I love most – investing into the next generation and the next!

In March of 2004, more than 300 YWAM leaders and their families from 52 nations converged onto the YWAM Guadalajara campus overlooking beautiful Lake Chapala, to participate in a Leadership Training School.

YWAM Guadalajara had done an amazing job of preparation and construction. More than 150 volunteer builders had worked long hours to prepare housing for the LTS. But when I and my international staff team arrived two weeks before the event, the three-story building meant to house everyone was only 85 percent finished. There were no toilets, showers or windows in place!

The LTS staff team prayed, and we set aside our classroom preparation and took on the agenda of the campus. We gave offerings to purchase toilets and building supplies; then we rolled up our sleeves and went to work!

Servant leadership is preparing the way for others, whatever it takes. Jesus was a carpenter – I'm sure that in a similar situation, that is exactly what He would have done!

YWAMers near and far also gave offerings and sent staff to help. By the end of the first week of the school we had toilets and cold showers on all three floors of the new building, thanks to the heroic and sacrificial efforts of many!

One day I was sitting in the Ohana Court in Kona, our multi-purpose sports and meeting place, chatting with a friend. A group of kids was playing basketball down on the other end of the court. Just then a little Asian girl approached me. "Are you Darlene Cunningham?" she asked. I nodded my head yes. She said, "Oh! You're important! You lead lots of people!"

I raised my eyebrows and asked, "Do you know what that means? It means I have more people to serve than anyone else." She looked a little shocked, but pleased. Hopefully she will grow up to understand that Jesus, the greatest leader, was also the greatest servant. We are to live and lead with Jesus as our model, serving others so that their gifts can be developed, and their destinies can be fulfilled.

III. We Value People

VALUES

Value the Individual (#14)
Value Families (#15)
Be Relationship Oriented (#13)
Practice Hospitality (#17)

YWAM values individuals as fellow image bearers of God. We trust and honor the word of the Lord in them. We believe in equal opportunity and justice for all, celebrating the contribution of people of all nations, and all ages and honoring the leadership gift-ings in both men and women. We are relationship oriented, living and serving in missional communities, bonded through Christ-like love, transparency and humility, rather than structures or rules. We affirm the importance of families serving God together in missions, with every member contributing their gifts in a com-plementary way. We joyfully practice hospitality as an expression of God's generosity and value for people.

Chapter Fourteen

Value the Individual
(Value 14)

YWAM is called to value each individual. We believe in equal opportunity and justice for all. Created in the image of God, people of all nationalities, ages and functions have distinctive contributions and callings. We are committed to honoring God-given leadership and ministry gifts in both men and women.

(Gen 1:27; Lev 19:13-16; Deu 16:18-20; Psa 139:13-16; Mar 8:34-37; Act 10:34-35; Gal 3:28; Eph 6:5-9; Heb 2:11-12; Jam 2:1-9)

Genesis 1:27 says, "God created man in His own image … male and female He created them." The idea that each person is a highly valued image bearer of the Creator is a cornerstone of our belief about God and humankind.

God created us to have a relationship with Him. We are reminded by the Psalmist and the Prophet Jeremiah that His plan and destiny for each life begins at conception. King David declared, "For you created my inmost being; you knit me together in my mother's womb. I praise you because I am fearfully and wonderfully made; your works are wonderful, I know that full well" (Psalm 139:13-14).

Jeremiah wrote: "The word of the Lord came to me, saying, 'Before I formed you in the womb I knew you, before you were born I set you apart; I appointed you as a prophet to the nations'" (Jeremiah 1:4-5). It goes on to say in verse 12, "The Lord said to me, '… I am watching to see that my word is fulfilled.'"

Wow! God has a design for each of us and watches to see it fulfilled! The gifts He plants within us always find expression, whether we know God or use the gifts to serve Him. As Romans 11:29 says, "God's gifts and his call are irrevocable."

Search for Treasure

One of the greatest joys of my life is helping people discern the unique and good gifts God has placed within them. He has given me faith to help them discover and develop their gifts for Kingdom purposes. I love being a "potential extractor." I believe this is not just a personal calling for me – it is part of God's anointing on YWAM. We believe everyone – staff, student, volunteer or visitor – has something to contribute.

In the early days of YWAM when it was just Cunningham and Cunningham, we didn't have staff to lead all our programs. We believed God would send us the skills needed within the people He brought, so we looked to them with faith and expectancy. When the participants arrived, I asked God to help me "see" them with His eyes. Then I would begin observing their character qualities, personal-interaction strengths, leadership gifts and practical skills. I also asked a lot of questions (and still do!) to find out their interests and what motivated them.

Then Loren and I would select a "point person" for each area – transportation, outreach, cooking. But we all shared the work. Everybody helped cook; everybody carried literature; everybody got to preach or share testimonies. Though we work in teams (one of our values), we learned early on how to spot and affirm leadership potential. Everybody's contribution is important.

If a student who comes to one of our schools has obvious God-given leadership abilities, I always encourage our leaders to let the student help lead the outreach! We want to allocate leadership roles according to character and God-given giftings. This is how we will grow.

From the beginning of YWAM, we have taught about the "priesthood of every believer" (Hebrews 7:23-28). This means we each take personal initiative in our relationship with God. We don't have to have a priest, pastor, or YWAM leader to act as a "bridge" between us and God. Each of us has direct and personal access to Him through Jesus.

Equal Opportunity in Christ

In YWAM we believe in justice and equal opportunity for all. We have a broad door of entry; we resist favoritism, and we love and value the diversity that God loves – all nations and ethnicities, all ages, and all roles and functions in both men and women.

We draw strengths from each of the 200+ nations that YWAMers come from! And while we celebrate cultural diversity, we always choose to honor Biblical principles above cultural preferences.

Part of equal opportunity and justice means we extend ourselves to allow all to have access to what they need. In 1981 Loren initiated what has become known as The Christian Magna Carta. It states:

Everyone on earth has the right to:

1. Hear and understand the Gospel of Jesus Christ,

2. Have a Bible available in his/her own language,

3. Have a Christian fellowship available nearby, to be able to meet for fellowship regularly each week, and to have Biblical teaching and worship with others in the body of Christ,

4. Have a Biblical Christian education available for their children,

5. Have the necessities of life: food, water, clothing, shelter, and health care,

6. Lead a productive life of fulfillment spiritually, mentally, socially, emotionally, and physically.

As a part of our call to justice, we seek to offer our training in more and more languages (the UofN presently teaches in 97 languages) and take initiative to get the Bible into all the Bibleless languages on earth.

YWAM Is Called to be Multi-Generational

YWAM is primarily made up of youth – and it should always be that way. But anyone who has a heart to champion young people is welcomed to be a part. God designed us to function as a multi-generational family, so that our young people have models and mentors to learn from. Many students entering our programs today come from broken homes and have never witnessed a marriage that succeeded. We want them to learn from successful, godly couples and families on our campuses. Youth who pursue the wisdom of these older believers may avoid making some big mistakes! And for the "more mature," being together with young people who are following Jesus gives them purpose and hope for the future.

My dear friend Russ, who in 2020 passed into the Lord's presence at age 95, was one of our oldest "youth" with a mission. He and his wife, Dorie, took early retirement in 1985 to do a Crossroads DTS and UofN counseling courses. For many years, they did marriage ministry in Kona, leading people to Jesus and seeing many marriages restored. Dorie passed away in 2019 (after 72 years of marriage), but Russ continued serving with the Family DTS.

I heard recently that a couple Russ and Dorie counseled had a son who planned to get engaged. The dad said, "Son, you should go talk to Grandpa Russ about marriage. He was a big help to your mom and me." So the young man made an appointment and spent a whole afternoon with the nonagenarian, who gave him Biblical pre-marital advice! Russ is a wonderful example to me of perseverance. He is often quoted as saying, "I didn't retire; I re-fired!"

Value Leadership Gifts in Both Men and Women

In YWAM, it's not the leader who is the "big deal" – it's "Joe or Jane YWAMer." It's Nadia from Brazil and Magdy from Egypt; it's YoungSook from Korea and George from Canada. YWAM was not to be built around the name recognition of one individual. Rather, "youth" was to be the distinguishing characteristic of our tribe: youth, with all their hidden gifts and untapped potential, waiting to be discovered. We knew the multiplication we sought would happen only if we highly value every individual God sends into our training courses!

We are also committed to honor God-given leadership gifts in both men and women. Loren began teaching on women in ministry early in the 1970s. Just as YWAM was considered "radical" for recruiting young people from all nations to short-term missions, so this concept of women having equal value to men and affirming God-given leadership gifts in them was controversial to many in the Church.

Later, Loren teamed up with David Joel Hamilton to address this subject in their book, *Why Not Women?* David is a leading Biblical scholar and has done much research on the Scripture passages pertaining to women. The enemy would love to silence the vast female resource of leadership for missions and ministry, but God does not want that to happen.

Loren has always seen and believed in my leadership. I had leadership roles in my college and nursing years, but when I came into YWAM, I had no great desire to lead publicly. I preferred to lead through influence. Then in the mid-1980s, many of YWAM's leaders began to say, "Dar needs to be on the eldership council." They wanted to acknowledge my leadership with a recognized role. I think they also wanted this because it aligned with our belief that men and women have equal value in God's eyes.

I acknowledged it was time to lead publicly as an example to my "younger sisters" whom God had also called to lead. I needed to be a door-opener for them because I had a leadership platform and support that many of them did not have. From that day to this, I have willingly and happily taken on other leadership roles in obedience to the Lord.

YWAM Is to be an Open Door for Door Openers

In our early days, if a kid came on outreach who said "I think God sent me. I'm a soccer player. Can God use me?" I would surmise, "Well, God must want us to have a sports team. Why else would He send us a soccer player?" Soon a fledgling sports ministry would be born. This led to a great diversity of ministries in YWAM. Nearly every ministry can fit somewhere within our three broad vision thrusts of Evangelism, Training and Mercy Ministry.

One of the most remarkable things about YWAM's journey is how God has placed skilled professionals in ministry roles they could never have imagined. Within our international family we have artists, scientists, coaches, doctors, dancers, accountants, carpenters, chefs, teachers, writers, farmers and other specialists all using their gifts for the Kingdom of God. They are like Oholiab, a highly skilled craftsman and designer who God summoned for construction of the Temple (Exodus 38:23).

One day, a middle-aged man named Doug McClure showed up at the Kona campus. He asked to meet with Loren, who had a "nudge" in his spirit that this meeting was important. As they met on the deck at our Kona GO Center, Loren discovered Doug was a professional cellist. We later learned that he had played for popes, presidents and prime ministers! Doug felt

God was calling him to use his gift within YWAM. We had no orchestra or concert hall on campus at the time.

Loren could have said, "Oh, sorry, we only accept young people." Or he could have said, "We don't have a place for a professional cellist." Or he could have said, "Come back in 10 years and we'll be ready to put your gift to use." But instead, listening to the urging of the Holy Spirit, he said, "Come join us and let's see what God wants to do."

Doug has since started a global ministry called Symphony of Hope. In India, he taught violin to children whose Christian parents were killed because of their faith. Doug formed an orchestra of 25 orphans who have played for many public events. Imagine how their sense of worth and self-confidence has grown!

In Hawaii, he formed Pacific Symphony of Hope, made up of 60 island youth ages 5-17 from Polynesia, Micronesia and Melanesia. Another Symphony of Hope was formed in Bad Blankenburg, Germany, to serve refugees from Afghanistan, Syria, Iraq, Yemen and other Middle Eastern countries. These refugee musicians were granted an audience to play Martin Luther's hymn, "A Mighty Fortress" for German Chancellor, Angela Merkel, to her delight and joy.

Because Loren determined, "If God is sending you, He must have a plan," all these doors have opened. Doug's story is an example that we shouldn't just be looking for people to fill slots in our organizational chart; rather we should always ask, "Why is God sending this person?" Be a door opener. You may be opening the door for a door opener.

Chapter Fifteen

Value Families
(Value 15)

YWAM affirms the importance of families serving God together in missions, not just the father and/or mother. We also embrace the inclusion of single-parent families. We encourage the development of strong and healthy family units, with each member sharing the call to missions and contributing their gifts in unique and complementary ways. We uphold and celebrate the Biblical view that God's intent for holy matrimony is between one man and one woman.

(Gen 2:21-24; Gen 18:17-19; Deu 6:6-7; Pro 5:15-23; Pro 31:10-31; Mal 2:14-16; Mat 19:3-9; 1Co 7:1-16; 1Ti 3:2-5; Heb 13:4)

Our curiosity was piqued! Loren and I were at an international staff conference in Colorado. Many second-generation YWAMers were in attendance – kids who grew up in YWAM and were now participating in the conference as college-age adults. About 30 of them rallied together, and they asked to meet with Loren and me.

Whatever did they want to meet with us about? I couldn't imagine, but we loved these young people, and made room in our solidly booked schedule to meet with them. I am so glad we did!

When we arrived for the meeting, there was a sense of anticipation in the room. We had known many of these young people since they were little (or even before they were born), so they greeted us warmly with hugs, but then they stepped back. They had appointed a spokesperson for their intended purpose, and he stepped forward.

"We asked to see you because we want to say 'thank you.' All of us were raised in YWAM. We have lived all over the world. Most of us speak two or more languages. We have lifelong friendships that span the globe – friendships with each other, with YWAM staff, and with the indigenous people where we served.

"We feel like we've lived in a whole different world than our peers at college. Many don't know one nation from another. They don't seem to want to talk about cultures and how they impact what people do. And we are just so grateful for our own special education in 'international studies' as YWAM kids."

Loren and I were speechless. Like proud parents, we were so delighted and thankful for these kids.

The young man went on to say they felt well equipped with the international awareness that is needed, not only to succeed in the 21st century, but to lead. Most of them were studying or working in missions or within spheres of influence like science, education and communications.

Our hearts rejoiced to hear their testimonies, but Loren wisely commented, "Well, I'm sure there must have also been a downside to growing up in YWAM?"

Their spokesman responded, "We have talked about this, but we all agree that any downside was small in comparison to all the benefits we have received! We want to thank you, because we know you will bless us, whether we use our talents in YWAM or whether we are called by God to work in the spheres. We know the Biblical truths we learned in YWAM apply to every area of life."

They encircled us to tell their stories. And of course, we prayed, blessed and "commissioned" them into their callings before we parted!

In YWAM, we believe in the importance of families serving God together in missions, with each one contributing their ministry gifts as they work together in teams. We believe that each family member is called by God – both the husband and the wife, not just one or the other. And as children come along, we want them to be included in ministry. According to their age and capacity, they should join in ministry decisions that impact the family. This is one of the benefits of being multi-generational and serving as families. It is often the children, like Samuel, who hear the voice of God most clearly because of their simple childlike faith! The second-generation YWAMers we met with in Colorado grew up this way.

The family is the basic building block of society, but it is under attack from all angles these days. Many nations of Europe, Eastern Europe and Asia are expected to have zero population growth (more deaths than births) between now and 2050. Society has pushed for more individual freedoms rather than valuing God's design of marriage, multiplication and creating healthy families. This will have a devastating impact in the decades to come. May our commitment to family in YWAM be ever strengthened as we seek to model and demonstrate God's design for society!

The YWAM concept of whole families serving as missionaries was foreign to the mission paradigm of the 1960s when YWAM was formed. At that time, many mission agencies only "hired the husband" – and the wife and any children were simply part of his dependents or entourage. Often, when children became school age, they were shipped off to boarding schools to be educated. This separation sometimes led to heartache and dysfunction in missionary families.

So where did YWAM's value of "whole families called to missions" come from? The roots of this principle emerged from the living example of both Loren's family and mine. We were both blessed with remarkable parents who loved God, loved His call to ministry, loved missions, and loved family. Our parents made us part of their team – even as children, we were encouraged to contribute.

As Loren and I look back, we realize neither of our families had much money, but we were rich in relationships, fulfillment and purpose. We felt like we had the most important job in the world!

We lived behind, below and above the church buildings where our parents pastored – often in unconventional housing. At one point Loren's family lived in a tent, making bricks with their hands to build a church building where they were pioneering. I don't remember ever once feeling like my family was "poor."

Our parents imparted to us an understanding that we were all doing something important. Because they loved what they were doing, it was contagious. We were not told to go sit in the back of the room and wait, while mom and dad did the "real" ministry. We were included in the work of God and our parents took time to nurture and develop our individual calling as part of how they walked out their own calling. As a family we joyfully gave our money and time to see the work of God grow and so it became a way of life.

From our beginning, YWAM has embraced each individual in every family as a missionary. We have tried to provide schools, have parents homeschool or create cooperative parent-led education programs and other ways to help families stay on the field together. Why? Because YWAM is called to do ministry *together* as family. Our children often get much more time with their moms and dads than many 21st century families. Especially in Western nations, both parents go off to work all day and get little time with their children.

We believe the Bible teaches that it is primarily the parents' role to disciple their children and teach them the ways of God. Psalm 145:4 (NASB) says, "One generation shall praise Your works to another, and shall declare Your mighty acts."

We raised our own children, Karen and David, to be part of our family missionary team. We taught them to listen to the voice of God and obey Him; to be generous in giving, to use Biblical principles for wise decision-making. We affirmed the unique gifts God had placed within them and invested in their development. We were also blessed for our children to be shaped by the extended YWAM family – godly men and women from a wide variety of backgrounds who invested in them their time, stories of transformation and talents. These friends had experiences and giftings that we did not have that deeply impacted our children.

Our God is kind and just in everything He does. And so, if a married couple is called to be in missions, you can rest assured that this call will be right for both spouses, and for each of the children, as God adds to the family. There is no better place to raise your kids than in the center of God's will. He won't call you to something that's horrible for your kids! We grew up understanding that raising families where faith was strong, and listening to God's voice, obeying and persevering was the way things were done. And that's what we have sought to impart into YWAM.

Children as Part of the Team

When we were praying for funds to buy the land for our Kona campus, God led the whole community to take up an offering. Loren and I personally heard God say we were to give everything – all the money we had – to purchase the 45-acre property. Our kids fully understood the vision for this land and this was not the first time they had witnessed a sacrificial offering. They were trusting God too.

The next morning, Karen and David came out with a towel and something wrapped up inside it. They said, "Well, if you and Daddy have given everything, then we think we should too." They had emptied their piggy banks. This was a big deal because they were saving to purchase bicycles. The bikes they wanted cost about $50 each, and the kids were about halfway to their savings goal. But they didn't want to be left out of the big offering.

Two weeks later, some of my childhood friends visited us in Kona. We had such a good visit. Before they left, they said, "Oh, we have a little gift for each of your kids." They were coin purses. I thanked them and said, "I'll put them under their pillows tonight and surprise them in the morning." When David and Karen found the purses and unzipped them, each had a $50 bill inside! Our friends did not know about the offering the kids had given, but God knew. And He was honoring their faith. Giving them a quick answer helped them to relate the two things – their obedience and God's generosity. I've often wished I could get answers as quickly!

I believe God delights to show His faithfulness to children. One of our single moms was praying for a Christmas tree and presents for her kids. She had no money, but she had faith and asked the kids to pray with her. Within just a few days, a Christmas tree was delivered to their home. Then packages began arriving in the mail from people the mom hardly knew. There was no Go Fund Me page, but the Holy Spirit had put it on people's hearts to bless this family.

God First; God Second; God Third ... God Over Everything

Several times, I've heard someone speak on having balance in family life. They will say, "God first, family second and ministry third." I know where their heart is coming from, but that is not what I believe, nor do I think it is Biblical. The Bible teaches God first, God second, God third, God last. He is the author and finisher. It's God over everything!

The Lord is far more committed to our families and our ministries than we are. Doing His will is always the highest and best for everyone. When God is in His rightful place, He orchestrates everything else. He would not call anyone to something that would cause them to neglect their children. But neither does He want our children to become idols in our lives.

Many times parents become concerned when their YWAMer sons and daughters, living without salaries in foreign lands, start having children. They wonder, "How are my grandchildren going to be provided for? How are they going to get a good education?" God knows their needs, and I know from decades of experience that He will provide what is needed for each child to fulfill his or her call. That is the testimony of the 30+ second-generation YWAMers we met with in Colorado. And that is our personal testimony as well.

Our son David felt early in his life that he was to be a filmmaker. He completed several courses at the University of the Nations, but then he needed more specialized training in filmmaking. David applied to the University of Southern California, and when he was accepted, two dear friends whose son had died years earlier felt the Lord direct them to give their son's college savings fund to David. He graduated from USC's top-rated School of Cinema-Television thanks to this gift that would enable him to fulfill his dream.

God is a debtor to no person. He is faithful and committed to family, which is the basic building-block of society that He initiated. When you obey His call, there is no end to the ways He pours out blessing – and grace for the hard times.

I have felt conviction about many things throughout my life, but never about neglecting my children for the ministry or neglecting the ministry for my children. This balance is something I could not have achieved in my own human wisdom. As I have walked hand-in-hand with the Holy Spirit, seeking Him in detail regarding my family, He has always been faithful to tell me what I should be involved with and what I should not. He has told me when I needed to include the children in my travels and when I should not; He's shown me when I needed to be home with the kids when they came home from school and when it didn't matter. There are seasons in life and in the lives of our children, and it's important that we listen to God in detail to know when they need us near, and when we need to give them space for their own development.

Families With A Mission

Since YWAM has consistently embraced the family, it's been a joy to see all the programs, schools, ministries and fruitfulness that have come out of this foundational value. We now have many family-based schools, camps, ministries and education programs around the world that are intent on building up families.

We've heard testimonies from couples that came to YWAM as their "last ditch" effort to save the marriage and save the family. Often the Lord does just that, as their hearts are committed to cooperate with Him. Our school staff members sometimes teach dads who have been absent in their homes due to heavy work demands, how to play with their children. Many have never known how to relate to their own children because they have not made time and had no godly examples to follow.

The Youngest Can Lead Us

King's Kids International, pioneered by Dale Kauffman, accommodates families going on outreach together, sharing the Gospel through music, drama, proclamation, construction and helps of all kinds. They work together in the spirit of Deuteronomy 6:6-7, "These commandments that I give you today are to be upon your hearts. Impress them on your children. Talk about them when you sit at home and when you walk along the road, when you lie down and when you get up."

King's Kids became a dynamic ministry, and they developed an effective curriculum to teach the participants about our amazing God and how to make Him known. As the children and youth came to know God more, their response was one of worship, and they amazed us all with their ability to hear from God in detail.

King's Kids International went viral when local churches picked up the concept and began to run with it. No one knows how many people have been involved with this endeavor around the world or how many people will enter heaven's gates because of meeting Jesus through their vital ministry.

Being Adopted into God's Family

Another ministry where we are seeing explosive growth and wonderful results is with YWAM families adopting or providing temporary foster care for needy children. Just as we are adopted into God's family, we know that it is important for children whose parents can't care for them due to death of both parents, drug or alcohol abuse, incarceration, economic hardship, etc. to be raised within a family, not within an institution.

One family I know of that has two biological children has taken in 11 additional children at various times over the past few years to protect and care for them until they can be returned to a safe permanent home environment. This family was contacted recently by the Department of Human Services who said, "We have three children that need a home immediately."

The YWAM family felt they were to receive these three siblings. They had bruises and human bite marks that their parents had inflicted. One day the three-year-old foster child became aggressive toward the couple's young daughter, attacking and scratching her. The wee-YWAMer responded, "Stop. I love you! We don't do that in our family!" The child stopped her attack. How many of us would have the Spirit of Jesus within us that strongly!

We have many proactive efforts around the world to protect the unborn, care for children abandoned by their parents, and facilitate placement in Christian homes. For as Psalm 34:18 says, "The Lord is close to the brokenhearted and saves those who are crushed in spirit."

Holy Matrimony

The last part of this value talks about marriage, which of course, is a covenantal starting place and foundation for a healthy family. YWAM historically has been a place where singles often discover their marriage partner – someone who is equally called, who has committed to listen, obey and go full time for God!

But not everyone is called to be married, and you don't have to be married to be fulfilled and productive in God's Kingdom. There are singles who are happily single, and we don't want to imply that everyone should be married or put pressure on them. There are also some who find themselves single for the second time, through death or divorce. God is the God who can create something new and beautiful, even out of devastation. There is room in YWAM for everyone who has a heart to serve God and many single individuals and single parents play significant ministry and leadership roles throughout YWAM.

But for those who *are* called to be married, it's important to know that YWAM upholds and celebrates the Biblical view that God's intent for [12]holy matrimony is between one man and one woman. In Genesis chapter 2, we see that God creates male and female (two sexually different beings).

---

12. See "Reflections on Value 15" by David Joel Hamilton: YWAMValues.com.

Marriage is clearly defined by their coming together in covenantal union that is intended to be for life. Genesis 2:24 says, "That is why a man leaves his father and mother and is united to his wife, and they become one flesh." Jesus also affirms this one flesh covenant of holy matrimony between one female and one male in Matthew 19:4-6.

Around the world there are many civic laws that now protect same sex marriages, and laws around gender and identity issues – that is within their domain of government. Within the domain of our YWAM mission and those who have chosen to join it, our unwavering commitment is to be in alignment with God's picture of gender and marriage, as defined in the Holy Scriptures.

Marriage and Ministry Roles

I have volumes of teaching on marriage and ministry roles, but let me just touch on one aspect here. Every person's ministry role is based on the specific callings, gifts and talents God gave them to steward. Many of our young leaders marry other young leaders. When a young woman marries, she retains the gifts and callings she had before she was married. It's the same for the man.

In Romans 11:29 (KJV), Paul says our gifts and callings are "without repentance" – that means, they don't change and we don't "lose" them. When children come along, the mother will have to allocate her time a bit differently. But I have been impressed at how, in young YWAM couples where both partners have strong leadership gifts, the husbands are making sure their wives have opportunity to contribute and lead.

I remember sitting in my office with a young couple who were sharing with me about their upcoming marriage. It was a cross-cultural relationship. I had been close to each of them as singles and was excited because I could see so much potential in them as a dynamic missions team. In our conversation, I remember saying to the young man, "I'm sure you know this, but you are marrying a remarkable person who has a great gift of leadership. She will never fight to express her leadership, but this is who she is. And if her gift is not allowed to be expressed, you will find you are married to a very different person than the one you *think* you are marrying."

I observed that he made a fully informed and conscious decision to support and highlight her leadership. I'm happy to report that, three children later, they are both loving Jesus and serving each other in their respective roles. Their family is thriving as both parents are fulfilling their leadership call.

My Heart Was Asleep…

Since our daughter Karen is a preschool teacher, she often comes home with humorous or insightful anecdotes from her day at school. One day she shared this story:

"Mom, you know how we have both YWAM kids and community kids in our preschool."

I nodded.

"And you know we always have a time when we give the kids an opportunity to invite Jesus into their lives, right?"

"Yes."

"Well, one of the 3-year-olds missed that 'decision day' in class because he was sick. So when he returned to school, I arranged for a teacher from another class to share with him at the level he could understand about salvation. I know that if I am the one to ask the children in my own class whether they want to receive Jesus, they will likely all say 'yes,' just because they love me and want to please me!"

I chuckled at that thought – it's true! Those kids think Karen is the most important person in the world, and they will bend over backwards to please her!

"When this little boy returned to my classroom after talking with the other teacher, he announced, 'I asked Jesus to come into my heart.' I asked him to explain to me what that meant to him. He said, 'Well, it's like my heart was asleep, and now it's awake.' I checked with the other teacher, and she had not used that illustration with the boy – it was his own heart revelation!"

What a delightful, insightful comment about meeting Jesus! I believe that when a whole family's hearts are awakened to Jesus' call together in missions, it will make a difference – in their family, in their community, and in the world!

Chapter Sixteen

Be Relationship-Oriented
(Value 13)

YWAM is dedicated to being relationship-oriented in our living and working together. We desire to be united through lives of holiness, mutual support, transparency, humility, and open communication, rather than a dependence on structures or rules.

(Lev 19:18; Psa 133:1-3; Pro 17:17; Pro 27:10; Joh 13:34-35; Joh 15:13-17; Joh 17:20-23; Rom 13:8-10; 1Jo 1:7; 1Jo 4:7-12)

Whenever I arrive to lead a leadership training event somewhere in the world where we are going to be living and learning together for some time, it is usually hosted by a local YWAM campus. Upon arrival, I always ask them to show me a list of the guidelines they plan to give to the participants because I want them to be able to teach me the principles behind the policies or decisions. I want them to take me down the Belief Tree, through the values to the beliefs the guidelines reflect about God, ourselves, our world, etc. I must know and understand the rationale behind a policy before I can support it.

Some things are obvious, like policies having to do with protecting the physical safety of those entrusted to our care. But others are not so clear.

At one location, they had a rule that men and women could not swim together. The place hosting our school had a sparkling turquoise Olympic-size pool right at the heart of the facility. I scratched my head, puzzled by this "no mixed swimming" idea. I wanted to learn where it had come from, so I began to ask questions:

"Is this something within the local culture?"

"No." I already noted that the venue didn't post distinct hours for men and women to swim separately. The local people swam together.

"Is this a standard imposed by church denominations in the nation?"

"No."

"Has there been some problem with immorality taking place because young men and women swam together?"

"No."

"So, where did this rule come from?"

In the end, I discovered that a female missionary (not from that nation) told the first YWAMers who arrived there not to allow mixed swimming. They honored her input by adopting her guideline. Year-after-year, the staff attended staff conferences in that country – often at places that had swimming pools – but were not allowed to swim together, even though it was swelteringly hot. I was shocked to learn that no one had ever challenged the "rule" and asked "why?" Those in leadership should always be able to answer the "why" question, giving Belief Tree responses for the policies they put into practice.

I said, "I'm sorry, but I cannot impose this rule in a school I'm leading because I can't explain the values or Biblical principles behind it."

The staff looked stunned. "Oh no, Darlene," they countered, "we need to keep this rule because ... well, this is the way we've always done it."

I said, "I won't publicly oppose the rule, but I also won't hand it out and endorse it. We will let our participants decide for themselves. Those who want to swim can swim. If it turns out by week two or three that I have caused division in the camp, then I will publicly humble myself."

Soon the pool was full of people. I watched with joy as mothers, fathers and children were able to enjoy family fellowship and fun in the pool together, alongside their single and married friends. No one ever came back to me with a complaint.

In YWAM we have always trusted young people and expected them to be trustworthy. We did not want to create a "culture of suspicion" toward others. We always want to treat our fellow YWAMers with respect, as peers. We want to help disciple, develop and grow people to be strong in the Lord and to live by His guidelines.

Live by the Law of Love

From the beginning of YWAM we wanted our teams to live as a family, not relate to one another as an organization or business. Our goal was that they be so in love with Jesus they would choose to be like Him in the way they related to one another – loving, kind, humble, truthful, upright, and full of grace and trust.

Jesus said, "A new command I give you: Love one another. As I have loved you, so you must love one another. By this all men will know that you are my disciples, if you love one another" (John 13:34-35). We are committed to this Great Commandment as well as the Great Commission.

So many times it is the love shown between members of our teams – with their multiple nationalities, languages, generations, denominations and other differences – that has had the biggest impact on those with whom they share Christ. It's not our words, but our actions that speak the loudest. People see that we love one another despite our differences.

Walking in Transparency with One Another

During our first schools in Switzerland, we would often spend hours together in small group huddles on the floor. As we talked and prayed, the Holy Spirit would convict us of sin toward God and one another, leading to repentance and forgiveness. This "clear conscience Christianity" wasn't something we demanded. It was the gentle but profound work of the Holy Spirit as people asked God to show them anything in their hearts that was unpleasing to Him.

We came to understand that we could not approach a holy God if we had sin in our hearts. Psalm 66:18-19 (NLT) says, "If I had not confessed the sin in my heart, the Lord would not have listened. But God did listen! He paid attention to my prayer." We also recognized that if our relationship with God was not clear, we could not have open and transparent relationships with one another.

"Holiness" is not a common word in our vocabulary today. But God is holy, and He wants us to be like Him. There is no compromise or trace of evil in His character. He hates sin because He knows it separates us from Him. Pursuing a life of holiness is only possible because of the work of Jesus on the cross. God is not unjust; He would not ask us to do something impossible, but it's only possible with His help.

It's my understanding that the number-one reason people leave the mission field is relationship problems. I believe this would not happen if mission co-workers lived a lifestyle of "clear conscience Christianity." When we meet to start our day, our teams need to be intentional in asking, "How is our unity?"

Starting with our very first schools, we made it a practice to check in with the Lord about whether we had offended God or others. He was faithful to bring conviction, understanding and correction whenever it was needed. As a result, we had tremendous levels of unity and lived the joy-filled life of repentance and forgiveness.

God would often tell us if we had spoken something hurtful to someone, even if we didn't realize it, and we could make it right. These misunderstandings can happen so easily, especially in a cross-cultural context like YWAM! I have determined "I will not pick up an offense." It doesn't mean that we don't talk together to sort things out. But we should never withhold our forgiveness. We know from Psalm 133 that "where there is unity, God commands a blessing" and we certainly saw that in terms of growth in those early years!

People who have transparent relationships will have "open doors" toward each other, allowing them to reconcile disagreements and live together in peace. If they do not have healthy relationships, people will resort to rules.

Occasionally in community, leaders will impose new rules on everyone because of what one or two people did wrong. They start putting up notes saying, "Don't do this or that" or make long announcements about the new rules. The result is that the whole group gets scolded for what one or two people did. If there is a problem, follow the reconciliation plan of Matthew 18. Come in love and humility to the person or persons involved and get the relationship and behavior going in the right direction.

Following *His* Guidelines

When I say that there should be "few rules," I don't mean we should be lawless; I mean that we should all follow one guidebook, the Bible, and we should live the Golden Rule, "So in everything, do to others what you would have them do to you, for this sums up the Law and the Prophets" (Matthew 7:12).

We need some guidelines for safety, order and to facilitate everyone moving in the same direction. But guidelines are meant to serve God's purposes, not to control people. There should be very few, because rules are the least effective way to motivate people toward positive action.

When a policy is given, such as the one on mixed-gender swimming, we need to be able to share the rationale behind it according to our Belief Tree teaching. When a decision is made at the policy level (the branches), we need to be able to explain what value it expresses (the trunk) and what belief about God it expresses (the roots).

In Lausanne, there was (and is) a rule that students can't burn candles in their rooms, even though the Swiss love the warmth and ambiance of candle-light. Why? Because the Canton of Vaud passed a law forbidding open flames in student dormitories. The law was made to protect people, not restrict them. And though it was a law made by the civic government, not YWAM, it was a law intended for our good, which reflects God's value for every individual.

If there is a violation of understood guidelines, this breach needs to be addressed in a "relational" way, which is transformational and brings life. If done in a transactional or "organizational" way, it can breed resentment and relational separation.

If people are only given rules, they often can conform to them for a season of time. But if they are not taught the beliefs and values behind the rules or policies, they can easily relapse into old patterns, habits or sins when they are no longer in that defined environment. In YWAM, we don't want people to comply with external rules or standards; we want them to have understanding and "ownership" and be governed by internal Biblical principles they have embraced.

While some believe "it is easier to control people by laws than trust them with freedom," that attitude does not bring lasting fruit, and it can set people up for failure. Rather, we want to be relational – we want to serve people as mentors and coaches, and believe in them and trust them as God the Father does. We want to teach them His ways and help to give internal-ized foundations for making wise decisions throughout their lifetime.

One of my co-workers tells the story of Rusty, a young worship leader from her home church. He went to Amsterdam to attend a DTS led by Maureen Menard (she later became the Director of the International DTS Centre and a Vice President for University of the Nations). My friend hap-pened to be visiting Amsterdam while Rusty was there, so she asked, "How is your DTS going?"

He said, "Oh, it's great – but it's so much different than I expected."

"In what ways?"

"Well, I thought DTS would be more like a military boot camp, with lots of rules and disciplines. When I first arrived, I went to Maureen and the other leaders and said 'I want to submit myself to you and your leadership. If there's anything in my life that you see that needs to be corrected, please feel free to come to me and tell me.' I was shocked by her reply! She said, 'Thank you. We want to give you the same invitation: if you see anything in our lives or leadership that you have questions about, or that you don't think is right, please come to us and talk to us.'"

This is being relationship-oriented, rather than being led by rules.

Instead of limiting Rusty's service during DTS, they recognized his giftings and godly character and began to involve him in leading worship in the school. They even asked him to lead worship at their citywide YWAM gatherings. He concluded, "Because I was trusted, I wanted to be trustworthy! I grew so much in relationship with Jesus, with others, and in my ministry giftings during the DTS!"

Bible-Based Conflict Resolution

You may ask, "How do I walk in open loving relationship with someone who has offended me?" The first thing I would encourage you to do is to ask God to search your own heart and show you if there is anything unpleasing to Him. Jesus asks, "Why do you look at the speck of sawdust in your brother's eye and pay no attention to the plank in your own eye? ... first take the plank out of your own eye, and then you will see clearly to remove the speck from your brother's eye" (Matthew 7:3-5).

Once your own heart attitude is good, Matthew 18:15-16 gives clear guidelines for how to go to them and resolve the situation in a Biblical way. Remember, the Bible says, our words are to be life-giving – like apples of gold in a setting of silver (Proverbs 25:11).

But, what if the "shoe" is on the other foot, and someone confronts you about an offense or sin they believe you have committed against them?

First, ask the Lord to show you if the charge is true, and be quick to repent if it is. But what if it isn't true? I have a good "lawyer instinct" in me, and if someone pulls out their "you-you-you" attack weapon, I'm ready to shoot back, "No – you-you-you!" But I try to look beyond the person's words and listen to their heart. Their approach may be harsh or unwise, but I find that if I'll take their complaint to the Lord in humility, I often learn something. Look for the truth. Even if the delivery is "off" or the accusation is unwarranted, there is nearly always some grain of truth to be discovered. One important question to ask yourself is, "What may have caused this person to perceive the situation as they did?" It could be as simple as a misunderstanding or a gap of information that needs to be corrected.

One indelible example in my life happened while I was leading operational areas at our Kona campus. One day, a woman came to me and said, "Darlene, I have seven things to talk to you about – five of them are negative and two are positive." She then blasted out all seven like a double-barrel shotgun. When she finished, I couldn't find the two positive things.

Prior to that meeting, I knew this woman was disgruntled. God impressed upon me that I didn't have to answer right away. I was to hear her and respond by saying, "Thank you for caring enough about me to bring this to my attention. I know I have a great deal to learn. I will take these things to the Lord and ask Him to show me my heart."

As soon as the woman left, I cried out to God, "Did you hear what she said about me?! Is that true?" He gently replied, "A little bit." But God's conviction was so much easier to receive than her accusation, and I followed up to obey God's conviction.

Assembling Face-to-Face

Youth With A Mission is not held together by structures or organization. Everyone who knows us well will confirm that! Rather, we are held together by vision, beliefs, values and relationships.

From the beginning of YWAM we realized that whenever we gathered our global family together face-to-face, God would speak corporate words of direction, correction and encouragement. It is so important that we are not independent or isolated from one another!

Hebrews 10:25 (GNT) says, "Let us not give up the habit of meeting together...." In the Original Testament, we see that the children of Israel assembled themselves for events such as Passover, Pentecost and the Feast of Tabernacles. At these family gatherings, the Jews strengthened their relationships with one another and heard the word of the Lord. They told their family history to future generations and maintained their calling and identity. They traveled long distances at great cost, time and effort to simply be together.

And so it is with YWAM. Our staff are spread around the world. And though we stay in touch with instant online communication, we make it a high priority to meet face-to-face in regional and ministry groupings, and from time-to-time in larger international events. Why? Because the relationships we form and the words of the Lord we receive at these gatherings bond us at a deeper level. For me and many other YWAMers, we have an automatic "yes" to participate in these family assembly times. Unless God specifically says not to attend, we must not let time, finances, travel or the hassle of getting to the location deter us from such gatherings.

The Scripture reminds us: "How good and pleasant it is when brothers live together in unity! ... For there the Lord bestows his blessing, even life forevermore" (Psalm 133:1, 3b).

Chapter Seventeen

Practice Hospitality
(Value 17)

YWAM affirms the ministry of hospitality as an expression of God's character and the value of people. We believe it is important to open our hearts, homes, YWAM locations and campuses to serve and honor one another, our guests and the poor and needy, not as acts of social protocol, but as expressions of generosity.

(Gen 18:1-8; 2Sa 9:1-11; Psa 68:5-6; Pro 22:9; Isa 58:7; Mat 25:3146; Act 28:7-8; Rom 12:13; Heb 13:1-3; 1Pe 4:9)

"I have made all the beds I want to make! I've flipped all the pancakes I want to flip! And I for sure don't want to show the city of Lausanne to ONE more person!" I blurted out those ungracious confessions to God during my not-so-quiet "quiet time" in the forest beside the YWAM center.

Every summer since I married Loren, we had been together, leading outreach teams to some exciting new frontier – except THIS summer! Our precious Karen Joy was now two years old. With a newborn, it was simple to continue traveling and ministering as we always had. But as Karen grew and became more active, I needed to adjust how we would live as a family committed to missions.

That summer, I stayed back at the YWAM center with Karen. I remember longingly watching busses full of young people pull out of our driveway, headed on exciting outreach adventures. Back at home base, I became the

Director of Maintenance, Head Chef, Director of Housekeeping, and Chief Tour Guide. I was basically the "leader" of everything, but with no one to lead. I was doing most of it myself, and I didn't like it one bit!

I had always known how to be hospitable from a social protocol point of view – both my family and Loren's family had always served and entertained a lot of guests, but this was "over the limit" for me.

As I stomped through the forest, I asked God how He felt about the great injustice I was suffering. He responded, "Darlene, why don't you see what My Word has to say about the *ministry* of hospitality?" I was dumbfounded. I had never thought of hospitality as a "ministry." I thought of it as social protocol. In my study, I was astonished to discover how much the Word has to say about hospitality (I found 36 references). It springs straight from the heart of God, who is the most generous and hospitable Being in the universe! It is part of His very essence, displayed abundantly through His character! And He calls us to be like Him.

1 Peter 4:9-10 says, "Offer hospitality to one another without grumbling. Each of you should use whatever gift you have received to serve others, as faithful stewards of God's grace in its various forms."

Galatians 6:9 says, "Let us not become weary in doing good, for at the proper time we will reap a harvest if we do not give up." And Hebrews 10:24 says, "… let us consider how we may spur one another on toward love and good deeds …."

The Love of Strangers

The word hospitality comes from a Greek word *philoxenos* that simply means "the love of strangers." In Paul's last letter, he reflected on the memory of a friend named Onesiphorus. He described him as someone who "… often refreshed me and was not ashamed of my chains" (2 Tim. 1:16). A spirit of hospitality refreshes people; it surprises them with goodness; it says to them, "We love and value you."

I learned so much about God's heart of hospitality from the Evangelical Sisterhood of Mary based in Darmstadt, Germany. When Loren and I lived in Switzerland, we occasionally visited their retreat center where a spirit of hospitality reigned. The anticipation of someone else's need, the proverbial cup of cold water for the thirsty, and the laying down of one's own comfort to serve others' wants and needs was all seen as ministry. Their example influenced us, and the vital ministry of hospitality became a part of the fabric of YWAM.

True hospitality is based on valuing others – setting aside your own agenda and embracing interruptions as possible "divine encounters." It is a way to reflect the love and kindness of God, even without words.

On one ministry trip, our family was housed in the home of a Polish farmer and his wife. Our hosts did not speak a word of English and we did not speak Polish, but we all became experts at sign language. We had many meals together around their table, and they showed our kids everything on the farm. After we said our sad goodbyes, I said to Karen and David, "Do you realize these people didn't know us, but they opened their home to us and shared everything they had. We don't speak the same language, but we love and serve the same God. Our hearts were knit together, and Jesus was glorified by their warm hospitality toward us."

Traveling YWAMers have experienced similar expressions of kindness many times. And because of that, we should be the most joyfully hospitable people on earth! As we have travelled and ministered, we have stayed in people's homes, eaten at their tables, ridden in their cars, boats, planes … or on their donkeys, and received their wisdom, prayers and financial support. We are truly a blessed people!

You Don't Get a Second Chance to Make a Good First Impression!

In the early days of YWAM Lausanne, we had a gathering every Sunday night for teaching and fellowship. It was open to visitors, and a man named Donald Hoke heard about the gathering and showed up one Sunday. The YWAMers had no idea who he was, but they were welcoming and hospitable to him, as they would be toward any guest. They served him coffee and cookies after the event and showed a sincere interest in him as a person.

Hebrews 13:1-2 says, "Keep on loving one another as brothers and sisters. Do not forget to show hospitality to strangers, for by so doing some people have shown hospitality to angels without knowing it."

Mr. Hoke went home and told his wife, "Martha, I've just met the nicest, warmest, most hospitable young people up at YWAM." He described how he had been welcomed and fed.

His wife countered, "Oh, they just acted like that because they know who you are – that you work with the Lausanne Congress on World Evangelization – and they just want a connection to Billy Graham."

"No – they have no idea who I am or what I do. Their hospitality is genuine!"

Martha Hoke decided she would go the next Sunday to see if she received the same warm hospitality from the YWAMers – and she did!

That encounter did lead to a strong link between YWAM and the Lausanne Congress. It later opened doors for Loren to become a friend of Billy Graham and to serve on one of the boards for his ministry. God opened that door through a warm welcome in Christ's name to two strangers.

True hospitality may take many forms. The Sisters of Mary taught us to anticipate what a guest might need. So if they have been traveling, they may be hungry. We often prepare for our guests a basket of fruit and snacks and a welcome card. The food basket is a thoughtful gesture of anticipating their need. We provide soap and towels for a shower, a clean bed for rest, and a WiFi password so they can let family know they arrived safely. But even this can become a formality – an "automated" ritual. Or it can be delegated to a department whose "job" it is to prepare welcome baskets. Hospitality is not a methodology, but an expression of God's heart.

Hospitality Requires Hard Work

Being hospitable is costly – in time, effort and finances. It involves planning, purchasing, preparing food or accommodations, decorating, etc. Often, on the final day of preparation for an event (thank God for our value of team!), I'll wonder, *What was I thinking? Why did I agree to do this event? It's exhausting!* And then, during cleanup, as I'm reflecting on all God did through the gathering – the depth of fellowship, the divine connections among the guests, the refreshment our work brought to others – I am always so glad I made the effort. The fruitfulness of the event refreshes my spirit, and God Himself restores me.

Hebrews 6:10 says, "God is not unjust so as to forget your work and the love which you have shown toward His name, in having ministered and in still ministering to the saints" (NASB).

We want our expressions of hospitality to always be fresh, life-giving, and personal – because that's how God is. I have been blessed so many times by welcome cards. Those who wrote the card had asked the Lord for a fresh word to encourage me, and it was deeply meaningful.

Hospitality Is a Requirement for Spiritual Leaders

In Titus 1:7-9, Paul tells Timothy to appoint elders over the Church in every town. He goes on to instruct him regarding who to choose: "Since an overseer manages God's household, he must be blameless – not overbearing, not quick-tempered, not given to drunkenness, not violent, not pursuing dishonest gain. Rather, he must be **hospitable**, one who loves what is good, who is self-controlled, upright, holy and disciplined. He must hold firmly to the trustworthy message as it has been taught, so that he can encourage others by sound doctrine and refute those who oppose it."

Right there amidst the "requirements" of being blameless, self-controlled and able to teach is a requirement to be **hospitable**! Why is it so important to God for leaders to express hospitality?

- Hospitality often bonds people into your personal life and family, as you invite them into your home.
- Hospitality expresses openness and transparency.
- Hospitality models inclusiveness; not exclusiveness.
- Hospitality reveals God's heart of generosity.

My friends and co-workers, David and Christine Hamilton, are some of the most hospitable and generous people I know. David is also known worldwide for his love of numbers. We jokingly call him "Count Hamilton" because he keeps a record of everything – the winning scores of his favorite soccer teams; the number of beds he has slept in during the past year; the number of flight miles he has flown. He also keeps track of the number of guest meals they serve in their home. They average serving around 1,700 guest meals every year. These are not covered by a YWAM expense budget; David and Christine trust God for the finances to serve visitors because it gives them great joy to do so!

YWAM must nurture the spirit of hospitality in all our ministries and locations. We must make it a priority both in personal and corporate finances. We urge our centers to allocate a generous amount in their budgets to this ministry. If we get narrow and stingy in this area, the blessing of God will grow thin. "Give and it will be given to you. A good measure, pressed down, shaken together and running over, will be poured into your lap. For with the measure you use, it will be measured to you" (Luke 6:38).

An Expression of Value

I've been so encouraged to see YWAMers in various cities host bountiful dinners on lovely tablecloths for the homeless, poor and needy. Afterward, they sit around and talk to the people, hear their life stories, and pray for them. After one of these meals, a man broke down and said, "No one has ever done anything like this for me. I have never felt so valuable before." That's exactly the point – God loves and values every individual He created. Hospitality expresses His inclusiveness.

Other YWAM teams have done manicure/pedicure/massage days for teachers in the local schools just to say, "We appreciate you." It communicates to them the love and value the Father has for them, and it opens other doors to minister to them.

A few years ago we were hosting an event with international leaders from several non-YWAM partner ministries. The white tent on the front lawn of our campus was adorned with flowers, and international students in their native attire served the meal. Afterward, I walked out of the tent alongside one of the visitors. I knew their previous gathering had been held at a five-star hotel, but the woman was exclaiming, "This was fabulous!" I replied, "Oh, but I know where you had your last event – it must have been so much nicer." The woman replied, "Oh, yes. It was nice. But that was produced by the corporate hospitality industry; this was true, heart-felt hospitality!"

Whether through acts of kindness or words of encouragement, we want all of our ministries to express to visitors, "It's good to have you with us. It's our pleasure and privilege to serve you."

Hospitality in Different Cultures

As I have travelled around the world, I have discovered that hospitality looks different from one culture to another.

One of my South American friends once said to me, "Yeah, it's nice to have a welcome basket and a card when I arrive to teach at a YWAM location. But I'm Latino – what I really want is for people to spend TIME with me!"

He said those from individualistic cultures may find it honoring to give their guest speaker a quiet room far away from everybody else. But as a Latino, he didn't want to be isolated. Whenever possible, try to learn how best to honor your guest – what blesses the extrovert may deafen the introvert; and what blesses the introvert may crush the extrovert. If you have a heart to bless, refresh and serve, you will seldom go wrong.

People can tell if you're just trying to act polite, or whether you genuinely care for them. Be sure to tell your face what your heart wishes to express. Until I had a revelation from the Lord in that Lausanne forest long ago, I'm sure most of my outward actions were "correct." But it's likely that perceptive visitors could read my inner turmoil.

If you are living and ministering outside your home country, consider how your expressed likes and dislikes reflect on the host culture. Missionaries can sometimes complain about the indigenous people and the way they do things; we sometimes grumble about the climate and long for food from our homeland, rather than being content with what we have. If we convey those perspectives to our visitors, we have done them a great disservice.

When people come to visit, it is an opportunity to express your love for the culture and food of the nation to which God has called you. I assure you, the host people love it when foreigners enjoy their traditions and cuisine. That's part of the bonding link of hospitality. That's what Loren did for me on our around-the-world honeymoon! He *loved the nations* and opened my eyes to appreciate the diversity of God's creation in each place.

Jesus Is our Perfect Model of Hospitality

Jesus performed the most generous act of hospitality and inclusion in all of history when He set aside the glories of heaven to become one of us! He cared for His disciples like a good shepherd. He anticipated their need for food and rest. He arranged a Passover meal; He prepared breakfast for them on the shores of Galilee; and even though He wasn't the host, Jesus supplied wine for a wedding feast. When His disciples were weary from walking, He washed their aching and dusty feet. He was practical in expressing hospitality!

Let's follow His example and reflect His love through hospitality to both believers and non-believers every day, everywhere.

IV. We Are a Global Missions Movement

VALUES

Be Decentralized (#7)
Practice Dependence on God (#16)
Function in Teams (#10)
Be International & Interdenominational (#8)
Communicate with Integrity (#18)

YWAM is a decentralized global volunteer movement. We are united by shared vision, core beliefs, foundational values and relationships. We organize ourselves in apostolic learning communities and ministry initiatives to serve the people and purposes of God. We do not depend on a formal hierarchy but count it a privilege and our spiritual responsibility to relate to eldership circles throughout the YWAM mission. We function in teams, recognizing our need for the gifts and callings of others to see all of God's purposes fulfilled. We practice dependence on God for our provision personally and for any YWAM team or community. We are international, welcoming every nation, ethnicity, culture and language into our movement. We are interdenominational. We fellowship and partner with all expressions of the body of Christ. We value truthful, accurate, timely and relevant communication, as it promotes and sustains healthy relationships and effective ministry.

Chapter Eighteen

Be Decentralized
(Value 7)

YWAM is a Christ-centered, faith-based global volunteer movement, united by shared vision, core beliefs, foundational values and relationships. We do not have a centralized structure. Every YWAM ministry has the privilege and spiritual responsibility to develop and maintain healthy relationships with appropriate authorities and circles of elders.

(Exo 18:13-26; Num 1:16-19; Num 11:16-17,24-30; Deu 29:10-13; Jos 23:1-24:28; Act 14:23; Act 15:1-31; 1Co 3:4-11; Tit 1:5-9; Heb 13:7,17)

Those outside YWAM often find it difficult to understand how we can operate with thousands of staff, in 200-plus countries, using the diverse themes of evangelism, mercy ministries, discipleship and university level training, without having typical administrative and organizational management structures in place. I am often amazed at how well it all works myself, but I shouldn't be, because it was God's design from the beginning.

In the *Starfish and the Spider*, a book by Ori Brafman and Rod A. Beckstrom, the authors articulate very well the concept and difference between centralized organizational structures (spider organizations) versus decentralized structures (starfish organizations). With a spider-structured organization, the strategy and decisions are centralized. Decisions are typically made at headquarters and then passed down throughout the organization. When you cut off the head of a spider-structured organization, it collapses and dies.

In contrast, a starfish-structured organization holds the DNA and the life of the entity in all its members. Uniquely, a starfish has the ability to multiply itself in every cell. Therefore, if you cut a starfish in half, it does not die; you now have two starfish – two living entities. The DNA and ability to reproduce is held within its cells.

The early Church was a starfish movement, functioning for 300 years with no centralized headquarters or formal hierarchical governance structure. The life of the movement was held in a very loose eldership structure and in each of its members. When persecution came and they were scattered geographically, the Church multiplied in those new locations, because each member carried the Church's DNA.

Having a defined structure is not wrong and often governments and nations require it of YWAM at local or national levels. Whatever structures we have in YWAM should serve the people and purposes of God. As a mission we are Spirit led, not board led. We should always be willing to adjust our structures when needed, and we should never try to use organizational structures to control the work of God or the people of God. I know many wonderful ministries and denominations with organizational structures very different from YWAM, and they are greatly used by God to accomplish His Kingdom purposes. But this is simply the way God has called YWAM to function.

I remember well some early intercessory prayer meetings in which the word of the Lord would come to a YWAMer and result in the birth of new ministries. Loren and I were the most experienced "senior elders" of YWAM, but still young ourselves. We would carefully process the "word of the Lord" with those who were hearing from God and encourage them to follow His leading.

"As Much Government as Necessary; as Little as Possible"

As YWAM grew in the 1970s, our leadership helped create appropriate legal structures to cover our new works according to the laws of the various nations where we were working and the needs of the YWAM movement. We never tried to centralize these legal structures or the assets or centralize our people. We always believed – and still do – in **as much governance as necessary and as little governance as possible**. Legal structures in YWAM are not connected or linked together but are completely separate in their governance and stewardship functions. We have worked hard to have good transparent and healthy relationships with our donors, with governments, and with others in the body of Christ. Since the founding of YWAM, we always sought out counsel from other Christian leaders.

As YWAM grew, God gave us a variety of leadership teams and formats around which to gather and make decisions, as we waited on God.

In 1972 we formed the International Council, to provide oversight and a spiritual covering for YWAM's rapid growth. Our senior leaders gathered together annually for an International Leadership Conference, which was later called the International Strategy Conference.

In 1995, with YWAM's continuing global expansion, a new geographic and thematic structure was created called the Global Leadership Team (GLT).

By 2002, YWAM had grown to more than 1,000 locations in 166 countries with over 14,000 full time staff. God brought to our attention areas of drift, and a need to "realign" our hearts with His ways. Our prayerful response also led to a realignment of our leadership structures to keep pace with God and the growing vision and purposes of YWAM.

At our 2009 GLT gathering in Lausanne, God spoke again, warning us not to copy any other government or church organizational structures, using the story in 1 Samuel 8, when the nation of Israel was tempted to reject God's governance over them. They declared that they wanted a "king," like all the other nations around them. The Israelites preferred a visible human king over an invisible, all-powerful divine King. As our global leaders stood together in prayer we cried out to the Lord, "We want no king but You, King Jesus."

As the prayer time quieted and we waited in silence, one of our senior leaders working in India shared a vision he had received from the Lord. He saw people on platforms of various heights connected by stairs. The people were moving up and down from one platform to another via the stairs with no strife or competition. The platforms kept increasing until there were too many to count. And as he watched the multiplication, the stairs between them vanished, and the platforms became all one height – no platform was higher than another. This vision and the 1 Samuel 8 Scripture were a huge confirmation to our senior leaders that God was about to radically shift and flatten our global governance structure. We began to use the term "eldership circles" to describe the leadership platforms our brother had seen.

God was calling us to function in circles of eldership in geographic and thematic areas throughout our YWAM movement. Eldership is not just about being older, but it is also a recognition of spiritual maturity. Timothy, a younger leader, was appointed to be an elder by the Apostle Paul. Some of the qualifications for eldership can be found in 1 Timothy 3 and Titus 1.

In 2014 we moved to a new global eldership structure called Area Circle Teams (ACTS). These included circles of elders who were to relationally and spiritually cover our YWAM movement. This shift created the possibility of unlimited decentralized growth, with new eldership circles being created as needed at various geographic and thematic levels, or for convening events and gatherings.

Growth and changing times will always require that we reassess what is needed, and that we maintain the flexibility to adapt our leadership structures.

One for All; All for One; All for All

Every individual, location and ministry should be committed to the whole of YWAM and not just to their specific area. Those serving in the University of the Nations should love, honor and protect those serving in Frontier Missions and vice versa; those working with Performing Arts or Sports should also embrace and champion those serving the poor and needy; those serving with YWAM Ships should wave the flag for those serving children, etc. We are decentralized but we are one global family!

A principle that has kept YWAM decentralized and fruitful has been God's leading us not to pay our workers, but to be a band of volunteer missionaries. This one decision has resulted in remarkable freedom for God to call and position people where they can have the greatest impact.

When Loren and I tried to pay the office secretary in the early 1960s, our motive was not to use the salary to control what she did but to be generous and supportive of her calling. However, God made it clear He did not want us paying our workers from a centralized fund. Had we persisted in trying to pay staff in the beginning, YWAM would be a small fraction of the size it is today.

Imagine with me for a moment that a YWAMer from Chile named Pedro wants to go on a six-month outreach to Africa. Pedro is embedded in a local YWAM community in Chile where he processes his guidance. He is also receiving his financial provision from family and friends who know him and who are called to support and pray for him. He is highly accountable to his supporters and to the YWAM community in which he lives and serves. Pedro will naturally communicate any updates and results of his Africa outreach to those he is serving with and to those who are supporting him.

Having each YWAMer be rooted in a mission community for decision-making and be responsible to their own network of supporters is a highly effective and multipliable model. These principles of guidance and dependence on God for financial provision, apply to all of our operating locations around the world. YWAM is a decentralized, accountable, united global mission!

The Three Cs: Circles, Cycles, Circuits

Some years ago, God spoke to Loren about YWAM functioning according to *circles, cycles and circuits*. This description was a helpful word for our movement. We've seen repeatedly that God gives us **circles** of relational influence, **cycles** or seasons of time in which to fulfill our assignments in God, and **circuits** of geography (places where He calls us to go and minister). This will only work when there are strong relationships and communication in place. Think of an image like the Olympic symbol, with the rings overlapping and intertwined.

My friends Maida and Magdy from Egypt are a good illustration of this principle at work. They live and serve with YWAM in Lausanne, Switzerland, leading schools and taking teams to the Middle East. But they also feel called to serve with me in our leadership development initiatives. During different seasons, they link teams from Kona to the Middle East. Their **circuits** of geography are Switzerland, the Middle East and Kona. They **cycle** through these places at different seasons because of their **circles** of relationship. Only the genius of God in how He designed YWAM to work as a decentralized movement could allow this to be possible.

When some people hear the term "decentralized," they picture everyone doing what they want, in a chaotic and unconnected way all over the world. That's not the reality of our YWAM movement. God has called us to be decentralized, but it is under the orchestration and leading of the Holy Spirit. We are united together primarily by these four things:

- Our shared vision
- Our Core Beliefs
- Our Foundational Values
- Our relationships and mutual submission to one another.

If you take away even one of these elements, over time YWAM will stop bearing fruit. Our true headquarters is in heaven, and we want no other king than Jesus to lead us.

Chapter Nineteen

Practice Dependence on God
(Value 16)

YWAM is a volunteer movement called to practice a life of dependence upon God for financial provision. For individuals and for any YWAM team or community, this comes primarily through His people. As God has been generous toward us, so we desire to be generous, giving ourselves, our time and talents to God with no expectation of remuneration.

(Gen 22:12-14; Exo 36:2-7; Num 18:25-29; Mal 3:8-12; Mat 6:25-33; Luk 19:8-9; 2Co 8:1-9:15; Php 4:10-20; Tit 3:14; 3Jo 5-8)

Why does God call YWAMers to practice a life of dependence on Him for finances? Because it keeps us humble and constantly aware of our need for Him. He is our provider and we cannot bear fruit without Him. God is the one who prompts people to give to our staff and ministries. This relationship-based approach to support allows anyone from anywhere to obey Jesus' call to go, funded through their own network of relationships, rather than a centralized organizational fund. This relational approach links family and friends of YWAMers together as active partners in God's work.

These partnerships between "goers" and "givers" are how God designed us to function as a movement. We cannot go without those who are willing to partner with us. Our victories are their victories; our challenges become theirs. In Matthew 6:21, Jesus said, "… where your treasure is, there your heart will be also." Those who give to us also pray for us, and their prayers, combined with their sacrificial giving and financial support, are powerful.

This living-by-faith dependence reinforces relationships and makes us accountable to those who give toward our ministry. We reciprocate their generosity through praying for them and their needs, reporting back to them about the ministry and often connecting them to teaching and other ministry resources.

God is the most generous Being in the universe. I could write volumes about the miracles of provision I have witnessed over the years. I see it happening in every DTS as students trust God for their travel needs, school fees and outreach expenses. It has become a lifestyle for many thousands of YWAMers, who give freely of themselves, seeking first the Kingdom of God.

I have seen firsthand God's abundant provision for personal and family needs such as children's education, medical needs, weddings, funerals, vacations, vehicles, musical instruments and basics like food and clothing and housing. I have also watched God provide corporately for our YWAM teams and communities in miraculous ways. We have experienced God's abundance as a mission and we have been blessed with many amazing properties all over the world.

A Call to Generosity

As God is generous with us and as we practice a life of dependence on Him, He often challenges us to give generously. One of my most memorable offerings in YWAM was in August of 1976, when 150 YWAMers met together in Eagle River, Wisconsin.

Just three years earlier at a similar gathering, God had corrected us and humbled us for sins we had committed as we pursued the purchase of a New Zealand ferry called the M/V *Maori*. In our enthusiasm about launching a ship ministry, God convicted us of idolizing a chunk of metal – the vessel itself – pushing Jesus into the shadows. It would be like the crowd in Jerusalem focusing on the donkey that carried Jesus rather than worshiping Jesus Himself, the King of kings!

We repented for robbing God of His glory and the Lord put before us this question: "Do you want a healing or a resurrection of the ship vision?" We chose to ask God for a resurrection, as we knew that would give Jesus the most glory. We forfeited the ship and the *Maori* was eventually towed away and sold for scrap metal.

Loren and I went city-by-city throughout New Zealand, publicly humbling ourselves and explaining how God was dealing with us and our pride. Many people around the world had given funds for the *Maori*, and even though the vision to buy that ship was now dead, we were still stewarding money designated for a future YWAM ship ministry.

Just prior to the Eagle River gathering, Loren said to me, "You know Dar, we still have $130,000 of funds we are holding for a future ship and Operation Mobilisation (OM) is raising money for their new ship, the M/V *Doulos*. They need $150,000. I wonder if God may want us to give our ship funds to them?"

I jerked my head up, looked Loren right in the eyes and said, "That would be the final death blow to our vision for a YWAM ship – so many YWAMers and friends gave that money sacrificially." Loren paused to think about the implications of such a decision. We were both willing to give away the funds if that was what God was leading us to do.

As we arrived at the Eagle River conference, we seated ourselves in folding chairs in a hot, dusty, white tent. If memory serves me right, the worship band was playing "Seek Ye First the Kingdom of God," as others filed in. Soon various leaders began pulling Loren aside asking, "I'm sensing we are supposed to give our remaining ship funds to OM. Could that be right?" No one knew Loren and I had discussed this idea and were praying about it.

Also, during the gathering a word was given that God was calling us to move into a new level of generosity as a mission and that God wanted to "rain down His blessings upon us."

Loren and I conferred with several of our International Council members and proposed giving our $130,000 to OM for their ship. They all confirmed it. Loren then shared with all the participants what God was saying to the leadership. "Let's each take a moment to ask the Lord if we're to give our $130,000 ship funds to OM." A hush fell across the tent. Then Loren asked, "What did God tell you?" There was a spontaneous, resounding, exuberant "YES!" from everyone. Loren then reported to the crowd that OM's full need was $150,000 and invited all of us to consider giving toward the remainder. We then took up an offering which brought the total up to the full $150,000 needed. When the amount was announced, everyone started laughing, jumping up and down and praising God. I don't think I have ever experienced an offering time that was more joyful.

As we broke into worship, I thought I heard rain. I looked outside, but I did not see any rain on the dry ground, so I walked outside to see what was making the rain noise. When I looked up, a rain cloud was hovering over us. It was raining only on our tent and nowhere else! It was God's encouragement to me that as we continued to move in generosity as a mission, He would continue to rain down His blessings on us.

I once heard it said, "If you're going to live by faith you have to give like crazy." God has called every YWAMer to a lifestyle of generosity. We are to freely give of our time, talents and our resources to others with no expectation of getting anything in return. It gives me such great joy to see this lived out by our mission all around the world.

Bring Vessels; Not a Few

Obeying God in detail is a necessary part of giving and receiving because He often provides for His people in specific ways. These encounters with God bring a deeper revelation to us of His character and how He operates.

I love the story in 2 Kings 4, which describes the prophet Elisha interacting with a widow who was in debt to creditors whom she could not pay. The creditors were about to enslave her two sons to cover what was owed. As the story unfolds, it reveals detail about the way God chose to provide. Elisha started by asking her what she had in her house. She replied, "a small jar of olive oil." Elisha then instructed her to ask her neighbors for empty jars and specifically told her, "Don't ask for just a few."

How many vessels would you go and get? According to the effort you put into being obedient, it will be measured back to you. I'm practical, so I would probably go to all the neighbors. I would not go at mealtime, and I'd plan storage space before I began asking. But I know Loren. He would go get trucks, oil tankers – whole reservoirs! And he would go at any time of the day or night.

God speaks "Gather vessels – and not just a few" – to me many times when I am trusting Him for provision of both people and financial resources. In the story in 2 Kings, as the widow obeyed the instructions from Elisha, every jar she got from her neighbors was filled. The family was able to sell the excess olive oil, pay off their creditor, and they even had money left over.

In Exodus 16, God provided daily manna for the children of Israel while they were in the wilderness. In Exodus 17, God provided water from a rock. In John 6, Jesus multiplied bread and fish for thousands of people who were listening to His teaching. In Matthew 17, Jesus instructed Peter to pay their Roman taxes with a coin pulled out of a fish's mouth. God is so amazing in all the creative ways He provides for us!

When Loren and I were first living in Lausanne, we had a tiny apartment. Our daughter Karen, who was about four years old, slept in a small bed next to ours and David was in a baby crib. Another family we knew needed a safe bed for their toddler. She would sometimes fall out of bed and hurt herself. Karen's bed had side rails, and I felt a nudge from the Lord to consider giving Karen's bed to the other family. I decided to ask Karen about giving her bed to the little girl in need. Karen paused only for a moment. "Yes, Mommy. I want to give her my bed!"

I knew Karen would be just fine as she was accustomed to sleeping on church pews and floors. She seemed able to sleep anywhere in her little sleeping bag. But I was so proud of her for sharing what she had with someone in need.

A few weeks later, a man drove up unannounced with the most beautiful child's bed in the back of his truck – and he gave it to us! It was custom-made with hand-carved woodwork, and it even had cute little curtains. Karen was delighted.

We don't give with a motive to get; we give because we desire to be more like Jesus. Our true reward in life is in becoming more like God in all our acts of generosity. As 1 Timothy 6:18 says, "Command them to do good, to be rich in good deeds, and to be generous and willing to share."

In YWAM we are known for taking a lot of offerings. Eliane, one of our first Swiss students, felt prompted by the Lord to give 60 francs during a School of Evangelism offering. She climbed the stairs to her room to get the money and found she only had a Fr.50 note and a Fr.20 note in her wallet. She looked for any other change but could not find any. She concluded God would not mind if she gave more than He had asked her to give, so she decided to give Fr.70.

A few hours later, Eliane came back to her room, opened her purse and was shocked to find a Fr.10 note inside. Just then, her roommate walked through the door. Eliane told her the story of giving the Fr.70 in the offering because she didn't have the right change. Her roommate smiled and responded, "Oh, now everything makes sense to me. When I prayed about what to give in the offering, God told me to give Fr.10 to *you* rather than give to the offering. It seemed strange to me, but I decided to obey God anyway, and I put the Fr.10 in your purse." Wow, God even gives change! He answers prayers in detail, and each time this happens, our faith is strengthened.

"Offerings" do not always have to be money. During a Leadership Training School in Nairobi, Kenya, we knew many of our 110 students (from 50 countries) had practical needs but almost no money. Someone proposed that we do a "blessing basket." We found a large woven African basket and set it out on the lawn. Each person was encouraged to ask the Lord what items he or she could put *into* the basket; and they also were welcomed to take anything *out* of the basket to meet their personal needs. We left the basket out for several days, and things kept being put into it, and other things taken out of it.

One of the stories from that offering reveals God's sensitivity to our needs, as well as His humor. A rather small Filipino man had bought new underwear before he came to the LTS. But when he opened the bag, he discovered he had bought a size that was way too large for him. He decided to put the underwear into the blessing basket. Also at the LTS was a large, muscular Polynesian man who said to his wife, "Well, you know what I need – I need underwear. But there's not a chance that anyone would put underwear large enough to fit my waist size in that basket." You guessed it – when he went to the blessing basket there was a bag of new underwear just his size!

Faith to Endure Tests

Living by faith isn't always easy. Some of our staff have gone out in obedience to God, freely giving of themselves and they have suffered greatly. They have been persecuted, and some have lost their lives for the sake of the Gospel. Hebrews chapter eleven, known as the faith chapter, links faith and obedience. It also links faith with times of testing. Hebrews 11:13-16 wonderfully reminds us that we are all "foreigners and strangers" here on earth. God calls us to live our lives in the light of eternity, as our true citizenship is in heaven. As Jim Elliot, a missionary who was martyred in Ecuador, wrote before he died. "He is no fool who gives what he cannot keep, for something he cannot lose."

I mentioned earlier my dear friend Paul, who pioneered a University of the Nations campus in Togo, and then moved to Port Harcourt, Nigeria, to start a campus there. During a leadership course I led in Port Harcourt in 2009, Loren and I lived in a small duplex next to Paul and Rachel and their two girls. I observed how tight their personal finances were, and I realized one day that they did not have money for laundry detergent. I said to him, "Paul, I'm so sorry that after so many years of serving in YWAM, you still don't have sufficient financial support."

He replied, "Oh, Darlene, don't you understand? Here in Nigeria, there is so much bribery and corruption. Many people want to attach themselves to Rachel and me as the leaders. We are offered favors and finances all the time, but often it is with manipulative 'strings' attached. They are expecting favoritism in return. So I am prayerful and careful about what gifts I accept. If I did not have a desperate financial need myself, turning down the bribes would mean little. But because I do have great need, every time I turn down a bribe, it is an act of spiritual warfare that brings defeat to the enemy." We have seen God use Paul in remarkable ways, and the local people trust him, because they have observed his life of integrity.

The God of Resurrection

A few years after our Eagle River gathering, God did resurrect the vision of YWAM ships and we purchased a large ship we named the M/V *Anastasis*. (*Anastasis* is the Greek word for resurrection.) Since that time, God has expanded the vision to use ships and boats of all sizes to reach coastlands, island nations and up-river tribes that otherwise could not be reached with the Good News. Today we have dozens of vessels of all sizes operating in the nations, and the ministry of YWAM Ships continues to grow and bear fruit.

Dependence on God and His people for finances keeps us connected to the true source of life. All glory to King Jesus, for His leadership, goodness, and abundant provision.

Chapter Twenty

Function in Teams
(Value 10)

*YWAM is called to function in teams in all aspects of ministry and
leadership. We believe that a combination of complementary gifts,
callings, perspectives, ministries and generations working together
in unity at all levels of our Mission provides wisdom and safety.
Seeking God's will and making decisions in a team context allows
accountability and contributes to greater relationship, motivation,
responsibility and ownership of the vision.*

(Deu 32:30-31; 2Ch 17:7-9; Pro 15:22; Ecc 4:9-12; Mar 6:7-13;
Rom 12:3-10; 2Co 1:24; Eph 5:21; Php 2:1-2; 1Pe 4:8)

In the mid-1990s, YWAM leaders in Europe asked Loren and me to return
to Lausanne, Switzerland to "re-pioneer" the work there. The campus had
closed for a season to renovate what we lovingly call "The Chalet," built
in 1903. Then the Swiss government stepped in and required them to do
much more than they had planned: restore the foundations, put in a new
dual-sewage treatment system, build firewalls throughout, etc. It was going
to take millions of dollars – and only a handful of YWAM staff remained.
They were not equipped to lead a project like that.

When Loren and I heard the news of our beloved YWAM Lausanne
being in such disrepair, we were deeply concerned. It was like Nehemiah
learning that the walls of Jerusalem needed to be rebuilt. It's not that we

worship a property or a building; it's that this was "devoted land – holy unto the Lord" (Ezekiel 48:14) and we sensed God's grief that it was now "out of service."

When we prayed, we knew instantly that we were to move back to Lausanne. We did not presume that any of the international team who were serving with us at that time would go with us. But they each sought God's direction, and nearly all came with us as a team to Lausanne. Other key leaders from around the world also laid down their responsibilities to give their support, and came to join our team, bringing their leadership gifts. One of them was Markus Steffen, who later became the President of the University of the Nations.

We had to "gut" the building and when the roof tiles were removed, you could see the sky. Loren's humor abounds in times of challenge, and he would say to visitors, "Some people have a 5-star hotel. We have a 1,000-star hotel!"

One of the first things we did was rent a large building nearby to begin running Discipleship Training Schools and other courses. You can't take a "sabbatical" from your calling! We also gave a generous offering – out of our own great need – for a YWAM property in Sweden that was in crisis.

God was faithful, and YWAM Lausanne survived. Today, 25+ years later, the campus is thriving and "bursting at the seams" with workers and new ministries. They are currently constructing new classrooms and housing accommodations on adjoining land. All glory to Jesus!

If Loren and I had not returned to Lausanne embedded in a team it would have been much more difficult. The strength of team was all-important in reclaiming our inheritance. We faced the challenges together, supported one another, received fresh direction from God together, and prayed through the challenges to victory. I cannot overemphasize the value of YWAM's call to function in teams!

What Is it about Team that Brings Success?

YWAM's value of functioning in teams relates directly to the value of the individual. Functioning in team involves the appreciation of individual gifts, the interaction of those gifts, personalities and perspectives, and the embracing of all of these things for God's purposes. Our teams are to be a mirror of the unity with diversity that exists within the Trinity. And people not only bring their personal strengths but also their cultural strengths.

Healthy teams are the strong legs that take us to the nations. No matter what the ministry focus is, we need our teams to pray and worship together, to seek God's guidance, to receive confirmation, to make decisions and to set out together to accomplish His will. We need all the expressions and gifts of the team members to succeed. And we need transparency and accountability within the team as a protection against accusations of any kind. There need to be checks and balances because we are human beings.

No one individual has all the giftings needed to accomplish the vision, and that's by God's design. When one member is down, the other can help to lift him or her up. God designed us to need each other relationally, and He wants us to seek out those with complementary gifts to succeed in the things He has asked us to do.

We don't want "group think" where everyone says "okay" to whatever the leader decides. Rather, we want to be as "iron sharpens iron" (Proverbs 27:17) where we benefit from varied perspectives and giftings.

Romans 12 is one of the most descriptive passages about the unique gifts God has planted within us: It says that, just as our physical body has many different parts that don't all perform the same function but are all a part of the body, so in team we all have different gifts that we should use in proportion to our faith: prophesying, serving, teaching, encouraging, generosity, leadership, showing mercy (Romans 12:4-7).

The chapter goes on to talk about love, and then continues in verse 16: "Live in harmony with one another. Do not be proud, but be willing to associate with people of low position. Do not be conceited." In other words, do not show preferential treatment!

All I've said about working in teams within YWAM should likewise be true of our working in team with other Christians. YWAM has been privileged to be a part of new cross-organizational partnerships. From the outset, a humble openness to learn from other parts of the body of Christ has added tremendous strength to global missions. Everyone bringing their strengths has allowed these partnerships to accomplish far more for the Kingdom of God than any one organization could have done separately.

Teamwork in Pioneering

In Acts 13:2-4, we see that the New Testament Church "set apart Barnabas and Saul" for the work to which God had called them. "After they had fasted and prayed, they placed their hands on them and sent them off." This is our model in YWAM, whether we're sending out short-term outreach teams or long-term pioneering teams. It is a key for success.

One example of this was from a time when I led a Mega DTS in Kona that had 205 students. As always, I had my "potential extractor" antenna turned on, and I spotted a young DTS staffer named Garth. He had a calling to the nation of Cambodia, and I could see his depth of character. Toward the end of the school, he said to me, "Darlene, after this I think I'm to move to Cambodia and start a YWAM work there."

I confirmed his call to Cambodia, but I said, "Garth, would you pray about staffing one more school in Kona, with the specific intention of building a team of staff and students to go with you to Cambodia on their outreach, then stay there and pioneer the new YWAM location with you?"

He agreed to co-lead the next DTS, and God brought a "bumper crop" of amazing staff who were captivated by God's call to Cambodia. They committed to go with him to pioneer in a city called Battambang. Garth could have gone alone, but it would have been a much bumpier road to success. With this multi-gifted, committed team, their launch went further and faster than imagined. Within the first few years, they were running a recurring DTS, educating 400 children daily in an after-school program, and serving the community in orphanages, hospitals and churches.

There is strength and multiplication through functioning in team! As Deuteronomy 32:30 says, "One can put a thousand to flight and two can put ten thousand."

No Lone Rangers

While we encourage people to discover their unique ministry giftings, we don't want to produce lone rangers or super stars. A person who tries to pioneer a new ministry all on their own, usually fails quickly. We work in teams because that is our anointing. In the New Testament we see that Jesus worked in a team. He nearly always had at least three and usually twelve disciples living, eating and ministering with Him. So why would we ever think we could "go it alone?"

One thing I tell those who come to work with me is this: "I am not a threatened leader. If you have an idea or a better way of doing things, offer it. If you think I may be missing the mark, ask me to explain the principle behind a decision. If I can't give the rationale based on my professed values and beliefs, then I *need* you to challenge me, because I need to be able to explain the rationale so that others can learn!" We should not be afraid of others' strengths, but rather welcome them and call them forth so that we can all do a better job for the Kingdom!

Yes, Let's Do It!

When Loren shared the vision for YWAM with his friends and mentors, Bob and Lorraine Theetge in early 1960, they did not say "that's a good idea, Loren. You should do it." They responded, "Yes, let's do it!" They included themselves in the team to help pioneer this radical new mission. And they did! They faithfully gave invaluable advice and support in the fledgling early years.

During YWAM's 50th anniversary, at the outset of each of the 44 events around the world, I would go to the stage and express how thankful we were to every individual who had helped YWAM be what it has become – pastors, teachers, supporters, parents, businessmen, doctors, government officials and so on – all those who so many times had responded to God's call, like Bob and Lorraine did. We would not have survived without them then – nor would we want to! We are so grateful for the close partnerships YWAM has with other missions, organizations and denominations. These are increasing, especially around global initiatives like Ending Bible Poverty.

Luminaries, Translators and Implementers

I use an illustration of team that many have found helpful. Think of our giftings like different sets of glasses. On one end of the spectrum are binoculars, with which a person can see far away. Next are distance lenses that enable us to read road signs. Then there are reading glasses that enlarge the print on a computer, phone or book. At the far end is a magnifying glass that allows us to see even the tiniest lines on a roadmap.

Loren's visionary gift is like binoculars. He sees things far out in the future. His vision for YWAM Ships and University of the Nations was like that. He joyfully carried these dreams in his head and in his heart for many years before he ever spoke about them.

Accountants and bookkeepers are good examples of people who are gifted to see through a magnifying glass. They want everything to be done with excellence and integrity down to the smallest detail. In the YWAM context, the visionary needs to appreciate the gift of the accountant and honor him/her by turning in receipts so that person can do their job well. And the accountant needs to appreciate the gift of the visionary who leads us into God's productive purposes.

I find myself in between these two extremes. I think of myself as a translator of the vision. I "get" what the visionary is seeing and can embrace it. But I also can see what the vision will "cost" in terms of man-hours, resources and finances. So I try to help the visionary to appreciate those who must get onboard to implement the vision; and I try to help the people understand the heart of the visionary, addressing the "why" and helping them to work out the "how." Nothing will quench vision faster than a naysayer who, upon hearing a vision proclaimed, shoots back ten reasons why it can't succeed. It is far better to listen to the vision, take it to the Lord in prayer, asking whether it is something you're to be a part of, and if so, how.

At an anniversary event in Kona, Dean Sherman said, "Look at Loren and Dar and the way they work together. I've been observing them for five decades. Loren gets the big 'what.' Darlene gathers the people around her and works out the 'who' and the 'how.'" It's true. All of us should listen for the word of the Lord, but Loren seems to hear Him in a broad-strokes way for the whole mission. I help to "translate it." I help people understand the "why" and the practical application of "how to do it." Add perseverance to all that teamwork, the "I won't quit" spirit, and that's how the vision gets accomplished, by the power of the Holy Spirit.

Cross-Cultural and Cross-Generational Communities

Teamwork presents special challenges when co-workers come from different cultures. They often have different concepts of personal privacy, ownership, time, correction, honoring elders, and a myriad of other topics.

Some cultures are very "direct" and will tell you exactly what they think, not to offend you, but to be truthful. Other cultures are more indirect. A question as simple as "would you like a cup of coffee" can be a problem in some cultures. To them, it would be impolite to say "yes" the first time you ask! You need to ask them in different ways. After they have been asked several times, if they really do want coffee, they will say, "Yes, please."

People from individualistic cultures often prefer "alone" time, whereas people from group cultures typically want to be with others much of the time.

When I first began working with one young Asian woman, she became irritated with me because whenever she brought a problem to me, I would ask her, "What do *you* think?" I recognized she had a strength of leadership that I wanted to draw upon. But I came to discover that in her culture, leaders do not seek opinions from their workers. My questions made her wonder, *Why is she asking me? She is the leader! It is her job to know the answer and to tell me what to do!* She has since become quite an experienced "critical thinker." Jesus often asked His disciples questions as a form of teaching. It's not Western thinking. It's a Biblical model!

Another thing to consider is, how do people in this culture relate to their elders? Some cultures have a strong respect for elders. This can be good, if they try to learn from those who are older and wiser. But it can be negative if the culture does not allow the younger to ask questions of the older.

How can we, from outside those cultures, know these things? It takes time, observation skills, and an unoffendable heart, where your motivation is to understand and know your brother or sister.

There Is More than One Way to Kill a Giant

In YWAM, we want to be multi-generational as well as multi-cultural, making adjustments to draw upon the benefits and strengths of everyone.

A good example of cross-generational communication is found in the Original Testament story of young David going out to confront Goliath. King Saul respected his bravery, but he tried to "protect" David by having him wear his armor. Saul had won many battles wearing that armor – so he assumed it would be good for David too. But there is more than one way to kill giant. Young David relied on his youthfulness and the fighting skills he learned tending sheep. David went into battle with a slingshot and five small stones.

A senior leader's job is to make sure the team is prepared for battle with the overall vision, beliefs and values. But the application may look very different in the next generation. Our senior leaders should be careful not to put "Saul's armor" on the next generation.

Don't Compare Yourself

Everything in our cultures and families sets us up for comparisons. In school our grades are compared, but also things like our dress, our size, our speed, our speech. And we've also seen ads that imply, "If you drive *this* car, you'll be cool" or "if you drink *this* diet drink, you will look like the swimsuit model in the ad." Those ads are empty promises. I could swim in diet cola, and I would never have her legs! If we compare ourselves and feel inferior, and we back down from contributing the gift God has placed within us, then the enemy has won a battle. He is fighting to defeat every individual and every organization committed to Jesus. He wants to keep us from accomplishing the great things God wants to do through us.

We are like an orchestra with many members, with very different skills, but all necessary for success. But on the day of the concert, what if the sound guy doesn't turn up? Or what if the janitor doesn't show up with the key to unlock the bathrooms? All these gifts are supposed to work together.

God the Father is the composer, and the Holy Spirit is the conductor, giving each of us the music to play as we keep our eyes on Jesus. Maybe I have a tiny little piccolo flute, which has a small but distinct sound. But what if I get jealous of the drummer because he has such a loud, emphatic sound to his drums? If I begin to focus on him, I will mess up the part I'm supposed to play. When the conductor gives me the cue to play my piccolo, I will miss my notes because I'm focusing on someone else's instrument. I cause disharmony in the orchestra and the music isn't what it is intended to be because my part is missing. Every contribution is important. God designed you to play a special part. Just use whatever gifts He gives you for His glory.

You can't create orchestra music alone. We need each other. And when we play in a beautiful spirit of unity, people will surely see and glorify Jesus.

Chapter Twenty-One

Be International and Interdenominational
(Value 8)

YWAM is international and interdenominational in its global scope as well as its local constituency. We believe that ethnic, linguistic and denominational diversity, along with redeemed aspects of culture, are positive factors that contribute to the health and growth of the Mission.

(Gen 12:1-4; Gen 26:2-5; Psa 57:9-10; Jer 32:27; Dan 7:13-14; Act 20:4; 1Co 12:12-31; Eph 4:1-16; Col 3:11; Rev 7:9)

My love affair with cultures and nations began when I was in my teens. My parents moved from the West Coast to Akron, Ohio, where my dad became the pastor of an established church. The city's huge Goodyear Tire factory attracted workers from many nations – Greeks, Italians, Ukrainians, Hungarians, Czechoslovakians, and Russians to name a few. Many people from these nations attended Dad's church.

I had never been around such a diversity of ethnicities! I loved their accents, their sometimes loud and animated conversations, their different ways of looking at things. And oh, I loved their foods! I got "adopted" into several immigrant families, and I embraced being "international." Sharing in these cultures made me "spoiled for the ordinary."

One evening after a message on missions at church, I sat frozen in my seat. I was 14 years old. My friends were waiting for me to join them for fries and Cokes™. But God was not done with me. I started to weep. In my mind, I was seeing the faces of people from India and God was sharing with me His compassion for them.

Out of the corner of my eye, I could see my friends waiting for me, but my encounter with God continued. He was imparting into me His heart for the nations. I eventually left with my friends, but I continued to weep in the back seat of the car, feeling the richness of God's love for *all* peoples. This experience with the Lord marked my life. I soon led two special friends to the Lord – Jeanie, an immigrant from Czechoslovakia, and Teresa, who was of African American descent.

I think to be a true YWAMer, one must have a love for the nations. Loving the nations is about seeing them as fellow image bearers of God – having a heart to reach them for Christ and to equip them to fulfill their God-given destiny.

We Are International in Scope and Constituency

On one of Loren's first international trips, he spoke to a group of young Nigerians about the Great Commission. He had challenged them to become missionaries. After the meeting, the Western missionary who was hosting Loren, pulled him aside, "Loren, you can't speak this way; these are natives; they can't be missionaries; *we* are the missionaries," he said, pointing to himself and Loren.

Loren gently responded, "But *their* Bible says the same as mine. It commands them, too, to 'go into all the world.'" The missionary thought for a moment. "You're right, I have never considered it that way." He was doing missions with the paradigm taught by other Western missionaries. But YWAM has become a truly international and interdenominational mission by welcoming all to participate.

Lily, a young Mexican YWAMer, mobilized a team of Mexican youth to partner with a Mexican pastor who had received many U.S. and Canadian teams. Upon arrival, she let the pastor know that the team of 15 missionaries had arrived.

The pastor welcomed Lily and said, "I want to go greet our guest missionaries!" He went to the van, looked inside, closed the door, and said, "I don't see the missionaries." Lily opened the van door again and said, "Here are the missionaries!" The pastor bluntly said to her, "They are not missionaries, they are Mexicans." Undeterred, Lily took the next few moments to explain to the pastor that the Great Commission of Christ was to be obeyed by all believers, including Mexicans.

YWAM is growing fastest in what used to be considered missionary receiving nations. There is a global acceleration around the world of waves of young people coming from everywhere and going to everywhere. Lily, now married, is serving as a missionary in Spain.

I get concerned whenever I observe that the primary make-up of staff and leaders at any given YWAM location is all from one language group, one nation or one culture. If I inquire about why their location lacks any international staff, they often respond, "Oh, we are international – we take teams to other nations." While such outreaches are part of what it means to be international, it's an incomplete picture of how God wants us to work. At any given YWAM location, the host nation will often be the majority (sometimes because of visa restrictions), but we need to keep making room for internationals to serve and be involved in leadership. We must be intentional in thinking of ways to draw them – language courses, bilingual DTSs, foods, etc. We can help the world get a bigger picture of missions.

YWAMers hold more than 200 passports, and we have had teams serving in every nation. Loren himself has been to every country on earth, and many of our other leaders have ministered in dozens of nations. We endeavor to follow the model of the Apostle Paul, who went to many nations and had different cultures, languages, ethnicities and nationalities on his missionary team.

God Redeems Cultures

In 1980 God raised up a ministry led by Pacific Islanders called Island Breeze. He was using them to redeem their culture's music, dance and celebration back to His purposes. If the Good News is to become relevant to all cultures, then it must be expressed appropriately in and by those cultures. I am not talking about syncretism, the blending of different religions and cultures, for we are called to worship the one true God, the God of the Bible. Our goal is to encourage indigenous peoples to worship Him using their own language, their own songs and instruments, and their own culturally relevant expressions.

Many early missionaries imported their own cultures and tried to impose it upon the "natives" as a part of their evangelism. In the South Pacific, where Island Breeze originated, the first missionaries imposed Western style of dress, Western forms of music (with printed hymnals) and stained-glass windows. These things were peculiar and irrelevant to the islanders the missionaries were giving their lives to reach. Forcing Western culture on people in the name of Christianity became known as "cultural colonization."

Island Breeze modeled for YWAM and others how God could redeem cultural expressions in all areas of life, while keeping Christ at the center. In Revelation 7:9, we read that a great multitude no one can count of redeemed people are gathered around the throne of Christ from every nation, tribe, ethnicity, and language. God wants to work through the culture and languages of the nations, and He wants to receive the glory embedded within them in worship. Island Breeze teams use cultural dress, dance and island-style music to worship God and to reach the lost. In their pioneering years, some pastors opposed this because these forms seemed so different from their own cultural norms. Some declared these cultural expressions as being "of the devil."

Island Breeze persevered in their belief that God was the creator of culture, language, art and music, and delighted in different forms of celebration and worship. In the early days, much of their time was spent in prayer, seeking God's heart and desiring to reflect His character in all that they did, especially His purity. They believed they had heard from God about "redeeming culture," they obeyed, and they didn't give up!

Of course, no culture is perfect, and if something is evil in a culture, we should stand against it. But a musical instrument, for example, is not bad just because historically it was used for pagan worship. That same kind of instrument can be used to worship Jesus, and that is what is happening around the world. I love seeing the Korean fan dance used to worship King Jesus, with all its grace and colorful beauty – or to hear the powerful sound of Korean drums. I love the beauty of African worship with all its creative dance and energetic voices lifted high in praise to God. I love the beauty and harmonies of Tongan "sweet song." I believe we are called to celebrate the beauty of the nations and their languages and cultures.

When YWAMers meet in different parts of the world, we always have translation, often in multiple languages. At Target World, prior to the Atlanta Olympics' outreach in 1996, 6,000 King's Kids came together from 100 nations. They had 21 translators to serve all 22 languages represented – our YWAM record. We do translation because we honor God's people and their languages. Our translators are some of the best in the world, and they play a significant role in helping multiply the work God is doing through YWAM.

As we embrace the richness of the nations and move across geographic, cultural and linguistic boundaries, God often uses creative cultural expressions to break strongholds that have held people in bondage to the evil one.

At our Viva Latin America conference in 2005, some 1,600 YWAMers from 80+ countries gathered in Belo Horizonte, Brazil. The hallways were filled with happy reunions, and there was much excitement as we met the first morning. But I was not prepared for what happened next.

Two indigenous people from the Amazon, Naru and Xagani, stood alone on the stage with painted faces and long orange feathers through their ears. There was no music band, no spotlights – just two people clothed in the unusual beauty of their culture. As they began to sing, a hush fell over the crowd. It was as if time stood still. Their voices blended and cascaded in wonderful foreign sounds, inviting the Holy Spirit to come and bless the conference. It was a holy moment – a sound from heaven never before heard outside of the Amazon, and I was a witness! Twenty years prior, their remote Amazon tribe had not known Jesus. Now through the ministry of YWAM, the Life Giver had come to dwell with them. This music was an expression of God's truth having permeated their culture. I will never forget that moment of being infused with sounds of heavenly wonder.

During one of our leadership schools in Tonga a student asked me in class, "Darlene, what should we embrace of our own culture and what should we discard as unrighteous?" This question needed a thoughtful answer. As I pondered how to respond, the student continued talking. "Also, what should we embrace of others' cultures and what should we avoid?"

Every eye was riveted on me, as I moved away from the podium and toward the class. I said, "I believe the Bible is our only textbook for defining what is godly or holy. It helps us to see what parts of culture came from God and can be redeemed by God." The context of my comments was to 200-plus students from 42 nations, speaking 60 different languages. The novelty of all these people and nations being together in tight accommodations and challenging circumstances had worn off weeks before, and I sensed the students may be letting their cultures become obstacles rather than bridges. The issue of culture in a mission as diverse as YWAM is complex. It involves the laying down of rights to see real breakthrough.

Sensing it was the right moment and empowered by the Holy Spirit, I said, "God intends our diversity of cultures to be blessings, not barriers, as we are called to serve the Lord Jesus together in this mission. YWAM is called to *be* international, not just to involve many nationalities. The very essence of our movement requires each one of us to wholeheartedly embrace our international identity – you can't truly be a YWAMer without this."

I paused for a moment to give the Holy Spirit time to bring revelation to each student. God began moving among us, and forgiveness and reconciliation began to take place. To my delight, God was doing more than just reconciling us. He imparted a deep appreciation for one another and our diversity of cultures. A new level of joy and grace was upon us all in understanding our call to be truly international.

Every human being tends to be ethnocentric. The language and culture we were brought up in seem "normal" to us, and it impacts how we think about the world and relate to each other. It can be challenging to become truly international. We all have cultural blind spots that affect the way we think.

I believe the key to redeeming cultures and the celebration of beauty of the nations is rooted in everyone first embracing "Jesus culture" as our standard. He is to be Lord over all cultures. In all our diverse missional communities around the world, we look to Jesus as our example for doing life together. In the places where we are most international and most embracing of Jesus culture, we have the most fruitfulness and joy in community life.

Racism is one of the most divisive and destructive forces in society today. We stand against racism by virtue of our lifestyle, which is a model of the unity found in Jesus. When He said to "love one another," He didn't mean to just love those who are like us. As Loren sometimes points out, the words "race," "racism" and "racial" are not found in Scripture. We are all part of *one* race – the human race. But within our race, we have the joy and beauty of many ethnicities and cultures.

We Are Interdenominational

Growing up as a pastor's daughter, I always loved the local church, but no one I knew worked interdenominationally. Pastors and their congregations tended to only relate within their own denomination. In rare cases around a major event like a Billy Graham crusade, pastors might connect with each other, but it was not the norm.

When we said we believed YWAM was to be interdenominational, Christian leaders told us we were making a huge mistake, and that it was never going to work. It was difficult to find a model to follow.

But when we launched our first School of Evangelism, we reached out to speakers from various denominations. Yes, there were minor theological differences, but our commitment to look to God's Word as our authoritative guide for life helped us to receive from one another. Many healthy discussions around the dinner table pushed us to be founded upon the Word rather than upon our own opinions.

We have received immense spiritual riches through different parts of the body of Christ from around the world. We love our Baptist friends with their emphasis on personal salvation and water baptism; the Lutherans and their contribution from their roots in the Reformation; the Methodists who help bring the Church a method for reading the Bible; the Pentecostals with their emphasis on the gifts of the Holy Spirit; the Congregationalists with their spirit of inclusion; the charismatics with their free-flowing worship and anticipation of signs and wonders. We love the beauty of the liturgy of the Anglicans, Orthodox and Catholics, especially when the Spirit of God breathes fresh life into those ancient paths. We love and benefit from the strength of a variety of denominational perspectives, both in our teachers and in our participants.

YWAM may not be a good fit for everyone, but for the millions of people around the world who have participated with us since it began in 1960, it is a glimpse of the unity we will have in heaven. We are so thankful for having been a melting pot of denominations and nations.

God has given us some wisdom and principles for how we do life together in YWAM. For example, you do not have to be a charismatic to be a YWAMer, but you cannot be anti-charismatic. All our staff are encouraged to attend a local church, and they are free to choose which denomination they want to fellowship with. The broader we spread into local churches, the better. This allows us to both receive from and fellowship with hundreds of different denominations around the world. And we are also known at a deeper level by the body of Christ because of the relationships we develop where we live and minister.

One key reason God called YWAM to be interdenominational is because we so often partner with others in the body of Christ to fulfill the Great

Commission. We love being used by God as a bridge, linking many groups together to accomplish His purposes. Often churches and denominations that don't know each other know YWAM. As these groups work with us, we often have the privilege of being the connector that brings them together. Over many decades, the Lord has used our YWAM leaders to convene and to host citywide, national and even global initiatives and events that help connect denominations, pastors and mission leaders. Our teachers regularly speak to other missions and in churches around the world. This cross-pollination in the global body of Christ brings life and unity among God's people.

One amazing incident happened at Amsterdam 2000's World Conference of Evangelists, sponsored by the Billy Graham Evangelistic Association, which drew some 10,000 evangelists representing many nations. Dr. Steve Douglass of Campus Crusade for Christ (Cru) and Mark Anderson of YWAM, were among them. During one of the breakout sessions, various mission and denominational leaders were gathered around 75 small tables to discuss the question, "What would it take to complete the Great Commission?" Dr. Douglass and Mark were seated together at Table #71. For 20 hours spread over several days, the 600 delegates had been shown a list of 253 unengaged, unreached people groups – ethnic groups from all around the world that had never received the Good News of Jesus in their language.

That day, the leaders present were asked to "adopt" one or more of these unengaged, unreached groups, and 140 of the 232 groups were adopted by organizations in attendance. But 92 of the most difficult-to-reach groups still needed to be adopted. The room grew silent with inactivity. That is when Dr. Douglass leaned over and asked Mark, "Why don't our two organizations adopt the rest?" With his mind spinning over the implications of such a partnership, Mark in faith agreed, and a whole new adventure began. Soon other organizational leaders from other tables came over to join Dr. Douglass and Mark as they formed a multi-denominational group called *Table 71* to work together in reaching every unengaged, unreached people group.

Several years later the Call2All Movement was launched under Mark's leadership. Their vision was to help the global body of Christ come into strategic unity with heaven to reveal Jesus on the earth, leading to the completion of the Great Commission. The Call2All Movement has strategically brought together tens of thousands of leaders from all over the world, representing more than 1,400 organizations, all united in the cause of reaching the least, the last and the lost.

Through these ongoing partnerships a new dimension of unity has developed in the body of Christ and God has privileged YWAM to be a key catalyst of this global movement.

I love Psalm 133, which says it is good and pleasant when God's people live together in unity. When we do, He **commands** a blessing!

Chapter Twenty-Two

Communicate with Integrity
(Value 18)

YWAM affirms that everything exists because God communicates. Therefore, YWAM is committed to truthful, accurate, timely and relevant communication. We believe good communication is essential for strong relationships, healthy families and communities, and effective ministry.

(Gen 1:3-5; Num 23:19; Pro 10:19; Pro 25:9-14; Zec 8:16-17; Mat 5:33-37; Luk 4:16-22; Joh 1:15; Col 4:6; Jam 3:1-18)

God is the master communicator! Everything exists because He communicates. He spoke, and the universe came into existence! John 1:1-4 tells us "In the beginning was the Word, and the Word was with God, and the Word was God. He was with God in the beginning. Through him all things were made; without him nothing was made that has been made. In him was life, and that life was the light of men."

Communication – the Cornerstone for Relationship

In the previous chapters, we have remarked that God is not only infinite but personal. He designed us for relationship with Himself, and relationship is based on two-way communication. This is a most remarkable thing about this God who loves us, and whom we can know, love and commune with.

Communication is not only the cornerstone for relationship with God, it is the bedrock for our relationships with one another, as stated in the second half of Value 18.

What Is Communication?

There are lots of definitions, but at its core, communication is conveying meaning from one person or group to another through commonly understood signs, symbols or rules – whether it is written, verbal, visual, sign language, body language or cultural norms. That's a broad definition. Then when you add in ethnic cultures, sub-cultures, generational cultures, etc., there is an added beauty and complexity to human communication. Communication doesn't "communicate" until it is not only sent, but it is taken in and understood by the receiver. When there is a consistent flow of two-way communication rooted in love and with mutual respect, people feel secure and valued.

God is consistent, faithful, truthful, creative and inclusive in His communication, and it is His standard of integrity in communication that we set as our goal in our families, in our ministries, communities and relationships.

We live in a time that is often referred to as the "communication age" when the mediums of communication and the capacity of our technologies are ever-expanding at an ever-increasing rate. Communication that once took months to get from one source to another by mule or ship can now be delivered in real time by satellite.

The emphasis on communication with integrity is increasingly vital in this social media age with its texts, Tweets and Facebook posts, etc. Words and photos uploaded in haste on social media cannot be "undone" and can have a monumental impact – both for good, like saving a life; or for evil, like destroying a friendship or someone's reputation. An example of a specific concern for us in YWAM is that a careless posting by someone on a short-term outreach can pose long-term danger to our workers or ministries on the field in that location.

We as a mission have long been reticent to communicate about ourselves. Many have said, "YWAM is the world's best kept secret." This can be both positive and negative. We have always tried to keep our focus on being faithful to the ministries God has called us to, keeping our profile as low as possible with the least amount of "spotlight" and therefore with less opposition and spiritual warfare.

But by the time of our 50th anniversary, millions had become part of our movement for a season or for life. We could no longer be "invisible." And with that reality, it has become more important that we personally

and corporately communicate the truth about God and ourselves before someone else tries to tell our story through a godless lens.

There are now hundreds of YWAM websites and blogs that tell our stories, state our values and present opportunities for involvement. With so many avenues of communication available, it is ever more critical that we be committed to truthful, accurate, timely and relevant communication, remembering to rightly reflect *all* that we believe and value.

What Is Integrity?

What we want to address in this chapter is not so much the methodology of communication, but the content of what we communicate and the character with which it is delivered. God's standard of integrity and truthfulness stand in stark contrast to the half-truths, self-promotions, exaggerations, manipulations and outright deceptions that mark so many forms of modern communication.

C.S. Lewis said that integrity is "doing the right thing, even when nobody is watching." Similarly, John Maxwell said, "Image is what people think we are; integrity is what we really are."

Integrity knows no compromise. It's hard to define, as it consists of so many elements that form a value, but going back to our Belief Tree illustration, integrity is when the fruits and the roots line up, with no "disconnect."

Think of it like this: Before our modern era, pillars of marble often supported the weight of a heavy structure. If a stonecutter was dishonest, he would fill a crack in the marble with wax to make it "look" whole, so that he could sell it for a good price. But if the stonemason was wise, when he came to choose the stones he used for pillars, he would heat the marble with a candle. If there was wax, the crevice would be exposed as the wax melted and ran out. When the stone had no wax and no cracks, he would proclaim "this stone has integrity." That's the way we want our lives to be – when the heat is on and the pressure comes, we want to unwaveringly communicate and act with unblemished integrity.

Integrity means that we behave in ways that are consistent with the beliefs, values and principles we claim to hold dear. The quality of the person you are is determined by how well you live up to the values that you say are most important to you. Live your life in such a way that when people think about integrity, they think of *you* – someone who doesn't take shortcuts or sweep things under the carpet.

We have a thriving functional fitness and sports ministry in Kona where YWAMers pursue excellence in health and fitness. One of their main ministries is trekking the Bible into remote Himalayan villages. They need their ultimate strength and fitness to do so. Their ministry is called "Respect the Corners." In other words, don't compromise – don't take short cuts. If you do, the "cracks" in your preparations will be revealed when you can't meet the physical demands required – like the wax in the stone melting to expose the areas of vulnerability. They disciple people to "respect the corners," not only in health and fitness, but in every aspect of life and ministry.

"You Can See My Spirit Move When I Can Trust You with Truth Itself"

In the area of communication, integrity means that we will always communicate honestly, no matter what the circumstances are. No "situational ethics."

God taught me about having integrity in communication long before I taught about YWAM's Foundational Values or the Belief Tree. His dealings with me were intense, and truthful communication became one of my first "life messages."

It began while Loren was on a trip to New Zealand. I had intended to accompany him, but to our shock, God said I was not to go. So, I remained in California.

The first day I was on my own, I was lying in bed reading about revival. I pulled the covers over my head and shouted "Lord, will revival always be hundreds of years ago and thousands of miles away? Will I never see You move like that in my lifetime?" The Lord answered immediately, in that still small voice you hear in your spirit – but it made a thunderous impression: *"You can see My Spirit move when I can trust you with truth itself."*

I was surprised and confused. I thought, *this message must have been intended for someone else.* I told God what a high value I placed on being truthful. Then, it was like God played back a movie in my head, allowing me to see and hear all the times I had exaggerated or was not careful with details. By nature, I am a positive person, and I wanted things to be seen in the best light – but I didn't concern myself too much with accuracy. It was not my intent to deceive – it just never occurred to me that my exaggerations were lying!

As God recalled scene after scene of my life, I realized that if there were 20 people present at an event and you asked me, "How many people were there?" I would likely say "25 or 30." I would often add a dimension that made it appear better.

Day after day, God continued with His laser-beam conviction. I read Proverbs 12:22, "The Lord detests lying lips, but he delights in people who are trustworthy."

God made this a very important lesson in my life. I knew that if I couldn't be trusted with being truthful about small details, God could never trust me with the big things I was asking Him for. In Luke 16:10, Jesus said, "Whoever can be trusted with very little can also be trusted with much," and also true … "whoever is dishonest with very little will also be dishonest with much."

The Lord also exposed other areas of my communication. He reminded me of times when I had said I would do something but did not keep my promise … Times when I had been unwise, and my words had been negative and hurtful … Times when I spoke my suspicions about people without godly discernment. I repented over each situation He brought to my remembrance. It seemed that God in His graciousness would not let even the smallest detail slip by.

I'd like to tell you that I do this 100 percent perfectly now and that no exaggeration or unrighteous response ever passes my lips. That's not true, but it happens much less now that I understand God's standards for communication and am committed to speaking that which is truthful, accurate, timely and relevant.

When God first began dealing with me about this, I compiled 84 scriptures on communication that have continuously guided my life, including these:

> *"Let the words of my mouth and the meditation of my heart*
> *be pleasing in your sight, O Lord, my rock and my Redeemer"*
> *Psalm 19:14 (NASB).*

> *"Death and life are in the power of the tongue, and those who*
> *love it will eat its fruit" Proverbs 18:21 (NASB).*

"The heart of the wise instructs his mouth and adds persuasiveness to his lips" Proverbs 16:23 (NASB).

Having been trained as a nurse, I wrote out all of the verses on index cards and divided them up like I would if I were assigning medications for someone who is sick. I placed them around our home so I could meditate on them throughout the day. Now, whenever I am confronted with a difficult situation, I have a grid of scriptures committed to memory that help me respond rightly. If there is some "hot" issue of concern I need to talk with someone about, I seldom do it immediately, lest I fall prey to the emotion of the moment. I pray out Psalm 141:3, "Set a guard over my mouth, O Lord; keep watch over the door of my lips."

Teeth Marks on my Tongue

I often say to others that I have "teeth marks on my tongue" from choosing NOT to speak when I am criticized or accused of something! Proverbs 10:19 says, "… he who holds his tongue is wise." I want to develop a higher standard of self-control, asking God to help me filter my words.

God's ideal for our communication is that our words bring grace, not condemnation. To those who wait upon Him, God will give wisdom on what to say and when. Part of self-control is looking not only for truth, but for the right timing to help that person receive more easily.

Jesus, the Great Communicator Incarnate

The most important message to communicate is the message of God's love, His desire for relationship with humankind, and His provision for reconnection.

Jesus, who is fully God and fully human, came to open the door of communication with the Father. And He is an example to us of how to communicate well. He walked in shoe leather, so that we could see how to live our lives. He was the great communicator incarnate. He told stories, He used examples of everyday things, He taught by asking questions, He provoked people to think, He chose to be silent; sometimes He spoke things in a way that the meaning was hidden and understanding came later with the light of revelation. His timing was perfect. He was always relevant, passionate, caring, moved with emotion. He knew when to confront and when to comfort. The stories He used to communicate were about everyday things, making it easy for people to understand.

Use Words, Symbols and Signs They Can Understand

We all have a heart language based on the culture in which we grew up. In reaching out to people of other cultures, we should communicate in ways that are not foreign to them. Our core message will remain the same, but it can be communicated in contextual ways that speak truth to each unique culture.

A YWAM ministry called Create International has been doing that effectively for more than 30 years. They have produced evangelistic films in the languages and cultural settings of over 100 unreached people groups, including the Banjara people of India. The Banjara movie told the story of the prodigal son, set in a Banjara village with local actors and culturally appropriate staging. The Banjara people embraced the story as their own and have since planted hundreds (perhaps thousands) of churches across India. In the ten years following the release of the film, more than two million Banjara became followers of Jesus.

The great Indian evangelist Sadhu Sundar Singh once said. "If an Indian man is thirsty, and you give him water to drink in a foreign bowl, he is going to reject it. But if you give him water to drink in his own Indian bowl, he will gladly accept it." The spiritually thirsty Banjara accepted the living water of the Gospel message because it was communicated in an Indian "bowl."

Creative Communication in Times of Crisis

During seasons of crisis, which can happen at local, national and global levels, the need for communication and relationship with one another is so important. This was highlighted during the COVID-19 global pandemic. Overnight, people found themselves in isolation from one another due to the restrictions placed by national and civic governments to confine the spread of the virus. Families were separated in far away lands due to airline shut downs and quarantine restrictions; often people could not be together with their loved ones as they died; even neighbors could not visit with those living next door, for fear of spreading the virus. People were desperate to "reach out and touch."

YWAM was faced with these same relationship restrictions – campuses and ministries shut down; those who remained were not able to meet together for fellowship. The enemy was trying to stop our "GO." But as always, what the enemy intended for evil, the Lord turned around and used for our good.

I was amazed at the creativity that arose out of this vacuum and began to reshape our communication. Tools like Zoom, Skype and WhatsApp, Internet meetings arose. Loren and I were in one three-day Founders' Circle meeting that spanned six continents – all from our living room while we were on lockdown! Online teaching sessions launched that crisscrossed the globe; spontaneous Zoom cooking and painting classes surfaced; 24/7 Moravian prayer groups, grassroots neighborhood Bible studies – all leading to greater opportunities than ever before. A Facebook prayer page emerged where people could connect real-time to share their needs, sorrows and victories. Cell phone choirs and symphonies were born. Drive-by graduations and drive-by weddings took place. Every initiative underlined our hunger for relationship, and fueled greater creativity in our communication.

Healing the YWAM Nervous System

"Communicate with Integrity" (Value #18) was the last value to be added to our YWAM Foundational Values. One of the challenges of being a decentralized mission has been a greater difficulty to communicate on a global scale. Because of the spread of our locations or the diversity of languages or the need for security, some international staff and ministries have felt isolated.

In 2014, God reminded our global leaders gathered in Singapore about a word He had initially given to us a decade earlier. In it, He stressed how important communication is to the health of YWAM, likening it to the body's nervous system. Even a simple daily task like seeing and then picking up a cup of coffee can be hindered if there are breakdowns or "gaps" in our central nervous system. So, it is with our YWAM family. If we have "gaps" in our communication, it will impact our overall effectiveness as a missions movement. In response to this word from God, as leaders we began to pray for the healing of our YWAM "nervous system" and many leaders around the world have devoted much of their life and ministry to teaching and modeling good communication at all levels of the YWAM movement both internally and externally.

God is the great communicator, and we want to be like Him. We've got wonderful stories to tell of His faithfulness. May all our individual and corporate communication – verbal reports, written articles, websites, videos, etc. – be truthful, timely, accurate and relevant. May they connect us together, enrich our relationships and give great glory to Jesus.

Going Forward...

I hope you have enjoyed this journey through the stories and the words of the Lord that led to YWAM's "Core Beliefs and Foundational Values." But more than enjoying them, I pray that you have been marked by what you have discovered, resulting in positive change. May you choose to live your life continually thinking of the Belief Tree, asking the question *"Does my fruit line up with the roots of what I say I believe?"* And may you walk forward in the light of the truths you have learned. Beliefs matter! Values matter!

When my kids were in middle school before the days of cell phones, they sometimes flew short distances unaccompanied to meet up with a relative or YWAM team. On the way to the airport, as a part of my "I love you," I would often give them a sheet of paper from my trusty yellow legal pad with the instructions for the journey that lay ahead: *"After you land, go out to baggage claim, and meet the YWAM leaders there." "If no one shows up right away, here's the name of a person and phone number you can call – and here's some money for the pay phone."* It was a part of valuing them by providing the communication they needed, or in the event of the unexpected.

I'd like to give each of you, my readers, a few instructions – things you already know – practical helps for how to strengthen your beliefs and values, and how not to lose your zeal, so that you can persevere and see the fulfillment of the purposes God has for your life, your leadership, your legacy ....

Galatians 6:9 instructs us: "Let us not become weary in doing good, for at the proper time we will reap a harvest if we do not give up." And Romans 12:11 says, "Never be lacking in zeal, but keep your spiritual fervor, serving the Lord." Perseverance that will see you through to a victorious end of the journey requires having an "I won't quit" spirit that fuels our faith. And living your beliefs and values along the way will make the journey smoother and more productive.

Remind yourself that you are not self-appointed nor YWAM-appointed – you are God-appointed.

Your life should be based on the values of knowing God and hearing His voice. YWAM and others can confirm what God is saying, but at the foundation, you must have the word of the Lord for yourself, and be God-appointed for your call. The truth is, we NEVER feel qualified. We often think *"I can't do this job."* But when we know we are God-appointed, we become God-anointed.

John 15:16: "You did not choose me but I chose you and appointed you to go and bear fruit – fruit that will last."

If you are only self-appointed or YWAM-appointed, you will seek approval from other people. But when we are God-appointed, Jesus said He would be with us and give us the authority to do everything He has called us to do (Matthew 28:18-20). Walk in the appointing and anointing of God.

Walk in lifestyle of gratitude and generosity.

The Bible tells us "give thanks in all circumstances; for this is God's will for you in Christ Jesus" (1 Thessalonians 5:18). Gratitude and faith go hand-in-hand; grumbling and complaining lead to unbelief.

Look for every opportunity to thank God and thank others. Have a spirit that exudes gratitude and generosity – as our value on hospitality encourages us to do. These are expressions of God's character and our valuing people. There's no creativity in a negative mind, but with gratitude comes the creativity to co-create with God. Be generous with those who are generous with you and those who are not. Give freely of yourself, your time and resources.

Be God loyal and give no room to self-pity.

When everything is falling down around you; when you're faced with horrible disaster and people are overwhelmed; when you're in the midst of huge personal disappointments; when the things you are believing for don't happen – remind yourself that God is in charge. When it would be easy to think, *"God, where are You?"* – *that* is exactly when you need to stir up your loyalty to Him and lean into your core beliefs of what you know to be true about His nature and character. He is always good, kind, just, loving, faithful and true. Your actions and your words reflect your beliefs about God. Declare: *"God, I don't understand any of the circumstances, but I want to declare that I am absolutely loyal to You. There is nothing wrong with You; there never has been, and there never will be. Even if I never understand, I will be loyal to You, trusting in Your nature and character."*

Nothing affects our loyalty to God like self-pity. It is the greatest robber of joy. If you begin to lose your joy, look to see if you discover self-pity in your heart.

What is root of self-pity? Pride. It is thinking, "I deserve better than this." *From who? Compared to whom?* Here is a helpful exercise to practice if you are feeling sorry for yourself: picture yourself seated at the foot of Cross, making your complaints – with Jesus, the most innocent, taking on the sin and abuse of the world! In both Peter and James, the Bible says that God is opposed to the proud but gives grace to the humble. When I let self-pity consume me, God actually opposes me, and there is no grace! That is a very scary scenario!

Resisting self-pity sounds easy, but it is not. It is hardest to resist self-pity when you have been victimized by true injustice. You made your marriage vows and stuck by them and your partner did not; you were righteous in business and others embezzled from you; you trusted your father and he violated you. We can become consumed with how wrong the other person was.

Be loyal to God. Self-pity is an attack on His character. If He says there is grace for every situation, then there is. When you and I stand before the Lord, He is not going to allow us to justify ourselves by saying "*but that situation ... but that person ... but this is what happened to me.*" Trust the God who sees everything and knows the hearts of everyone to judge righteously.

Forgiveness should never be an issue – it should be automatic. Even if the person who wronged us or victimized us or judged us never asks for it, we should grant them our forgiveness.

We must say, "*God, I am devastated ... disappointed ... I have no idea how I'm going to cope. But I am giving this situation to You – I nail it to the cross. I believe Your Word when You say that the God of all the earth will judge righteously. I'm going to concentrate on being a man or woman of God, and I leave the judgment to You.*" Joy will return and grace will be there, because He is that kind of God.

Don't pick up an offense.

Picking up offenses against others is exhausting! It will wear you out and everyone else around you.

Think of our YWAM values: we value relationships, individuals, families and teams. We need the gifts and contributions of others. Then consider a family with the same mother and father, the same upbringing, who all speak the same language. Is there ever miscommunication or misunderstanding? Of course. Then consider the fact that in YWAM, we often come from vastly different cultures and are trying to sort things out in a second or third language. Sometimes we don't give others the attention or affirmation we should. It happens. The part that is sin is when we pick up and carry an offense against someone because of miscommunication, misunderstanding or misjudgment. Or sometimes we can pick up an offense on behalf of someone else whom we love, and long after they have gotten the issue resolved, we may still be carrying the weight of that offense.

Nothing offends us more than when our motives are questioned. We don't intend to hurt and offend one another, but sometimes we do. We need to have enormous respect for Jesus in each other. Yes that guy really did irritate you … yes, that leader really did handle that situation poorly. But Jesus in you is enough to overcome the situation.

If I were the devil – and I am not! – tempting people to pick up offenses would be my strategy to slow down the effectiveness of the Kingdom. When we are offended, there is no unity; there is junk in our hearts, and the enemy has won.

Leaders are too often consumed with trying to put out fires and judge between those who are offended, mad, depressed and down. I really get tired of endless discussions about who said what to whom; who did what; who was right and who was wrong. To me the discovery we need to pursue is to ask the Lord to measure our lives by the Belief Tree standard, weighing our beliefs, values, decisions and action: *Where was a Biblical principle violated? What did we do to step into someone else's domain? How did we offend the Holy Spirit?* When we can discern those things and make them right, we can move on quickly, walking forward in truth.

Here is the advice a prophetic friend gave to me awhile back: "I try to handle offenses thinking like this: *Jesus is in me and Jesus is in you. So what part of Jesus in me just got offended?*" Usually I discover it is not JESUS in me that got offended at all – it's Darlene. Extend grace and remember, the joy of the Lord is your strength.

Be with people who celebrate you and don't just tolerate you.

Appreciate one another. Have fun. Enjoy each other. This is part of the joy of valuing each other and the teams God has called us to work in. Another way of saying it is, *"Hang out with people who love the 'smell of fish' because, like you, they are called to be fishers of men."* Be with other people who enjoy the call of God – who eat, sleep, breathe, talk and live it. Spend time together with people who celebrate one another's gifts and callings.

Serve for the glory of God, not for yourself or for the mission.

If you don't serve for the glory of God, you will never get enough affirmation or credit. Remember the story I shared with you in the chapter on servant leadership from the life of Abigail, when God called me to be a "footwasher of those who wash the feet of the king." It is a freeing thing if you can wake up in the morning and say "It doesn't matter if no one ever notices – I'm doing whatever I do for Your glory, Lord." Then you will thrive.

Love the Lord with all your heart, mind, soul and strength.

Don't just worship with your emotions, but with your mind. Be a thinking person. Ponder how things line up with a Biblical Christian worldview (Value #9). You need to know what you believe and why you believe it; what you don't believe and why you don't believe it.

Walk in God's authority and anointing. Be God loyal. Serve for His glory. This is how we faithfully live out the purposes, beliefs and values God has called us to live by. Be a person who brings joy to God's heart because you listen, obey and won't quit!

Beliefs & Values Discovery Starters

By David Joel Hamilton

Introduction

You have just finished reading stories about the experiences and words of the Lord that led YWAM to embrace our six Core Beliefs and 18 Foundational Values. These "discovery starters" are just what the name implies. David Hamilton invites you to dig deeper, exploring and discovering more about each one, anchored firmly in its Biblical basis, which will help you to make them your own.

As you have seen in *Values Matter*, each belief and each value has 10 Scripture passages that undergird and support it – four to six from the Original Testament and four to six from the New Testament. Each of the following Discovery Starters focuses on just *one* of those verses or passages, as a place to begin to unpack the richness. Don't stop with just this one. The Scriptures are full of inspiration and wisdom to spur you on in your pursuit. Begin now on a new adventure of discovery for yourself!

More Beliefs and Values Discovery Starters focusing on different Scripture verses/passages are available on YWAMValues.com to help you go further in your studies.

– Darlene Cunningham

Beliefs Matter
Discovery Starters

Belief #1 – Worship: Worship Only God

Biblical Foundation:

For the Lord had made a covenant with the descendants of Jacob and commanded them: "Do not worship any other gods or bow before them or serve them or offer sacrifices to them. But worship only the Lord, who brought you out of Egypt with great strength and a powerful arm. Bow down to him alone, and offer sacrifices only to him. Be careful at all times to obey the decrees, regulations, instructions, and commands that he wrote for you. You must not worship other gods. Do not forget the covenant I made with you, and do not worship other gods. You must worship only the Lord your God. He is the one who will rescue you from all your enemies" (2Ki 17:35-39).

Discovery Starter:

Hebrew is a very concrete language. Its verb-centric vocabulary results in a very action-oriented, tactile, experiential form of communication. The word *shachah* (Strong's #7812) which is translated as "worship" literally means "to bow down" or "to prostrate oneself." The word creates a visual picture of intense desire and total devotion. It embodies the act of surrender and service, of alignment and allegiance, of honor and esteem. Not only can you imagine the respectful obedience of a subject who bows in homage before a king; you can also envision the passionate love of a young man who kneels down on one knee to ask his beloved for her hand in marriage.

We are all worshipers. We all give allegiance to someone. We all desire something. Every one of us. The question is not whether or not we will worship.

The question is whom or what will we worship. Will we worship the living God or will we long after some substitute pleasure, some alternate goal? The answer we give will focus our attitudes and our actions. Worship drives us. It sets the course of our life. It determines the direction of our existence. We live for what we treasure, for what we worship.

As worship gives expression to our deepest desires, it also shapes our destiny. It is a powerful factor in discipleship. We are told in the Scriptures that those who pursue ungodly passions are shaped by their misaligned, idolatrous devotion. People become like the gods they worship. So, "those who make idols are just like them" (Psa 115:4-8; 135:16-18) – deaf, mute, powerless, lifeless. But the good news is that those who worship the living God "in Spirit and in truth" (Joh 4:23)will be transformed in their character to be more and more like him. John writes, "Dear friends, we are already God's children, but he has not yet shown us what we will be like when Christ appears. But we do know that we will be like him, for we will see him as he really is. And all who have this eager expectation will keep themselves pure, just as he is pure" (1Jn 3:2-3).

Keep Going:

Pick a psalm or two. Read them out loud. Meditate on the character qualities of God highlighted in what you have read. Turn your reflections on the Word into a response of worship. You may want to bow down – literally, physically – as you speak out the words of your devotion to God.

Belief #2 – Holiness: Made Holy

Biblical Foundation:

So I brought them out of Egypt and led them into the wilderness. There I gave them my decrees and regulations so they could find life by keeping them. And I gave them my Sabbath days of rest as a sign between them and me. It was to remind them that I am the LORD, who had set them apart to be holy (Eze 20:10-12).

Discovery Starter:

Ezekiel makes it clear that God's <u>purpose</u> for us is that we be holy. God's <u>reason</u> is because he is holy (Lev 11:44-45; 19:2) and he wants to conform us to his image (Rom 8:29) in order that we might walk in close fellowship with him (1Co 1:9). He wants us to share in his character and have uninterrupted friendship with him. A call to holiness is not a call to limit us, but an invitation to pursue the imitation of God in order that we may enjoy intimacy with God.

God's <u>means</u> of making us holy is rooted in himself. His redemptive work in our lives is what makes the difference – that is why we are repeatedly told that he is the one who makes us holy (Exo 31:13; Lev 20:8; 21:8,15,23; 22:9,16,32). It's not that God does this independently from us. God exhorts us to put all his "decrees ... into practice" precisely because he is the one "who makes ... holy" (Lev 20:8). Our response of obedience to his acts of deliverance allow us to live as God intends us to live.

Jesus' exhortation "to be perfect, even as your Father in heaven is perfect" (Mat 5:48) in the Sermon on the Mount, and the parallel "be compassionate, just as your Father is compassionate" (Luk 6:36) in the Sermon on the Plain echo the command, "You must be holy because I, the Lord your God, am holy" (Lev 19:2). God is to be our standard of how we should live our lives. Oftentimes moral excuses are made with the phrase, "Well, we're only human." Let us not forget that we were designed by a holy God for holiness. Jesus came to restore us to that original design by showing us what it means to be truly human. He embodies the new normal by living a life which matches God's way of living life. Jesus "faced all of the same testings we do, yet he did not sin" (Heb 4:15). Paul enjoins us: "Imitate God, therefore, in everything you do, because you are his dear children. Live a life filled with love, following the example of Christ" (Eph 5:1-2).

Keep Going:

When God wants to say something with emphasis, he underscores his words with "I am the Lord." This declaration can be found 158 times in 70 chapters across 14 books of the Original Testament. The chapter that most frequently repeats this phrase is Leviticus 19, often considered the heart of

"The Law of Holiness" which comprises the last third of Leviticus. Consider the statements that climax with "I am the LORD" in this chapter:

19:3	honor your parents and the Sabbath
19:4	do not participate in idolatry
19:10	care for the poor
19:12	do not use dishonest words and thereby dishonor God
19:14	care for those with disabilities
19:16	care for those whose life is at risk
19:18	love your neighbor as yourself
19:25	take care of your physical environment
19:28	do not participate in pagan practices to honor the dead
19:30	honor God's sanctuary and the Sabbath
19:31	do not participate in pagan practices to contact the dead
19:32	care for the elderly
19:34	care for the refugees, immigrants, foreigners in your midst
19:35	do not use dishonest weights and measurements
19:37	obey all of God's decrees

How do these statements help you understand holiness? What are repeated themes? What are the inner heart issues and the outward social issues addressed in this passage? How do integrity, love and compassion display holiness?

Belief #3 – Witness: Peter's Conversion

Biblical Foundation:

And we are witnesses of all that he did both in the country of the Jews and in Jerusalem. They put him to death by hanging him on a tree, but God raised him on the third day and made him to appear, not to all the people but to us who had been chosen by God as witnesses, who ate and drank with him after he rose from the dead. And he commanded us to preach to the people and to testify that he is the one appointed by God to be judge of the living and the dead. To him all the prophets bear witness that everyone who believes in him receives forgiveness of sins through his name (Act 10:39-43 ESV).

Discovery Starter:

Shouldn't the title be "Cornelius' Conversion"? Hold on for just a bit... Peter's opening statement at Cornelius' house reflected his reluctance to be among Gentiles. "You know it is against our laws for a Jewish man to enter a Gentile home ... tell me why you sent for me" (Act 10:28-29). It had not occurred to him to preach the gospel! Cornelius had to coach him how to proceed. Then Peter misquoted Jesus. Peter stated that Jesus "commanded us to preach to the people." The word translated here is not *ethnos* (the word Jesus used in Mat 28:18-20), but *laos*. Whereas *laos* was used to describe exclusively the Jewish people, *ethnos* denoted all other people – the Gentiles. Though Jesus said one thing, Peter had heard another. Like Peter, we're often deaf to words which challenge our cultural paradigms.

Acts tells the story of the expanding reach of the gospel. At first all the followers of Jesus were Aramaic-speaking, Jewish "men of Galilee" (1:11). Then they included women (1:14) and non-Galilean Jews (2:5-11). The growing number of Greek-speaking believers even included one ex-Gentile (6:1-6)! The story continues with the inclusion of half-Jews (Samaritans in 8:1-25) and a wanna-be Jew (an Ethiopian in 8:26-39). That brings us to the two central conversions in the book: Paul's (9:1-22) and Peter's (10:1-47). So why call it Peter's conversion? Well, Cornelius obeyed immediately (10:7) but Peter did not. When God visited him his immediate response was, "No, Lord" (10:14) – two words which should never be used together. If he's Lord, shouldn't the answer always be "Yes"? But after three visions and one prophetic word, Peter finally obeyed. So though both changed, it was Peter's "conversion" that required the greater effort.

Let's step back and look at the big picture. Acts is built around the stories of Peter and Paul. Their respective conversion stories are each retold twice (Peter's in 11:4-18; 15:7-11; Paul's in 22:3-21; 26:2-23). The telling and retelling of these two iconic stories occupies one eighth of Acts. They embody its central message: all who desire to follow Jesus are to be included! And for that reason we must all bear witness to all.

Keep Going:

Consider Peter's situation. Seven years after Jesus' instructions to preach the gospel to every person (Mar 16:15), he still was only moving in familiar, culturally-comfortable circles. How about us? Are there changes God wants to make in the way we think and live like he did in Peter's life? Are we moving beyond the known and the familiar to reach those who are culturally different from us? Are we sharing good news with those who were born elsewhere and speak a different language? Are we communicating redemption to those who are outside our day-to-day activities? Take time to consider how you can move beyond your relational circles to share the gospel with those who are different from you. How can you include them? How can you reach them? Take time to listen to God about your role in extending his kingdom with a commitment to say, "Yes, Lord" when he speaks.

Belief #4 – Prayer: A Tragic Day

Biblical Foundation:

"I looked for someone who might rebuild the wall of righteousness that guards the land. I searched for someone to stand in the gap in the wall so I wouldn't have to destroy the land, but I found no one. So now I will pour out my fury on them, consuming them with the fire of my anger. I will heap on their heads the full penalty for all their sins. I, the Sovereign LORD, have spoken!" (Eze 22:30-31).

Discovery Starter:

The interplay of justice and mercy is one of the overarching themes of the Scriptures. Both are attributes of love. Therefore, a loving person will always be just. Injustice has no place in the life of a loving person. Similarly, a loving person will seek every opportunity to be merciful. A lack of mercy is contrary to love. Because "God is love" (1Jn 4:8), he does everything "in justice, in steadfast love and in mercy" (Hos 2:19 ESV). As a just God, equity is his standard, so he makes sure that no one gets less than they deserve. But as a merciful God, grace is his goal, so he looks for every opportunity to give us better than we deserve.

The prophets of old prophesied with this framework. They understood that the actions of a just and merciful God take our actions into account. Certain actions on our part require a response of justice on God's part. Other actions on our part make possible a merciful response on God's part. This principle is at the heart of Jeremiah's vision at the potter's house (Jer 18:1-11) and Ezekiel's description of God's heart (Eze 18:1-32). You can count on God always being just and yet always looking for an opportunity to show mercy. This is the story line behind the iconic events found in Exodus 32:7-14; Jonah 3:4-4:2; and 2 Kings 20:1-7. Prayer, fasting, repentance, intercession – freely undertaken by humans – gave God the just reason to replace expected punishment with unexpected redemption. These stories climax in a grand finale as "mercy triumphs over judgment" (Jam 2:13 NIV).

But not so in Eze 22:30-31. The situation merited divine judgement. But – as always – God would have preferred mercy over justice. He looked for someone who through their prayers would give him a just cause to stay judgment. But he found no one. Therefore, he could not justly extend mercy. He had to bring upon them the deserved punishment. With a broken heart God had to withhold the mercy he desired. Our actions are significant. Prayer does indeed change things. On this day there was none, so no change was possible. What a tragic day!

Keep Going:

Take time to read the book of Jonah through from beginning to end. It only takes about seven minutes. After this quick overview go back and consider the different prayers prayed in the book. Reflect on who prayed; what was the content of their prayer; what was the result of their prayer; what difference did those prayers make; and how was God's justice and mercy reflected in his response to each prayer. Note particularly:

- The sailors' prayers in Jon 1:14
- Jonah's prayer in Jon 2:2-9
- The Ninevites' prayers in Jon 3:6-9
- Jonah's prayer in Jon 4:3

Belief #5 – Fellowship: Radical Koinonia

Biblical Foundation:

And all the believers met together in one place and shared everything they had. They sold their property and possessions and shared the money with those in need.

They worshiped together at the Temple each day, met in homes for the Lord's Supper, and shared their meals with great joy and generosity – all the while praising God and enjoying the goodwill of all the people. And each day the Lord added to their fellowship those who were being saved (Act 2:44-47).

Discovery Starter:

The Greek words *koinonia* and *koinonos* may conjure up images of delicious dinners and cozy sofas where we can hang out and "fellowship" with one another. This is not what came to the mind of first-century believers. A *koinonos* referred to a voluntary association of human beings. It was a purposeful corporation formed for political, educational, religious, athletic, or commercial reasons. Plato, in his *Republic* speaks of the *koinonos* as the smallest, most basic building block of society. When the early church described itself as a *koinonos* it was a bold, counter-cultural declaration, affirming that they were a new society which challenged the existing world order.

Jesus did not call us to himself in an individualized manner. He called individuals into a body with Jesus at the center. This is what he did with the first twelve that followed him. This is also what he does with those of us who follow him today. Jesus promises, "where two or three gather together as my followers, I am there among them" (Mat 18:20). We're called into a *koinonia*. Paul writes how the "meetings of God's holy people" (1Co 14:33) should be conducted to "build up the church" (Eph 4:11-13). The main point is that everyone has something to contribute – like partners in a *koinonos* – and that "everything that is done must strengthen all of you ... so that everyone will learn and be encouraged" (1Co 14:26,30). Indeed, believers are admonished, "Let us think of ways to motivate one another to acts of love and good works. And let us not neglect our meeting together, as some people do, but encourage one another" (Heb 10:24-25).

But the gathering of God's people is not only for edification and encouragement; it is also to equip for external expansion. Peter writes, "for you are a chosen people. You are royal priests, a holy nation, God's very own possession. As a result, you can show others the goodness of God, for he called you out of the darkness into his wonderful light" (1Pe 2:9). This chosen people is called a *koinonos* because as a counter-cultural movement that is committed to expanding the kingdom of God on earth.

Keep Going:

Do some research. Dig into history. Explore a time in the past when the church was the catalyst for some disruptive innovation that ushered in transformative change in society. Read some books. Watch some videos. Consider how you can contribute to the people of God in this generation. How can you be a part of an activated *koinonos*, expanding the kingdom of God in powerful redemptive ways? Gather with a group of friends in Christ. Seek his face. Pray. Read the Scriptures. Listen to his voice. Help each other grow. Encourage one another. Dream big. Get practical. Serve your community. Discover how you can extend the kingdom of God. With others be a truly radical *koinonia*!

Belief #6 – Service: When the City Rejoices

Biblical Foundation:

The whole city celebrates when the godly succeed; they shout for joy when the wicked die. Upright citizens are good for a city and make it prosper, but the talk of the wicked tears it apart (Pro 11:10-11).

Discovery Starter:

What a stunning statement! Why does the city celebrate when the godly succeed? Usually people rejoice only when they, or their team, succeeds. What is different here? The Hebrew word for "the godly" is *tsadikkim*. They are the ones "who are willing to disadvantage themselves for the community, while the wicked are those who put their own economic, social, and personal needs ahead of the needs of the community" (Timothy Keller, quoted in Sherman, *Kingdom Calling*).

Jesus said that the "entire law and all the demands of the prophets are based" on two commandments: to love God and to love neighbor (Mat 22:37-40). The two sins most frequently addressed in the Scriptures are idolatry (not loving God) and social injustice (not loving neighbor). In the law, the essence of loving neighbor is exemplified in this exhortation:

"True justice must be given to foreigners living among you
and to orphans, and you must never accept a widow's garment

213

as security for her debt. Always remember that you were slaves
in Egypt and that the LORD your God redeemed you from
your slavery. That is why I have given you this command"
(Deu 24:17-18).

The prophets continue this theme:

"This is what the LORD of Heaven's Armies says: Judge fairly,
and show mercy and kindness to one another. Do not oppress
widows, orphans, foreigners, and the poor. And do not scheme
against each other" (Zec 7:9-10).

Throughout the Scriptures, God expects his people to act kindly towards the most disadvantaged. The marginalized in our midst are often described as "widows, orphans, foreigners, and the poor." God is described as a "Father to the fatherless, defender of widows" (Psa 68:5). Because God's people are to reflect his heart, "You must not exploit a widow or an orphan" or any other "at-risk" person (Exo 22:22-23). This imitation of God's goodness towards the "least of these" (Mat 25:31-46) must be part of our everyday lives. We are called to holistic service: an integrated, two-handed gospel proclaiming the truth of God and demonstrating the love of God to all those in need. When we do this the city will indeed rejoice!

Keep Going:

It is estimated that by 2030 over 3.2 billion people will be living in 700 cities of a million or more. Many "widows, orphans, foreigners, and the poor" will occupy these needy urban landscapes. The following list of passages addresses the issue of these precious individuals who are most at risk in our society. These passages are a Biblical sampling of commands, proverbs, exhortations, and portrayals of God's heart for "the least" among us. This is a long list, because the Bible has much to say on this subject. Don't rush through these references. Pick a few. Read them slowly. Meditate on them deeply. Ask God to reveal his heart to you. In light of these passages, ask him how he wants you to respond. What is your heaven-sent assignment?

Listen, obey and don't give up.

- Exo 22:21-24; 23:3,6,9-11
- Lev 19:9-10,15,33-34; 23:22; 25:35-38
- Deu 10:17-19; 14:28-29; 15:7-11; 24:12-15,17-22; 26:12-13; 27:19
- Job 29:11-17; 31:16-23,31-32
- Psa 10:17-18; 12:5; 35:10; 68:5; 72:1-2,4,12; 82:3-4; 94:4-9; 107:41-43; 109:15-17; 113:5-9; 146:9
- Pro 14:21; 15:25; 19:17; 21:13; 22:9,16,22-23; 23:10-11; 28:8,27; 29:7; 31:8-9,20
- Isa 1:17,21-23; 10:1-2; 11:1-5; 25:4; 61:1
- Jer 5:26-29; 7:5-7; 22:3,15-17; 49:11
- Eze 16:49; 18:10-17; 22:6-12
- Dan 4:27
- Amo 2:6-7; 4:1-2; 5:10-12; 8:4-7
- Zec 7:10
- Mal 3:5
- Mat 19:21; 25:31-46
- Mar 10:21; 12:38-40
- Luk 3:11; 4:16-21; 6:20; 11:39-41; 14:12-14; 18:22; 19:8-10; 20:45-47
- Act 10:2-4,31
- Rom 15:26
- 1Co 13:3
- 2Co 9:9
- 1Ti 5:3-7
- Heb 13:2
- Jam 1:9-11,27; 2:1-7
- 3Jo 5

Values Matter
Discovery Starters

Value #1 – Know God: Pursuing Relational Revelation

Biblical Foundation:

"I had only heard about you before, but now I have seen you with my own eyes" (Job 42:5).

Discovery Starter:

Walking through the bustling street market, I heard a local vendor address her young child, "I have to leave the stand for a few moments. Don't you dare move from this chair while I'm gone. If you do, God will see you and he will get you." I cringed. The mother's threatening tone evoked in my mind images of a story-book ogre who took delight in punishing wayward children. Imagine what these words must have produced in the spirit of that young, impressionable child? What mark did they leave on his heart? Was God really like that? Does he sneakily spy on fidgety kids, cackling with sinister delight when they mess up so he can "get" them?

So many things are said about God. Some of them are true. Many are not. We see this even in the book of Job. At the end of the story, God says that Job's three friends had not "spoken accurately" about God and his ways. He said this not only once, but twice (Job 42:7,8)! This is shocking, for the words of Eliphaz, Bildad and Zophar occupy nearly one fifth of this dramatic book. Steer clear of their words – even those which seem fairly orthodox – for they do not meet with God's approval.

The point is this: second hand "facts" about God should be shunned. We don't want mere information about God. We want him. We want a deeply intimate, experiential encounter with the living God. For this reason, Job resisted his friends' pat answers and their religious platitudes. Amidst his pain, he passionately pursued God with hard-hitting questions until he reached a relational revelation; until he could say to God, *"I have seen you with my own eyes."* This kind of knowledge is truly transformational. This kind of knowledge is not accidental. It comes to those who – like Job – earnestly yearn for God. Job's hunger for God was unquenchable, his pursuit of God was unstoppable. He declared his undying hope, *"I will see God! I will see him for myself. Yes, I will see him with my own eyes"* (Job 19:26-27). May this be our undying goal as well.

Keep Going:

Read the following verses and consider how you can passionately pursue God:

- Deu 4:29
- 1Ch 28:9-10a
- Act 17:27
- Heb 11:6

Value #2 – Make God Known: Tell Everyone

Biblical Foundation:

"Publish his glorious deeds among the nations.
Tell everyone about the amazing things he does.
Great is the LORD! He is most worthy of praise!
He is to be feared above all gods.
The gods of other nations are mere idols,
but the LORD made the heavens!
Honor and majesty surround him;
strength and joy fill his dwelling" (1Ch 16:24-27).

Discovery Starter:

Tell everyone! God does not want anyone to be left out. He tells Abraham that he wants to bless every family across the face of the earth (Gen 12:1-3). David confirms that it is God's intent that "the whole earth will acknowledge the LORD and return to him. All the families of the nations will bow down before him" (Psa 22:27). God wants "to save all the oppressed of the earth" (Psa 76:9). Indeed, God "desires all persons to be saved and come to a knowledge of the truth" (1Ti 2:3-4). He does not want "anyone to perish, but all to come to repentance" (2Pe 3:9). Everyone. All. Every. This has always been God's desire.

So how is God's forever dream to be accomplished? Through us. As Abraham was blessed to be a blessing, so also it is to be with us. Jesus says, "Give as freely as you have received!" (Mat 10:9). So all of us who have come to know God by his gracious acts in our lives are called to make God known. All of us. Not just some of us. To everyone. We must tell of God's redemptive deeds to everyone who has not yet experienced the amazing love and transforming grace of God.

Remember, we are exhorted to "tell everyone about the amazing things he does." The focus is to be on God's actions. His deeds are to be the centerpiece of our proclamation. It is for this reason that the psalmist tells us, "How amazing are the deeds of the LORD! All who delight in him should ponder them. Everything he does reveals his glory and majesty" (Psa 111:2-3). We are to share what he has done with everyone. Why? So they too can come to know this awesome God. For, "how can they believe in him if they have never heard about him? And how can they hear about him unless someone tells them?" (Rom 10:14). Because God has redeemed you, you are to "… show others the goodness of God, for he called you out of the darkness into his wonderful light" (1Pe 2:9).

Keep Going:

Keep growing in your intimacy with God by intentional meditation in the Word of God. The Bible is a treasure trove of revelation, telling us what God has done so that we can tell everyone. In the Bible there are over 1200 distinct verbs which describe God's amazing actions, his wonderful works. Some are just used once or twice, some many hundreds of times. Pick one of the following Psalms: 4, 18, 25, 68, 103, 118, 139, 145. As you read it, highlight every verb or phrase which describes an action of God. Ponder on these passages and worship God for his wonderful works in the Scriptures and in your life. Then commit yourself to tell someone this week about what God has done. Are there more people you could tell about God's awesome deeds?

Value #3 – Hear God's Voice: God is Speaking

Biblical Foundation:

Samuel did not yet know the LORD because he had never had a message from the LORD before. So the LORD called a third time, and once more Samuel got up and went to Eli. "Here I am. Did you call me?" Then Eli realized it was the LORD who was calling the boy. So he said to Samuel, "Go and lie down again, and if someone calls again, say, 'Speak, LORD, your servant is listening'" So Samuel went back to bed. And the LORD came and called as before, "Samuel! Samuel!" And Samuel replied, "Speak, your servant is listening" (1Sa 3:7-10).

Discovery Starter:

Radio waves fill the air. Music to suit every ear; sporting events, news, talk shows, public announcements. They are all around us, but we do not hear them unless we get a radio. Still we hear nothing. So we plug it in to an outlet. Still we hear nothing. So we make sure it's turned on. Still we hear nothing. So we check the volume. Still we hear nothing. So we dial our favorite station. Now we hear clearly. The radio waves were there all the time, but we couldn't hear because our radios weren't tuned in. God is speaking. Are we tuned in?

This story of Samuel begins with a tragic commentary about that moment in history. We are told, "The word of the LORD was rare in those days" (1Sa 3:1 NRSV). The problem was not a lack of communication on God's part, but a shortage of listening on the part of his people. Of all the things the Bible tells us about God, his capacity to communicate is the action most frequently mentioned! In the Original Testament, we are told that God speaks (Hebrew *'amar*) over 1400 times. In the New Testament, God is said to speak (Greek *lego*) over 500 times. These – and many other words – are used to describe God's great communication skills. He answers, asks, assures, calls, commands, declares, directs, explains, instructs, mentions, orders, promises, replies, responds, reveals, says, speaks, swears, tells, warns, etc. All told, God's great ability to communicate is mentioned nearly 3000 times in the Bible!

No one communicates more abundantly than God. But are we listening? Are our radios tuned in? Do we need to posture ourselves, like Samuel, to hear with a servant's heart? God declares, "Oh, that you had listened to my commands! Then you would have had peace flowing like a gentle river and righteousness rolling over you like waves in the sea" (Isa 48:18). Again God shares his heart, "Oh, that my people would listen to me! ... How quickly I would then subdue their enemies! ... I would feed you with the finest wheat. I would satisfy you with wild honey from the rock" (Psa 81:13-16).

Keep Going:

Read Psalm 81:8-16 several times. Take your time to savor it and reflect on it slowly. Listen with your heart. What stands out to you? Note what it says about listening. What is the result of paying attention to God? What are the consequences when we fail to heed him? What is God wanting to do for his people when they listen to him? Ask God to help you cultivate a listening heart, like Samuel's, to hear and obey the word of the Lord.

Value #4 – Practice Worship and Intercessory Prayer: Spiritual Warfare

Biblical Foundation:

Therefore, put on every piece of God's armor so you will be able to resist the enemy in the time of evil. Then after the battle you will still be standing firm. Stand your ground,

- *putting on the belt of truth*
- *and the body armor of God's righteousness.*
- *For shoes, put on the peace that comes from the Good News so that you will be fully prepared.*
- *In addition to all of these, hold up the shield of faith to stop the fiery arrows of the devil.*
- *Put on salvation as your helmet,*
- *and take the sword of the Spirit, which is the word of God.*

Pray in the Spirit at all times and on every occasion. Stay alert and be persistent in your prayers for all believers everywhere. And pray for me, too. Ask God to give me the right words so I can boldly explain God's mysterious plan that the Good News is for Jews and Gentiles alike. I am in chains now, still preaching this message as God's ambassador. So pray that I will keep on speaking boldly for him, as I should (Eph 6:13-20).

Discovery Starter:

We are impressed with God, the lover of our soul. "Who is like you among the gods, O LORD—glorious in holiness, awesome in splendor, performing great wonders?" (Exo 15:11). No one! Only our God is rightly called "Wonderful" (Isa 9:6) for he alone fills us with enduring wonder. We are not the only ones amazed by such a remarkable God! "The highest angelic powers stand in awe of God. He is far more awesome than all who surround his throne. O LORD God of Heaven's Armies! Where is there anyone as mighty as you, O LORD? You are entirely faithful" (Psa 89:7-8). God's unparalleled capacity and his spotless character deserves our undivided admiration.

We are not impressed with Satan, the enemy of our soul. Now, we don't discount Satan or ignore his activity. But neither are we awed by him, for he is a defeated enemy. God is great; Satan is not. The story of Simon the Sorcerer (Act 8:9-13) illustrates that even when the enemy seeks to amaze people with counterfeit efforts; only God's work is genuinely amazing. We are not intimidated by the enemy for "we use God's mighty weapons, not worldly weapons" (2Co 10:4). Indeed, "we use the weapons of righteousness in the right hand for attack and the left hand for defense" (2Co 6:7).

Spiritual warfare surrounds us, but God "has rescued us from the kingdom of darkness and transferred us into the Kingdom of his dear Son" (Col 1:13). God invites us to participate with him in the retaking of planet earth. For this reason, we are to "put on all of God's armor" (Eph 6:11) and take a stand with God. We are to arm ourselves with his mighty acts – with the truth, righteousness, peace, faith and salvation which come from God, relying on Holy Spirit and the Word of God for victory. Then we will be counted among those who "sing for joy as they lie on their beds" because they have "the praises of God ... in their mouths, and a sharp sword in their hands" (Psa 149:5-6) to establish God's good and kind purposes in our world.

Keep Going:

Time and again we are told in the Original Testament that God astounds people "with amazing wonders" (Isa 29:14). The Gospel writers do the same when they record how people were astonished and amazed with Jesus' words and actions. Take some time to look at the following passages: Mat 7:28; 12:23; 13:54; 19:25; 22:33; Mar 1:22; 2:12; 5:42; 6:2,51; 7:37; 10:26;

11:18; Luk 2:47-48; 4:32; 8:56; 9:43; 24:22. Ponder on those things which most amaze you about God. Set your heart to praise him for his extraordinary capacity and excellent character.

Value #5 – Be Visionary: Do the Right Things Right

Biblical Foundation:

Then the LORD *said to me, "Write my answer plainly on tablets, so that a runner can carry the correct message to others. This vision is for a future time. It describes the end, and it will be fulfilled. If it seems slow in coming, wait patiently, for it will surely take place. It will not be delayed"* (Hab 2:2-3).

Discovery Starter:

What is vision? It is – as Habakkuk states – that which "describes the end," the grand goal, the ultimate target. Without vision we are directionless. We flounder. We are purposeless. We are lost. Unless you have a vision of your future, you cannot live your today well. A God-inspired vision is essential to live a fruitful and fulfilled life. It enables you to know what is the right thing to do.

But it is not enough to know simply "what" to do; we must also know "how" to do it. We must understand the right way to get the right thing done. It is important to get both the end (the "what") and the means (the "how") right. Doing one without the other always results in destructive foolishness. We see this in the story of Saul's failed battle against the Philistines (1Sa 13:1-14). He got the "what" right – he knew victory was possible if he sought God's favor. But he got the "how" wrong – he took matters into his own hand and foolishly killed the sacrifice lamb himself instead of waiting patiently for the prophet, violating God's commands. As a result, his dynasty came to a premature end. How unnecessarily tragic! Had he proceeded with obedient integrity, history would have been different. But Saul's life unfortunately illustrated the proverb: "As dead flies cause even a bottle of perfume to stink, so a little foolishness spoils great wisdom and honor" (Ecc 10:1).

Jesus sets out the ultimate vision when he teaches us to pray, "May your Kingdom come soon. May your will be done on earth, as it is in heaven" (Mat 6:10). This is the grandest of all grand goals. The question each person must ask is, "What is my part in this God-inspired vision?" We should not expect to get a blueprint for our future so that we can take off in our own strength, hoping to meet God at the destination. No – <u>how</u> we get there is vitally important. We are to pursue the vision relationally with God; engaging with Emmanuel continuously as we travel from its inspired inception to its fruitful completion.

Keep Going:

As you seek to understand God's vision for your life, consider the following. Like Habbakuk, look at a given situation around you and ask God for spiritual insight, to discern if it brings joy to God's heart or if it breaks God's heart? If the former, ask Holy Spirit what you can do to cooperate with and strengthen that situation. If the later, ask the Lord to show you how to collaborate with him to change that situation. Commit yourself to listen carefully, get God's vision and obey God's instructions without ever giving up.

Value #6 – Champion Young People: Despise Not Youth

Biblical Foundation:

Don't let anyone think less of you because you are young. Be an example to all believers in what you say, in the way you live, in your love, your faith, and your purity. Until I get there, focus on reading the Scriptures to the church, encouraging the believers, and teaching them. Do not neglect the spiritual gift you received through the prophecy spoken over you when the elders of the church laid their hands on you. Give your complete attention to these matters. Throw yourself into your tasks so that everyone will see your progress. Keep a close watch on how you live and on your teaching. Stay true to what is right for the sake of your own salvation and the salvation of those who hear you (1Ti 4:12-16).

Discovery Starter:

As Paul writes to his "true son in the faith" (1Ti 1:2), two things are of paramount concern to the apostle:

- the well-being of Timothy, and
- the well-being of the Church.

This dual concern is reflected in the very structure of the letter. Paul goes back and forth between these two topics. At times he instructs Timothy about his life as a minister of the Gospel. At other times he focuses on the nature of the ministry in the church. This literary "interchange" can be portrayed as follows:

A_1	1:1-4	Charge to Timothy
B_1	1:5-17	Focus on the Church
A_2	1:18-20	Charge to Timothy
B_2	2:1-4:5	Focus on the Church
A_3	4:6-5:2	Charge to Timothy
B_3	5:3-20	Focus on the Church
A_4	5:21-23	Charge to Timothy
B_4	5:24-6:10	Focus on the Church
A_5	6:11-16	Charge to Timothy
B_5	6:17-19	Focus on the Church
A_6	6:20-21	Charge to Timothy

Everything he writes in this letter reflects his love for and his trust in Timothy to act as an anointed minister of the Gospel. Timothy is a young leader who is being mentored by Paul and who in turn is mentoring other emerging young leaders. In our foundational passage, part of the longest of the six "Charge to Timothy" segments, Paul gives eight imperatives to Timothy: two regarding what he should not do; six about the priority items for a young leader:

- 12a ***despise not*** youth
- 12b ***set*** an example
- 13 ***pay attention*** to the public reading of Scripture, preaching and teaching
- 14 ***neglect not*** God's gift
- 15a ***devote*** yourself to these things
- 15b ***immerse*** yourself in these things
- 16a ***keep a close watch*** on yourself and on your teaching
- 16b ***persevere*** in these things

The instructions that Paul gives to a younger leader underscore his confidence in Timothy's ability to be able to make spiritually mature choices. You entrust a charge to someone who is trustworthy, and that is a character issue; not an age issue. Paul confidently delegates to Timothy a leadership role in the church. These are encouraging words of endorsement.

Keep Going:

Meditate on the eight commands/instructions Paul gives to Timothy. What do you like about them? What do you find challenging? On which of them do you feel like God would want you to focus? How can you cultivate more the spiritual gift not only in yourself, but also in those around you? Are there any younger leaders near you that you can encourage like Paul did with Timothy? How can you endorse them in their ministry contribution?

Value #7 – Be Decentralized: Authority Dispersed

Biblical Foundation:

The next day, Moses took his seat to hear the people's disputes against each other. They waited before him from morning till evening.

When Moses' father-in-law saw all that Moses was doing for the people, he asked, "What are you really accomplishing here? Why are you trying to do all this alone while everyone stands around you from morning till evening?"

Moses replied, "Because the people come to me to get a ruling from God. When a dispute arises, they come to me, and I am the one who settles the case between the quarreling parties. I inform the people of God's decrees and give them his instructions."

"This is not good!" Moses' father-in-law exclaimed. "You're going to wear yourself out—and the people, too. This job is too heavy a burden for you to handle all by yourself. Now listen to me, and let me give you a word of advice, and may God be with you. You should continue to be the people's representative before God, bringing their disputes to him. Teach them God's decrees, and give them his instructions. Show them how to conduct their lives. But select from all the people some capable, honest men who fear God and hate bribes. Appoint them as leaders over groups of one thousand, one hundred, fifty, and ten. They should

always be available to solve the people's common disputes, but have them bring the major cases to you. Let the leaders decide the smaller matters themselves. They will help you carry the load, making the task easier for you. If you follow this advice, and if God commands you to do so, then you will be able to endure the pressures, and all these people will go home in peace."

Moses listened to his father-in-law's advice and followed his suggestions. He chose capable men from all over Israel and appointed them as leaders over the people. He put them in charge of groups of one thousand, one hundred, fifty, and ten. These men were always available to solve the people's common disputes. They brought the major cases to Moses, but they took care of the smaller matters themselves (Exo 18:13-26).

Discovery Starter:

Though Moses had a heart to serve his people well, his father-in-law Jethro recognized that he had unwisely centralized decision-making around himself. This centralized leadership style was clearly "not good" and would have negative effects on both Moses and the people (vv 17-18). Jethro urged Moses to disperse authority, not concentrate it. Today's leaders should likewise think of how to empower others, instead of amassing power unto themselves.

To this end, Jethro encourages Moses to do several things that every leader should take to heart:

- 18:19 – Continue to stand before God, interceding on behalf of the people. Prayer for those whom you are leading is a hallmark of every godly leader.
- 18:20 – Teach, teach, teach. To lead people into godly decision-making, godly leaders must take time to instruct them in the ways of wise living. When people are governed by a clear internal understanding of what is right, then the need for centralized, external government is diminished.
- 18:21 – Select and appoint other responsible leaders, delegating authority to them. These leaders must be people of competence and character. Competency has to do with their capabilities and skills. Character has to do with their integrity and trustworthiness

Psalm 119 is the only other chapter in the Bible which uses the same Hebrew words used by Jethro to describe these "<u>honest</u> men who <u>fear</u> God and hate <u>bribes</u>" (Exo 19:21). The Psalmist...

1. prays for the integrity/truthfulness which comes from being shaped by the Word of God, saying, "Do not snatch your word of truth from me, for your regulations are my only hope" (Psa 119:43).

2. prays that he will align himself with all those who fear God. He says, "Let me be united with all who fear you, with those who know your laws" (Psa 119:79) and "May all who fear you find in me a cause for joy, for I have put my hope in your word" (Psa 119:74).

3. prays that the love of walking in God's ways will keep him from the covetousness that would make him susceptible to bribery, saying, "Give me an eagerness for your laws rather than a love for money!" (Psa 119:36).

Keep Going:

A phrase the Bible regularly uses as a shorthand description of a life of integrity is "the fear of the Lord." It is used most often in the book of Proverbs, a very practical book about how we should live. Consider the following passages: Pro 1:7,29; 2:5; 8:13; 9:10; 10:27; 14:26,27; 15:16,33; 16:6; 19:23; 22:4; 23:17. As you read through them, ask Holy Spirit how he wants to grow these character qualities in your life.

Value #8 – Be International and Interdenominational: Paul's Missionary Band

Biblical Foundation:

Several men were traveling with him. They were Sopater son of Pyrrhus from Berea; Aristarchus and Secundus from Thessalonica; Gaius from Derbe; Timothy; and Tychicus and Trophimus from the province of Asia (Act 20:4).

Discovery Starter:

Luke notes seven who traveled overland with Paul from Ephesus to Troas on his third missionary journey. These are just some of those who served alongside Paul in the spread of the gospel. According to Eusebius, the famous 4th century church historian, Paul "had innumerable fellow-laborers, or fellow-soldiers, as he called them ... for he gave enduring testimony concerning them in his own epistles" (*Ecclesiastical History* 3.4.4).

Indeed, Paul used nine different terms to identify 39 individuals as his companions in ministry. He described each as an apostle (*apostolos*), deacon (*diakonos*), fellow-servant (*sundoulos/doulos*), fellow-prisoner (*sunaichmalotos*), fellow-soldier (*sustratiotes/stratiotes*), fellow-worker (*sunergos*), laborer (*kopiao*), partner (*koinonos*), and/or as a sister/brother (*adelphe/adelphos*). The passages in which Paul describes his 39 partners in ministry are:

Achaicus	1Co 16:17
Andronicus	Rom 16:7
Apollos	1Co 3:5-9; 4:6-9,12; 16:12
Apphia	Phm 2
Aquila	Rom 16:3
Archippus	Col 4:17; Phm 2
Aristarchus	Col 4:10-11; Phm 24
Barnabas	1Co 9:5-7; Gal 2:9
Clement	Php 4:3
Demas	Col 4:11,14; Phm 24
Epaphras	Col 1:7; 4:11-13; Phm 23
Epaphroditus	Php 2:25
Euodia	Php 4:2-3
Fortunatus	1Co 16:17
James	Gal 2:9
John	Gal 2:9
Junia	Rom 16:7
Justus	Col 4:11
Luke	Col 4:11,14; Phm 24
Mark	Col 4:11; 2Ti 4:11; Phm 24
Mary	Rom 16:6
Onesimus	Col 4:9; Phm 10-13,16
Onesiphorus	2Ti 1:16-18
Persis	Rom 16:12
Peter/Cephas	Gal 2:9
Philemon	Phm 1,6-7,10-13,17,20
Phoebe	Rom 16:1
Priscilla	Rom 16:3
Quartus	Rom 16:23
Silas	2Co 1:24; 1Th 2:6

Sosthenes	1Co 1:1
Stephana	1Co 16:17
Syntyche	Php 4:2-3
Timothy	Rom 16:21; 1Co 16:10; 2Co 1:1,24; 3:3-6; 4:1; 6:3-4; 8:19-20; Php 1:1; Col 1:1; 1Th 2:6; 3:2; 1Ti 4:6; 2Ti 2:3-6; 4:5
Titus	2Co 2:13; 8:16-9:5
Tryphaena	Rom 16:12
Tryphosa	Rom 16:12
Tychicus	Eph 6:21; Col 4:7
Urbanus	Rom 16:9

This list illustrates how remarkably diverse Paul's team was. It includes Africans, Asians and Europeans, as well as both men and women. The group includes some wealthy individuals as well as slaves; the politically powerful and prisoners; Jews and Gentiles; the learned and the uneducated. Paul did not just surround himself with people like himself. He reached out to many who came from backgrounds very different from his own and included them in his Great Commission activities.

Keep Going:

Paul, a Jew, championed Gentiles. He promoted others who were not like himself. Spend some time in prayerful reflection. Is there someone who comes from a different background, a different nation, a different ethno-linguistic group, that you could champion? How could you work with them in spreading the good news of Jesus? What concrete steps can you take this week to reach out to others who are not like you?

Value #9 – Have a Biblical Christian Worldview: Think and Act!

Biblical Foundation:

And now, dear brothers and sisters, one final thing. Fix your thoughts on what is true, and honorable, and right, and pure, and lovely, and admirable. Think about things that are excellent and worthy of praise. Keep putting into practice all you learned and received from me—everything you heard from me and saw me doing. Then the God of peace will be with you (Php 4:8-9).

Discovery Starter:

As Paul gets ready to draw this lovely "thank you letter" to a close he has two final commands (excluding the charge to greet one another in 4:21): to think and to act. Paul introduces this dual command as "one final thing" – because they are two sides of the same coin. Let's take a look.

Paul urges his hearers to think about eight things, about whatever is:

1. true
2. honorable
3. right
4. pure
5. lovely
6. admirable
7. excellent
8. worthy of praise

What an amazing list! The Greek verb is *logizomai* (Strong's #3049) and it is used as an imperative five times in the New Testament. Apart from this passage in Philippians you can find it in Rom 6:11; 1Co 4:1; and 2Co 10:7,11 (take a look; discover more!). Paul's point is that we are not to give this list a quick once over. We are to reflect on it very deliberately in order that we might give ourselves to these good things. When we truly value these things, we will no longer see them merely as an external standard which we strive to attain. They become an internal delight that we gladly embrace because we consider them to be both desirable and beneficial.

Paul doesn't stop with the "think about" command, because Biblical truth is actionable. It should make a difference in our lives. We should conform our actions to align with God's revelation. The goal of discipleship is truth understood and applied. Revealed truth must reshape the habits of our lives. So Paul's next imperative is *prasso* (Strong's #4238): "Keep putting into practice all you learned ..." Paul used this same word earlier, when he was testifying before Herod Agrippa. Paul begins his defense saying, "I preached first to those in Damascus, then in Jerusalem and throughout all Judea, and also to the Gentiles, that all must repent of their sins and turn to God – and prove they have changed by the good things they <u>do</u>" (Act 26:20). When we repent and follow Jesus, we do not only think about good things; we do them! This is the transformative power of the gospel in action.

Keep Going:

So, here's a gift that will help you think and act as Paul exhorted: it is a list of all the occurrences in the New Testament of the eight words that we are to "think about" and "put into practice." There's plenty here for you to keep discovering more of what God wants to teach you. So, get started and may you lean into Holy Spirit as you seek to make these things your default way of thinking and doing life:

- "whatever is **<u>true</u>**" – *alethes* (#227) occurs 25 times: Mat 22:16; Mar 12:14; Joh 3:33; 4:18; 5:31,32; 7:18; 8:13,14,16,17,26; 10:41; 19:35; 21:24; Act 12:9; Rom 3:4; 2Co 6:8; Php 4:8; Tit 1:13; 1Pe 5:12; 2Pe 2:22; 1Jo 2:8,27; 3Jo 1:12.

- "whatever is **<u>noble</u>**" – *semnos* (#4586) occurs 4 times: Php 4:8; 1Ti 3:8,11; Tit 2:2.

- "whatever is **<u>right</u>**" – *dikaios* (#1342) occurs 81 times: Mat 1:19; 5:45; 9:13; 10:41a,41b,41c; 13:17,43,49; 20:4,7; 23:28,29,35a,35b; 25:37,46; 27:19,24; Mar 2:17; 6:20; Luk 1:6,17; 2:25; 5:32; 12:57; 14:14; 15:7; 18:9; 20:20; 23:47,50; Joh 5:30; 7:24; 17:25; Act 3:14; 4:19; 7:52; 10:22; 22:14; 24:15; Rom 1:17; 2:13; 3:10,26; 5:7,19; 7:12; Gal 3:11; Eph 6:1; Php 1:7; 4:8; Col 4:1; 2Th 1:5,6; 1Ti 1:9; 2Ti 4:8; Tit 1:8; Heb 10:38; 11:4; 12:23; Jam 5:6,16 1Pe 3:12,18; 4:18; 2Pe 1:13; 2:7,8a,8b; 1Jo 1:9; 2:1,29; 3:7a,7b,12; Rev 15:3; 16:5,7; 19:2; 22:11.

- "whatever is **<u>pure</u>**" – *hagnos* (#53) occurs 8 times: 2Co 7:11; 11:2; Php 4:8; 1Ti 5:22; Tit 2:5; Jam 3:17; 1Pe 3:2; 1Jo 3:3.

- "whatever is **<u>lovely</u>**" – *prosphiles* (#4375) occurs only one time, here in Php 4:8.

- "whatever is **<u>admirable</u>**" – *euphemos* (#2163) occurs only one time, here in Php 4:8.

- "if anything is **<u>excellent</u>**" – *arete* (#703) occurs 5 times: Php 4:8; 1Pe 2:9; 2Pe 1:3,5a,5b.

- "or **praiseworthy**" – *epainos* (#1868) occurs 11 times: Rom 2:29; 13:3; 1Co 4:5; 2Co 8:18; Eph 1:6,12,14; Php 1:11; 4:8; 1Pe 1:7; 2:14.

Value #10 – Function in Teams: Two by Two

Biblical Foundation:

And he called his twelve disciples together and began sending them out two by two, giving them authority to cast out evil spirits. He told them to take nothing for their journey except a walking stick—no food, no traveler's bag, no money. He allowed them to wear sandals but not to take a change of clothes.

"Wherever you go," he said, "stay in the same house until you leave town. But if any place refuses to welcome you or listen to you, shake its dust from your feet as you leave to show that you have abandoned those people to their fate."

So the disciples went out, telling everyone they met to repent of their sins and turn to God. And they cast out many demons and healed many sick people, anointing them with olive oil (Mar 6:7-13).

Discovery Starter:

When Jesus called his disciples he called them into community. They did life and ministry together as a team. So when he sent them on their first missionary adventure, he sent them out in small teams, "two by two." Earlier, Mark tells us that Jesus "appointed twelve that they might be with him and that he might send them out to preach ..." (Mar 3:14-15). Discipleship had a dual purpose: They were called to have a relationship with Jesus and to help others have a relationship with Jesus. And they were to do this together, as a team.

In many ways it was an unlikely team. Among them was Judas Iscariot. Not only was Judas known to be a thief (Joh 12:6), but we are told that he indignantly chastised his team leader – Jesus! – in public (Joh 12:4-5). That must have created some interesting team dynamics! But that was not all. Jesus had picked both Matthew (who, as a tax-collector, was a pro-Roman collaborator) and Simon (who, as a zealot, was an anti-Roman revolutionary) to be on his team. They must have had some heated arguments coming from opposite sides of the political spectrum! Even so, Jesus opted to minister with a team, rather than go it alone. He saw diversity not as a liability but as an asset, providing a unique opportunity for "sandpaper discipleship," as one rubbed against another, smoothing off the rough edges. The unlikely love between natural enemies would be a powerful witness to the transforming power of the gospel. He taught his team, "Your love for one another will prove to the world that you are my disciples" (Joh 13:35). In AD 197, Tertullian would write that the critics of the church recognized in awe, "how they love one another!'" (Tertullian, *Apologeticus* 39.114).

We don't grow in relational grace in isolation, nor do we advance God's relational goals ministering as lone rangers. Emmanuel Jesus modeled "withness" as a foundation for "witness." Jesus chose to minister with a team, and Peter – one of Jesus' original team members – reminds us that Jesus "is your example, and you must follow in his steps" (1Pe 2:21).

Keep Going:

The following is a list of over 100 verses in Mark that explicitly talk about Jesus being with his disciples and doing something together with them as his team. The record of his "withness" is found in every chapter. Are you walking with Jesus in this degree of "withness"? Are you doing "team" with your colleagues like Jesus did with his disciples? Consider the following: Mar 1:17-21,29,38; 2:14-15; 3:7,13-14,20,34-35; 4:10,34,36; 5:24,37,40; 6:1,7,30-33,35,45,48,50-51,53-54; 7:17; 8:1-2,6-7,10,13-14,27,32; 9:2,5, 8,14,28,31-33,35; 10:10,13-14,23,27-30,32-42,46; 11:1,11,14,19-22,27; 12:43; 13:3-4; 14:14,17-20,22-26,28,33-34,37,40-41,45,47,67; 15:41; 16:19.

Value #11 – Exhibit Servant Leadership: Justice, Mercy, Humility

Biblical Foundation:

O people, the LORD *has told you what is good, and this is what he requires of you: to do what is right, to love mercy, and to walk humbly with your God* (Mic 6:8).

Discovery Starter:

God is our ultimate model for leadership. Ethan the Ezrahite declares to God, "Righteousness and *mishpat* are the foundation of your throne; *hesed* and faithfulness go before you" (Psa 89:14). The two words transliterated from Hebrew describing God's rule are the same words that Micah uses in our foundational passage. *Mishpat* is the word we commonly translate as justice, and speaks of the governance of a judge who equitably executes the law and its consequences. *Hesed* is translated as mercy or loving-kindness or compassion. It is used to describe the quality of heart that maintains an enduring, covenantal relationship of love.

When it comes to justice and mercy, how can we be imitators of God? In the Ten Commandments, God makes it clear that the law carries consequences. He states, "I do not leave unpunished the sins of those who hate me, but I punish the children for the sins of their parents to the third and fourth generations. But I lavish my love on those who love me and obey my commands, even for a thousand generations" (Exo 20:5b-6; Deu 5:9b-10). To get the full impact of these words, we have to do a little math. Whereas justice reaches to 3 or 4 generations, mercy extends to 1000 generations! In other words, though God will always be just, he's about 250 to 333 times more desirous displaying mercy! God <u>does</u> justice, but he **LOVES** mercy. What a contrast that is with the way I often respond. When someone has done me wrong, my natural inclination is to exact justice, not extend mercy – certainly I don't wish for mercy over justice to the tune of 250+ times!

If we are going to be servant leaders who imitate God in doing justice and loving mercy, the third quality listed by Micah is absolutely vital! We will only have grace to walk in a servant-hearted manner if we "walk humbly with God." We can't do it on our own. We can do it with God. It is in the context of relational intimacy with God, that we find the grace to relinquish our rights and serve others in a Christ-like manner.

Keep Going:

The following seven passages from Psalms all contain the Hebrew words *mishpat* (justice) and *hesed* (mercy). Read through them and ponder the extraordinary character of God who blends them so artfully, indeed beautifully, in his every action.

- Psa 25:8-10
- Psa 33:5
- Psa 36:5-7
- Psa 48:9-11
- Psa 101:1
- Psa 103:6-12
- Psa 119:41-43

In your time of meditation, reflect on what steps you can take to grow in *mishpat* (justice) and *hesed* (mercy) as you "walk humbly with God." As you finish, invite God to work in your life in these areas so you can better reflect his servant heart to those around you.

Value #12 – Do First, Then Teach: A Three-Step Approach

Biblical Foundation:

This was because Ezra had determined to study and obey the Law of the LORD and to teach those decrees and regulations to the people of Israel (Ezr 7:10).

Discovery Starter:

When Ezra enters the story (Ezr 7:1-10), it twice states that "the gracious hand of his God was on him" (7:6,9). Why? It was not accidental. It was because (as various translations say ...) "Ezra had determined to ... had prepared his heart to ... had devoted himself to ... had set his heart to ... had committed himself to ... had resolved to ... had directed his heart to ... had devoted his life to ..." do three things:

- Study
- Obey
- Teach

The focused passion and intentional commitment displayed by Ezra is inspirational. Ezra modeled something that is worthy of imitation. His intense hunger for God shaped his priorities, and calls us to do likewise.

Luke says that the Gospel he wrote was "about everything Jesus began to do and teach" (Acts 1:1). Do and teach. Jesus' actions fully embodied his teaching. He walked the talk and that is why his words rang so true! We should model ourselves after his example. When our words are a confirming echo to our deeds, then our teaching has a deep and lasting, transformative impact. But lofty words fall lifeless from the lips of those who do not practice what they preach. We are told that Jesus "was a prophet mighty in deed and word before God and all the people" (Luk 24:19 ESV) and he's at work to establish in us "every good work and word" (2Th 2:16-17 ESV). Our doing and our teaching are to go hand-in-hand.

Back to Ezra. He obeyed and taught, but those actions were preceded by study. The same Hebrew word, *darash*, is also used in these passages:

1. David said to Asaph, "Search for the LORD and for his strength; continually seek him" (1Ch 16:11).

2. Josiah instructed Shaphan, "Inquire about the words written in the scroll that has been found" (2Ch 34:21).

3. Isaiah exhorts his readers, "Search the book of the LORD, and see what he will do" (Isa 34:16), and "Seek the LORD while you can find him. Call on him now while he is near" (Isa 55:6).

Study, search, inquire, seek. This is just a sampling of *darash*. It's a call to set your heart to the thoughtful and passionate pursuit of God.

Keep Going:

Ezra's intense pursuit of God led him to a place of intimacy with God. What he knew about God was not second-hand knowledge, but resulted from a rich relational encounter with the living God. The record of his devotional life reflects this intimacy. For him God was not a distant divinity but – in his words – "my God." He tells us, "I fell to my knees and lifted my hands to the LORD my God. I prayed, 'O my God ...'" (Ezr 9:5-6). When God becomes "my God" through pursing passion and relational obedience, we like Ezra will have transformative teaching to share with those around us.

The Hebrew phrase translated "my God" is used not only by Ezra, but by other Biblical notables like: Asaph, Caleb, Daniel, David, Elijah, Ethan the Ezrahite, Habakkuk, Hosea, Isaiah, Jacob, Jonah, Joshua, Micah, Moses,

Nehemiah, Ruth, Solomon, and Zechariah. But of all of them, David is the one who utters "my God" more frequently than anyone else. Take time to read through these passages in which David speaks of "my God" – 2Sa 22:7,22,30; 24:24; 1Ch 11:19; 17:25; 21:17; 22:7; 28:20; 29:2,3a,3b,17; Psa 3:7; 5:2; 7:1,3; 13:3; 18:2,6,21,28,29; 22:1a,1b,2,10; 25:2; 30:2,12; 31:14; 35:23,24; 38:15,21; 40:5,8,17; 59:1; 63:1; 68:24; 69:3; 86:2,12; 109:26; 140:6; 143:10; 145:1. As you reflect on these passages, I encourage you to pray and set your heart to seek God, so you too can join the list of those who know him as "my God." May you keep discovering more and more about this amazing God in deeply personal ways. And may your hunger for him lead you continuously to study, obey and teach about your God.

Value #13 – Be Relationship-Oriented: So What's New?

Biblical Foundation:

So now I am giving you a new commandment: Love each other. Just as I have loved you, you should love each other. Your love for one another will prove to the world that you are my disciples (Joh 13:34-35).

Discovery Starter:

What's new about this commandment? Prior to Jesus, the moral high ground was to love neighbor as self. Because every individual has been created by God in God's image, all people are equally valuable and we should love each accordingly. But then Jesus came. He loved like no one else had loved before. He introduced a "greater love" (Joh 15:13). Paul says, "But God showed his great love for us by sending Christ to die for us while we were still sinners" (Rom 5:8). Jesus' loving sacrifice on our behalf has forever raised the bar. He has changed the narrative of history.

Our love for neighbor is no longer to be measured by how much we love ourselves, but by how much Jesus has loved us. Jesus is the new reference point for defining true love. We are to have the same rights-relinquishing, servant-hearted "attitude that Jesus Christ had" – and which is the glorious theme of an early Christian hymn (Php 2:5-11). Jesus' example calls us to prefer our neighbors as Christ preferred us. We're to follow this new example. Therefore,

"Don't be selfish ... Don't look out only for your own interests ... Don't just pretend to love others. Really love them ... Love each other with genuine affection, and take delight in honoring each other" (Php 2:3-4; Rom 12:9-10).

This other-preferring, self-sacrificing love is not due to some unhealthy dysfunction. Jesus experienced no coercion. He says, "No one can take my life from me. I sacrifice it voluntarily" (Joh 10:18). Jesus' servant-hearted love was rooted in his wholeness as a person. On his final evening with his closest friends, "Jesus ... loved his disciples ... to the very end ... Jesus knew that the Father had given him authority over everything and that he had come from God and would return to God. So he got up from the table, took off his robe" and washed their feet (Joh 13:1-5), a graphic prelude to what he would do on the cross. Because he was secure in his identity, and knew where he had come from and where he was going, he could voluntarily serve with the greatest love ever displayed. Jesus is the new standard.

Keep Going:

Eight times we are given the positive command to love (*agapao*) in the New Testament. Three of these are about loving our enemies; three are about husbands loving their wives; and two are about how we are to love our brothers and sisters in the body of Christ. Consider these passages in the light of how Jesus' life has redefined the meaning of true love.

- Mat 5:44 But I say, <u>love</u> your enemies! Pray for those who persecute you!
- Luk 6:27 But to you who are willing to listen, I say, <u>love</u> your enemies! Do good to those who hate you.
- Luk 6:35 <u>Love</u> your enemies! Do good to them. Lend to them without expecting to be repaid.
- Eph 5:25 For husbands, this means <u>love</u> your wives, just as Christ loved the church. He gave up his life for her
- Eph 5:33 So again I say, each man must <u>love</u> his wife as he loves himself, and the wife must respect her husband
- Col 3:19 Husbands, <u>love</u> your wives and never treat them harshly.
- 1Pe 1:22 so now you must show sincere love to each other as brothers and sisters. <u>Love</u> each other deeply with all your heart.

- 1Pe 2:17 Respect everyone, and <u>love</u> the family of believers. Fear God, and respect the king.

Take time to linger over these passages. Thank God for his immeasurable love. Ask him to show you how he sees the relationships you have – where can you go deeper in love? Ask him to show you steps you can take to grow in Christ-like love. Determine to take those steps which lead you to serve others around you and find new ways to express honor towards them. Take time to tell someone how much you value your relationship with him or her.

Value #14 – Value the Individual: No Partiality!

Biblical Foundation:

Slaves, obey your earthly masters with deep respect and fear. Serve them sincerely as you would serve Christ. Try to please them all the time, not just when they are watching you. As slaves of Christ, do the will of God with all your heart. Work with enthusiasm, as though you were working for the Lord rather than for people. Remember that the Lord will reward each one of us for the good we do, whether we are slaves or free.

Masters, treat your slaves in the same way. Don't threaten them; remember, you both have the same Master in heaven, and he has no favorites (Eph 6:5-9).

Discovery Starter:

Paul's words seem to be an uncomfortable endorsement of slavery. Is he just perpetuating the continuance of an unjust system? But wait! Though his words initially reflect the accepted perspective of his society ... Paul had a transformative surprise up his sleeve! After rehearsing the expected obligations of a slave, Paul unexpectedly turns to the masters and tells them to treat their slaves "in the same way"! In the course of that brief sentence he turned unjust social hierarchy on its head and established egalitarianism as the new gospel norm. It is impossible to enslave someone if you are expected to serve them in the same way they serve you. They are no longer your slave, but your brother.

Paul anchors this thought in the most solid of all foundations: in the character and nature of God. Paul's concluding punch line is that this is so because our "Master in heaven ... has no favorites." He is building upon Moses' understanding that "the great God, the mighty and awesome God ... shows no partiality and cannot be bribed. He ensures that orphans and widows receive justice. He shows love to the foreigners living among you and gives them food and clothing. So you, too ..." (Deu 10:17-19; see Rom 2:11; Gal 2:6; Col 3:25).

So you too ... Because God sees all people as valuable, so must we. Whenever our societies divide people into categories and value one more than another, they do not reflect God's perspective. Whether "Jew or Gentile, slave or free, male and female" (Gal 3:28) – all people are valuable. This is true, even though all people have sinned and "fall short of God's glorious standard" (Rom 3:23). Right belief and right behavior is not a pre-condition for being valued. God valued and loved us all even when "we were still sinners" (Rom 5:8). Every human being is valuable, because each one is created by God in his image (Gen 1:25-27; 9:6; 1Co 11:7; Col 1:15-17; Jam 3:9). Every individual has inestimable worth (Psa 72:14; Mat 6:26; 10:31; 12:12; 16:26), created with specific gifts and talents, which are to be discovered and developed for that individual's God-given potential to be fully realized.

Keep Going:

Have you ever considered yourself better than – or worse than – others because of nationality, education, socio-economic standing, or any other reason? If so, what needs to change? Take time to repent and ask God to help you see people as he sees them. Ask God to help you see yourself as he sees you. What steps can you take this day to communicate to someone else their incredible value?

Value #15 – Value Families: Doing Family and Ministry Together

Biblical Foundation:

So a church leader must be a man whose life is above reproach. He must be faithful to his wife. He must exercise self-control, live wisely, and have a good reputation. He must enjoy having guests in his home, and he must be able to teach. He must not be a heavy drinker or be violent. He must be gentle, not quarrelsome, and not love money. He must manage his own family well, having children who respect and obey him. For if a man cannot manage his own household, how can he take care of God's church? (1Ti 3:2-5).

Discovery Starter:

When our children were aged 15, 13, 11 and 9, God spoke to my wife Christine and me that he wanted to do something new with us as a family. After two decades serving on YWAM bases we felt we were to go "on the road" – visiting some of the most far-flung, least-visited YWAM communities in Africa, Asia and the Pacific. We called our children together to discuss the implications and seek the Lord. We did not rush the decision. Over the next several weeks we talked and prayed together often. When we were sure of the word of the Lord, we embarked on a new Great Commission adventure. Over the next 44 months we traveled and ministered together in 189 YWAM bases in 91 countries. All of us played a key part. Midway through our travels, a mission leader approached Sarah, my pre-teen daughter, and asked her, "How do you feel about your parents dragging you around the world?" Surprised, she looked him square in the eye, "What do you mean? I'm dragging them," she retorted. She clearly "owned" the ministry we were doing together as a family.

Some have proposed that God's priority is, "God first, family second, ministry third." Though well-intentioned, this formula is not found in Scripture. God's instructions are simpler: God first. Period. There should be no conflict between family and ministry if we listen carefully to God, for he is the source of both. He who called you into ministry has not forgotten that he also called you to family. These two callings complement one another. It's simple: seek God on every occasion and embrace his guidance together. He is Lord. As a family we are to hear and obey.

In Paul's instructions to Timothy we see that leadership responsibilities and family life are interwoven together seamlessly. Marital and parental dynamics are really important. In fact, Paul's final point is that how a person does family qualifies them for leadership in God's family – the church. Family and ministry go hand in hand. We hold family in high regard and celebrate the fact that we can display the kingdom of God with our family.

Keep Going:

Jesus, quoting Psalm 8:2, defended the role of children in ministry when he spoke to religious leaders (Mat 21:15-17). When Jesus spoke to his disciples (most of whom were single), he underlined the importance of children in his eyes. Jesus wanted to make sure that children were included in what he was doing (Mat 19:13-15; Mar 10:13-16; Luk 18:15-17). Take time to read these passages and – whether you are married or single – consider how you can take Jesus' words to heart and not only include children in ministry, but place them front and center as Jesus did. Ask God to lead you to develop ministry expressions which honor and celebrate family.

Value #16 – Practice Dependence on God: A Generosity Contest

Biblical Foundation:

"Should people cheat God? Yet you have cheated me!

"But you ask, 'What do you mean? When did we ever cheat you?'

"You have cheated me of the tithes and offerings due to me. You are under a curse, for your whole nation has been cheating me. Bring all the tithes into the storehouse so there will be enough food in my Temple. If you do," says the LORD of Heaven's Armies, "I will open the windows of heaven for you. I will pour out a blessing so great you won't have enough room to take it in! Try it! Put me to the test! Your crops will be abundant, for I will guard them from insects and disease. Your grapes will not fall from the vine before they are ripe," says the LORD of Heaven's Armies. "Then all nations will call you blessed, for your land will be such a delight," says the LORD of Heaven's Armies (Mal 3:8-12).

Discovery Starter:

Test God? It seems inappropriate considering Jesus' response to Satan. Jesus quoted Deuteronomy 6:16, "You must not test the LORD your God" (Mat 4:7). But in Malachi the circumstances are different, and God urges the people, "Put me to the test!" He is challenging them to a generosity contest. People had not been giving the triennial tithe (Deu 14:28-29; 26:12-14), which was designed to create a "storehouse" fund to help the Levites, widows and orphans in times of economic distress. God challenged them to try to out-give God himself.

If you accept God's challenge, know that you are up against the most generous of givers! In Genesis, the three verbs that God uses most frequently to describe his actions are: *nathan* (gives: 26x), *barak* (blesses: 14x), and *'asah* (makes: 11x). Above all else, God wanted us to know that he is a generous God! He is a God who gives to people lavishly, frequently, unexpectedly, caringly, abundantly, personally, thoughtfully, consistently ... For this reason, even in the leanest of times, we can be generous givers as we accept his challenge and seek to imitate him! This is a (con-)test that God welcomes.

Because of this, I have come to love YWAM offerings! One of my favorites was during the Leadership Training School in South Africa in 1998. There were 124 students from 52 countries. While praying for finances to birth a new ministry one person felt led to give his guitar as a gift. It was an act of unexpected generous obedience that released a remarkable spirit of giving. As people prayed, one by one they slipped away to their rooms and came back, adding their gifts to the growing pile. For nearly two hours people laid their treasures – big and small – before the Lord. The one who first gave wrote:

> *I gave my guitar, they gave their shoes.*
> *I have much, they gave their last possessions.*
> *I live a life of comfort with occasional faith, they live a life of daily provision.*
> *I gave with great sorrow, they gave with joy.*
> *I gave my most precious possession, they gave their last.*
> *I know what tomorrow holds, they know God.*

Keep Going:

Take time today to consider how you can accept God's challenge to a generosity contest. Determine to give something to someone you've never given to before, someone who would not be expecting anything from you. Your expression of generosity might involve money or an object, or it might simply consist in an action or a word which brings unexpected blessing. Make it as lavish as you can. As you give, remember Paul's words, "This most generous God who gives seed to the farmer that becomes bread for your meals is more than extravagant with you. He gives you something you can then give away, which grows into full-formed lives, robust in God, wealthy in every way, so that you can be generous in every way, producing with us great praise to God" (2Co 9:9-11 MSG).

Value #17 – Practice Hospitality: Close Encounters of the Divine Kind

Biblical Foundation:

The LORD appeared again to Abraham near the oak grove belonging to Mamre. One day Abraham was sitting at the entrance to his tent during the hottest part of the day. He looked up and noticed three men standing nearby. When he saw them, he ran to meet them and welcomed them, bowing low to the ground.

"My lord," he said, "if it pleases you, stop here for a while. Rest in the shade of this tree while water is brought to wash your feet. And since you've honored your servant with this visit, let me prepare some food to refresh you before you continue on your journey."

"All right," they said. "Do as you have said."

So Abraham ran back to the tent and said to Sarah, "Hurry! Get three large measures of your best flour, knead it into dough, and bake some bread." Then Abraham ran out to the herd and chose a tender calf and gave it to his servant, who quickly prepared it. When the food was ready, Abraham took some yogurt and milk and the roasted meat, and he served it to the men. As they ate, Abraham waited on them in the shade of the trees (Gen 18:1-8).

Discovery Starter:

The story of Abraham's hospitality to the three strangers sets the context for the exhortation we read in Heb 13:2, "Don't forget to show hospitality to strangers, for some who have done this have entertained angels without realizing it!" Because of this story the ancient Jewish rabbis taught that "Abraham introduced ... hospitality" into the world (*Midrash Tanhuma Yelammedenu,*

Noach 14.2) and therefore hospitality was called "the Abrahamic virtue" (*Chizkuni*, Genesis 21.21.1).

Although Abraham's household was a very large enterprise (from within its ranks he could muster "318 trained men" according to Gen 14:14), when it came to serving these unexpected guests he did not delegate it out to his servants. He welcomed these strangers himself. Consider the many verbs which describe his actions: Abraham "was sitting, looked up, noticed, saw, ran to meet, bowing low, said, [found favor, asked, asked], let me prepare, to refresh, ran back, said, ran out, chose, gave, took, [prepared], served, and waited on" his angelic guests. Abraham's intentional activity modeled the heart and function of hospitality. We read: "*let me prepare some food to refresh you*" – this described the activity (*prepare*) but also the purpose of hospitality (*to refresh*). Three times it mentions that Abraham "*ran*" underscoring his diligence. His actions embodied an over-the-top generosity when he asked Sarah to "*Get three large measures*" (the equivalent of 28 cups worth!) "*of your best flour.*" He certainly wasn't simply meeting a minimal cultural requirement. He lavished hospitality on the three strangers and did it in a servant-hearted way as he personally "*serve*d and *waited on*" them.

The three strangers are called *xenos* in the Greek Septuagint translation: foreigners, outsiders. In English we speak of *xenophobia*: the fear of those who are different from us. It is important to note that when Paul lists the characteristics of a Christian leader in Titus 1:7-8, he mentions five things that a leader must avoid before proceeding to six things that a leader must embrace. The first of these positive requirements is that the leader must be *philoxenos*: a lover of the stranger, who graciously welcomes the outsider into the family of God in very practical ways. This is true hospitality.

Keep Going:

As Abraham saw strangers passing by his house he invited them to partake in a generous meal. Are there strangers in your neighborhood whom you could invite to join you in breaking bread? How else could you reach out to someone in your community that you do not know, and display the welcoming love of God? Why not take the time to pray with those in your household and develop a plan to show hospitality to someone who is a *xenos* to you this week?

Value #18 – Communicate with Integrity: Radical Honesty

Biblical Foundation:

You have also heard that our ancestors were told, 'You must not break your vows; you must carry out the vows you make to the LORD.' But I say, do not make any vows! Do not say, 'By heaven!' because heaven is God's throne. And do not say, 'By the earth!' because the earth is his footstool. And do not say, 'By Jerusalem!' for Jerusalem is the city of the great King. Do not even say, 'By my head!' for you can't turn one hair white or black. Just say a simple, 'Yes, I will,' or 'No, I won't.' Anything beyond this is from the evil one (Mat 5:33-37).

Discovery Starter:

At an early age I learned to avoid telling lies, or – at least – avoid being caught! The punishment for telling lies was to have my mouth washed out with soap. The lye left an indelible imprint on my taste buds. Though effective to a degree, the soap did not cleanse my heart. I soon learned to tell "the truth" with an intent to mislead. For example, when an argument with my younger sister resulted in an "accidental" punch, I knew I would be in trouble. So I would try to dissuade her from running to Mom. If my efforts did not work, and she took off down the hallway, I'd yell after her in an attempt to stop her with desperate irritation. "Ok ... I'm sorry!" I'd fume. Unmoved by my angry and unrepentant tone of voice she proceeded to tell Mom. Soon I heard my name being called. "Yes," I confessed, "I did hit her, but just barely, and besides she started it." And then I'd add, as sweetly as possible, "And I said 'I'm sorry.'" My feigned angelic demeanor covered up the reality. I had mastered the art of being technically honest while being intentionally deceitful. And thus I avoided the dreaded bar of soap.

In this passage, Jesus teaches us about radical honesty – when words, actions and heart match 100%. His teaching is rooted in the Torah: "Do not bring shame on the name of your God by using it to swear falsely." (Lev 19:12). This is one of six passages in Leviticus which warns against those sins which cause God's holy reputation to be tarnished in eyes of the lost. They are when:

- one says one thing while intending to do something else (Lev 19:12)
- the people do not keep God's commands in holy obedience (Lev 22:31-33)

- priests do not fulfill their functions with integrity (Lev 21:5-6; 22:2)
- anyone sacrifices their child by fire to Molech (Lev 18:21; 20:2-5)

This last point was viewed as the most despicable, unimaginable sin. And the lack of radical honesty is likened unto it. Sobering.

Lord, please apply your soap not only to my tongue, but to my heart as well.

Keep Going:

Psalm 15 details the characteristics of those who live in intimacy with God. From verse 2 through the second line of verse 5, there are ten descriptive statements. Five of them – that's half! – have to do with radical honesty and integrity with the tongue. Read through the psalm and meditate on the five lines in italics. Ask God to show you any area which you need to make right. Is there something of which you need to repent? Is there an act of restitution that you need to make? Is there someone you need to go to in order to restore a relationship? Listen to God and do as he tells you.

15¹ Who may worship in your sanctuary, LORD?
Who may enter your presence on your holy hill?
² Those who lead blameless lives and do what is right,
speaking the truth from sincere hearts.
³ *Those who refuse to gossip*
or harm their neighbors
or speak evil of their friends.
⁴ Those who despise flagrant sinners,
and honor the faithful followers of the LORD,
and keep their promises even when it hurts.
⁵ Those who lend money without charging interest,
and who cannot be bribed to lie about the innocent.
Such people will stand firm forever.

Appendix 1

The Statement Of Purpose, Core Beliefs And Foundational Values Of Youth With A Mission (May 2020)

This document presents YWAM's sincerely held purpose, core beliefs, foundational values and practices which have been compiled in response to specific directives given by God since YWAM's beginning in 1960. They are recorded here in order to pass on to successive generations that which God has emphasized to us. This shared purpose and our YWAM beliefs and values are the guiding principles for both the past and future growth of our Mission. Some are common to all Christians everywhere; others are distinctive to Youth With A Mission. The combination of this purpose, beliefs, values and practices makes up the unique family characteristics of YWAM – our "DNA." They are the framework we hold in high regard for they help us determine who we are, how we live and how we make decisions. A YWAMer is someone who has completed a YWAM Discipleship Training School and who joyfully embraces our Statement of Purpose, Core Beliefs, Foundational Values, Legacy Words and Covenants. **Please copy and share this document in its entirety as presented here.**

YWAM's STATEMENT OF PURPOSE

Youth With A Mission (YWAM) is an international movement of Christians from many denominations dedicated to presenting Jesus personally to this and future generations, to mobilizing as many as possible to help in this task, and to the training and equipping of believers for their part in fulfilling the Great Commission. As citizens of God's Kingdom, we are called to love, worship, and obey our Lord, to love and serve His body, the Church, and to love all peoples everywhere, which includes presenting the whole Gospel for the whole person throughout the whole world.

We of Youth With A Mission believe in God – Father, Son and Holy Spirit – and that the Bible is God's inspired and authoritative Word, revealing that Jesus Christ is God's Son; fully God and fully human; that people are created in God's image; that He created us to have eternal life through Jesus Christ; that although all people have sinned and come short of God's glory, God has made salvation possible through the incarnation, life, death, resurrection and ascension of Jesus Christ; that repentance, faith, love and obedience are fitting responses to God's initiative of grace toward us through the active ministry of the Holy Spirit; that God desires all people to be saved and to come to the knowledge of the truth; and that the Holy Spirit's power is demonstrated in and through us for the accomplishment of Christ's last commandments, *"Go into all the world and preach the Good News to everyone"* (Mark 16:15 NLT) and *"Go and make disciples of all the nations ..."* (Matthew 28:19 NLT).

YWAM's CORE BELIEFS AND FOUNDATIONAL VALUES

A. YWAM's Core Beliefs

Youth With A Mission (YWAM) affirms the Bible as the inspired and authoritative Word of God and the absolute reference point for every aspect of life and ministry. Based upon God's Word, who He is, and His initiative of salvation through the atoning work of Jesus (His death, burial and resurrection), the following responses are strongly emphasized in YWAM:

- **Worship**: We are called to **praise and worship God alone** (Exo 20:2-3; Deu 6:4-5; 2Ki 17:35-39; 1Ch 16:28-30; Neh 8:2-10; Mar 12:29-30; Rom 15:5-13; Jud 24-25; Rev 5:6-14; Rev 19:5-8).
- **Holiness**: We are called to **lead holy and righteous lives** that exemplify the nature and character of God (Lev 19:1-2; Psa 51:7-11; Jer 18:1-11; Eze 20:10-12; Zec 13:9; Luk 1:68-75; Eph 4:21-32; Tit 2:11-14; 1Pe 2:9,21-25; 1Jo 3:1-3).

- **Witness**: We are called to **share the Gospel of Jesus Christ** with those who do not know Him (Psa 78:1-7; Isa 40:3-11; Mic 4:1-2; Hab 2:14; Luk 24:44-48; Act 3:12-26; Act 10:39-43; 1Co 9:19-23; 2Co 2:12-17; 1Pe 3:15-18).

- **Prayer**: We are called to **engage in intercessory prayer** for the people and causes on God's heart, including standing against evil in every form (Gen 18:20-33; Exo 32:1-16; Jdg 3:9,15; 1Ki 8:22-61; Eze 22:30-31; Eze 33:1-11; Mat 6:5-15; Mat 9:36-38; Eph 3:1421; 2Th 3:1-5).

- **Fellowship:** We are called to **commit to the Church** in both its local nurturing expression and its mobile multiplying expression (2Ch 29:20-30; Psa 22:25-28; Psa 122:1-4; Joe 2:1517; Mat 18:19-20; Act 2:44-47; Act 4:32-35; 1Co 14:26-40; Eph 2:11-18; Heb 10:23-25).

- **Service:** We are called to **contribute toward God's Kingdom purposes** in every sphere of life (Deu 15:7-11; Deu 24:17-22; Psa 112:4-9; Pro 11:10-11; Zec 7:8-10; Mat 5:14-16; 2Th 3:13; Tit 3:4-8; Heb 13:15-16; Jam 2:14-26).

B. YWAM's Foundational Values
1. KNOW GOD

YWAM is committed to know God, His nature, His character and His ways as revealed in the Bible, the inspired and authoritative Word of God. We seek to reflect who He is in every aspect of our lives and ministry. The automatic overflow of knowing and enjoying fellowship with God is a desire to share Him with others (2Ki 19:19; Job 42:5; Psa 46:10; Psa 103:7-13; Jer 9:23-24; Hos 6:3; Joh 17:3; Eph 1:16-17; Php 3:7-11; 1Jo 2:4-6).

2. MAKE GOD KNOWN

YWAM is called to make God known throughout the whole world, and into every arena of society through evangelism, training and mercy ministries. We believe that salvation of souls should result in transformation of societies thus obeying Jesus' command to make disciples of all nations (1Ch 16:24-27; Psa 68:11; Psa 71:15-16; Psa 145:4-7; Mat 28:18-20; Mar 16:15; Act 1:8; Act 13:1-4a; Rom 10:8-15; Rom 15:18-21).

3. HEAR GOD'S VOICE

YWAM is committed to creating with God through listening to Him, praying His prayers and obeying His commands in matters great and small. We are dependent upon hearing His voice as individuals, together in team contexts and in larger gatherings, as an integral part of our process for decision-making (1Sa 3:7-10; 2Ch 15:2-4; Psa 25:14; Isa 6:8; Amo 3:7; Luk 9:35; Joh 10:1-5; Joh 16:13-15; Heb 3:7-8,15; Rev 2:7,11,17,27; 3:6,13,22).

4. PRACTICE WORSHIP AND INTERCESSORY PRAYER

YWAM is dedicated to worship God and engage in intercessory prayer as integral aspects of daily life. We also recognize the intent of Satan to destroy the work of God and we rely upon God's empowering presence, the Holy Spirit, to overcome his strategies in the lives of individuals and in the affairs of nations (1Sa 7:5; 2Ch 7:14; Psa 84:1-8; Psa 95:6-7; Psa 100:1-5; Mar 11:24-25; Act 1:14; Eph 6:13-20; 1Th 5:16-19; 1Ti 2:1-4).

5. BE VISIONARY

YWAM is called to be visionary, continually receiving, nurturing and releasing fresh vision from God. We support the pioneering of new ministries and methods, always willing to be radical in order to be relevant to every generation, people group, and sphere of society. We believe that the apostolic call of YWAM requires the integration of spiritual eldership, freedom in the Spirit and relationship, centered on the Word of God (Num 12:6; 1Sa 12:16; Pro 29:18; Eze 1:1; Hab 2:23; Mar 1:35-39; Luk 9:1-6; Act 16:9-10; Act 26:19; 2Pe 3:9-13).

6. CHAMPION YOUNG PEOPLE

YWAM is called to champion youth. We believe God has gifted and called young people to spearhead vision and ministry. We are committed to value, trust, train, support, make space and release them. They are not only the Church of the future; they are the Church of today. We commit to follow where they lead, in the will of God (1Sa 17:32-50; Ecc 4:13-14; Ecc 12:1-7; Jer 1:5-10; Dan 1:17-20; Joe 2:28; Joh 6:9; Act 16:1-5; 1Ti 4:12-16; 1Jo 2:12-14).

7. BE DECENTRALIZED

YWAM is a Christ-centered, faith-based global volunteer movement, united by shared vision, core beliefs, foundational values and relationships. We do not have a centralized structure. Every YWAM ministry has the privilege and spiritual responsibility to develop and maintain healthy relationships with appropriate authorities and circles of elders (Exo 18:13-26; Num 1:16-19; Num 11:16-17,24-30; Deu 29:10-13; Jos 23:1-24:28; Act 14:23; Act 15:1-31; 1Co 3:4-11; Tit 1:5-9; Heb 13:7,17).

8. BE INTERNATIONAL AND INTERDENOMINATIONAL

YWAM is international and interdenominational in its global scope as well as its local constituency. We believe that ethnic, linguistic and denominational diversity, along with redeemed aspects of culture, are positive factors that contribute to the health and growth of the Mission (Gen 12:1-4; Gen 26:2-5; Psa 57:9-10; Jer 32:27; Dan 7:13-14; Act 20:4; 1Co 12:12-31; Eph 4:1-16; Col 3:11; Rev 7:9).

9. HAVE A BIBLICAL CHRISTIAN WORLDVIEW

YWAM is called to a Biblical Christian worldview. We believe that the Bible – the textbook for all of life – makes a clear division between good and evil; right and wrong. The practical dimensions of life are no less spiritual than the ministry expressions. Everything done in obedience to God is spiritual. We seek to honor God with all that we do, equipping and mobilizing men and women of God to take roles of service and influence in every arena of society (Deu 8:1-3; Deu 32:45-47; 2Ki 22:8; Psa 19:7-11; Luk 8:21; Joh 8:31-32; Php 4:8-9; 2Ti 3:1617; Heb 4:12-13; Jam 4:17).

10. FUNCTION IN TEAMS

YWAM is called to function in teams in all aspects of ministry and leadership. We believe that a combination of complementary gifts, callings, perspectives, ministries and generations working together in unity at all levels of our Mission provides wisdom and safety. Seeking God's will and making decisions in a team context allows accountability and contributes to greater relationship, motivation, responsibility and ownership of the vision (Deu 32:30-31; 2Ch 17:7-9; Pro 15:22; Ecc 4:9-12; Mar 6:7-13; Rom 12:3-10; 2Co 1:24; Eph 5:21; Php 2:1-2; 1Pe 4:8).

11. EXHIBIT SERVANT LEADERSHIP
YWAM is called to servant leadership as a lifestyle, rather than a leadership hierarchy. A servant leader is one who honors the gifts and callings of those under his/her care and guards their rights and privileges. Just as Jesus served His disciples, we stress the importance of those with leadership responsibilities serving those whom they lead (Deu 10:12-13; Psa 84:10; Isa 42:1-4; Mic 6:8; Mar 10:42-45; Joh 13:3-17; Rom 16:1-2; Gal 5:13-14; Php 2:3-11; 1Pe 4:10-11).

12. DO FIRST, THEN TEACH
YWAM is committed to doing first, then teaching. We believe that firsthand experience gives authority to our words. Godly character and a call from God are more important than an individual's gifts, abilities and expertise (Deu 4:5-8; Ezr 7:10; Psa 51:12-13; Psa 119:17-18; Pro 1:1-4; Mat 7:28-29; Act 1:1-2; Col 3:1217; 2Ti 4:1-5; 2Pe 1:5-10).

13. BE RELATIONSHIP-ORIENTED
YWAM is dedicated to being relationship-oriented in our living and working together. We desire to be united through lives of holiness, mutual support, transparency, humility, and open communication, rather than a dependence on structures or rules (Lev 19:18; Psa 133:1-3; Pro 17:17; Pro 27:10; Joh 13:34-35; Joh 15:13-17; Joh 17:20-23; Rom 13:8-10; 1Jo 1:7; 1Jo 4:7-12).

14. VALUE THE INDIVIDUAL
YWAM is called to value each individual. We believe in equal opportunity and justice for all. Created in the image of God, people of all nationalities, ages and functions have distinctive contributions and callings. We are committed to honoring God-given leadership and ministry gifts in both men and women (Gen 1:27; Lev 19:13-16; Deu 16:18-20; Psa 139:13-16; Mar 8:3437; Act 10:34-35; Gal 3:28; Eph 6:5-9; Heb 2:11-12; Jam 2:1-9).

15. VALUE FAMILIES

YWAM affirms the importance of families serving God together in missions, not just the father and/or mother. We also embrace the inclusion of single-parent families. We encourage the development of strong and healthy family units, with each member sharing the call to missions and contributing their gifts in unique and complementary ways. We uphold and celebrate the Biblical view that God's intent for holy matrimony is between one man and one woman (Gen 2:21-24; Gen 18:1719; Deu 6:6-7; Pro 5:15-23; Pro 31:10-31; Mal 2:14-16; Mat 19:3-9; 1Co 7:1-16; 1Ti 3:2-5; Heb 13:4).

16. PRACTICE DEPENDENCE ON GOD

YWAM is a volunteer movement called to practice a life of dependence upon God for financial provision. For individuals and for any YWAM team or community, this comes primarily through His people. As God has been generous toward us, so we desire to be generous, giving ourselves, our time and talents to God with no expectation of remuneration *(Gen 22:12-14; Exo 36:2-7; Num 18:25-29; Mal 3:8-12; Mat 6:25-33; Luk 19:8-9; 2Co 8:1-9:15; Php 4:10-20; Tit 3:14; 3Jo 5-8).*

17. PRACTICE HOSPITALITY

YWAM affirms the ministry of hospitality as an expression of God's character and the value of people. We believe it is important to open our hearts, homes, YWAM locations and campuses to serve and honor one another, our guests and the poor and needy, not as acts of social protocol, but as expressions of generosity (Gen 18:1-8; 2Sa 9:1-11; Psa 68:5-6; Pro 22:9; Isa 58:7; Mat 25:3146; Act 28:7-8; Rom 12:13; Heb 13:1-3; 1Pe 4:9).

18. COMMUNICATE WITH INTEGRITY

YWAM affirms that everything exists because God communicates. Therefore, YWAM is committed to truthful, accurate, timely and relevant communication. We believe good communication is essential for strong relationships, healthy families and communities, and effective ministry (Gen 1:3-5; Num 23:19; Pro 10:19; Pro 25:9-14; Zec 8:16-17; Mat 5:33-37; Luk 4:16-22; Joh 1:15; Col 4:6; Jam 3:1-18).

HISTORICAL NOTE: This document includes the YWAM *Statement of Purpose* and the *Core Beliefs and Foundational Values* of Youth With A Mission.

The YWAM *Statement of Purpose* was written in the early 1960s. We purposefully never wrote a "Statement of Faith" because we are "an international movement of Christians from many denominations" and wanted simply to clarify why God had called this movement into being.

YWAM's *Core Beliefs and Foundational Values* were birthed through a multi-decade process of hearing God and listening to one another. The process of identifying our values was initiated by Darlene Cunningham in 1985 at the time of YWAM's 25th anniversary, in order to pass them on to successive generations. The document was then approved six years later by the International Council in 1991.

At that time the International Council (IC) was the recognized global eldership of the mission. Since that time the senior circle of global elders has functioned under several different names. First it was the International Council (IC). It was later called the Global Leadership Team (GLT) and then was known as the Global Leadership Forum (GLF). This body was disbanded in Singapore 2014 in order to put in place a flatter, movement framework at the trans-local level in the place of what was becoming an increasingly hierarchical organizational structure. Now there are many circles of spiritual eldership around the mission – many of them known as Area Circle Teams (ACTs). A senior group of elders has been convened by Loren and Darlene Cunningham and is known as the Founders' Circle (FC).

Throughout these many decades, a primary role of the body of global spiritual elders (whether the IC, GLT, GLF or FC) has been to confirm, steward and safeguard the foundational documents of the mission. Though the FC does not have the governmental oversight of earlier leadership frameworks, it does carry this role of protecting and clarifying our foundational documents.

A history of YWAM's Values, since first presented by Darlene in 1985 and approved by the IC in 1991, include updates by the GLT in 2003 and the GLF in 2011, 2014. The FC confirmed an update in 2017 during the UofN Workshop in Costa Rica regarding the inclusion of "Service" as one of our responses to our Core Beliefs; and an update in 2018 during YWAM Together in Thailand, which clarifies Value 15. At that same time this new format was adopted so that our Purpose, Core Beliefs, Foundational Values, and the supporting scriptural references would be presented as a singular document. The above document, approved by the Founders' Circle in May 2020, clarifies wording in the Statement of Purpose and Values 4, 7, 16 & 17.

This updated document plus the following six covenantal documents form the foundational documents of Youth With A Mission:

- 1988: The Manila Covenant,
- 1992: The Red Sea Covenant,
- 2002: The Nanning Covenant,
- 2010: The Jubilee Covenant,
- 2014: The Singapore Covenant, and
- 2014: The Covenant to End Bible Poverty.

YWAM's identity and mission is further clarified by what we know as the *"Four Legacy Words"* given by God to Loren Cunningham through the years regarding the "alls" and the "everys" of our call. These are the major words of the Lord, which over our history have guided us and shaped our inheritance as a mission. They include

1. The Covenantal Vision of the Waves, which Loren received in June of 1956 in the Bahamas shortly before his 21st birthday.
2. The Call to Disciple Nations through the Seven Spheres of Society (1975),
3. The Christian Magna Carta (1981), and
4. The Commitment to End Bible Poverty Now (1967 & 2014).

All of these are rooted in the early days of the mission's story, and we continue to grow in our understanding and application of these *Four Legacy Words*.

Appendix 2

The Belief Tree

by Darlene Cunningham with Dawn Gauslin

Jesus' strategy to evangelize the world was to multiply Himself into His disciples, who would reproduce men and women of like vision and values, who would multiply disciples, and so on (2 Tim 2:2). The goal was and is to preach the Gospel to every creature (Mark 16:15), to disciple all the nations (Matthew 28:19) and to produce fruit that will remain (John 15:16). This is the call of Youth With A Mission and University of the Nations, and should be the goal of every disciple.

How is good and lasting fruit produced? How do we reproduce in others the vision and values God has given to YWAM? It is not enough to be well organized and pass on information: we need to have ingested the foundational beliefs of the faith and the values of the Mission in order to pass them on to successive waves of learners. If this is not done, we will only copy a model and we will never be able to answer the "why" questions.

We need to know what we *do* believe and why; and we need to know what we do *not* believe and why.

The Bible uses many illustrations of trees, soil, vines, pruning, fruit, leaves and seeds to speak to us about our lives, ministry and fruitfulness. I first heard the analogy of the "Belief

Belief Tree

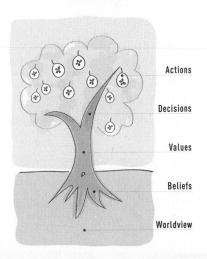

Actions

Decisions

Values

Beliefs

Worldview

Tree" from Darrow Miller, of Disciple Nations Alliance, who speaks on Biblical Christian worldview. He teaches that "ideas have consequences" – that there is a direct link between roots and fruit; what we believe and how we behave. I have since developed the illustration and use it as a foundation for nearly everything I teach. This simple illustration can provide a reference point – a measuring rod – for making decisions and evaluating the fruit of your ministry both individually and corporately. I trust that God will use it to bring insight and impart life to you in such a deep way that it becomes a part of your "toolbox" as well.

As you consider a tree, the soil represents our worldview; the roots represent our foundational beliefs; the trunk represents our values; the branches represent our decisions; the fruit represents our actions. The seeds represent the genetic code for reproducing life. And of course, the DNA of that First Seed was/is Jesus Himself, living in us! In order for there to be cycles of healthy life, the DNA must flow from the roots, through the trunk, along the branches and into the fruit ... the seeds in the fruit start the process all over again.

SOIL = WORLDVIEW

One of the first things it is important to identify about ourselves and/or others is, "What is the environmental worldview that I was raised in....and what is the worldview of those I'm relating to?" Even though you may have come to Christ through the work of the cross, what is the background that has influenced your family, your culture and your thinking - even in subtle ways? This is the soil in which your "tree" grows. Is it Animistic? ... Hindu? ... Muslim? ... secular humanism? This will affect the glasses through which you see everything. Much of the Western world has a Judeo-Christian background, but it has declined into a worldview of secular humanism: "It's all about me. If it feels good, do it. Truth is relative – it's whatever I think is right for me." Even in the way we present the Gospel, it is important that we do not feed this lie. We value the individual, but we don't worship the individual! It's all about Jesus!!

Often the errors in the worldview in which we have been raised need to be transformed to align with a Biblical Christian worldview, which then forms the taproot of our beliefs. The first four foundational truths below describe the shared presuppositions of all the Biblical writers. In YWAM we learned of this Biblical framework from Dr. Francis Schaeffer, founder of L'Abri. We have added a fifth presupposition that affirms the purpose of mission for which God has created us:

1) GOD IS INFINITE AND PERSONAL. He is absolutely limitless and cannot be measured; He is uncreated and has no beginning or ending. And He is a personal/relational being with an intellect, will and emotions. Only the God of the Bible is both infinite and personal.

2) MEN AND WOMEN ARE FINITE AND PERSONAL. We are made in God's image as personal beings (with intellect, will and emotions), created for relationship with Him and others. But we are finite – we have a beginning point and definable limits.

3) TRUTH IS CONSTANT AND KNOWABLE. Truth doesn't change; it is absolute. And we can know truth ("You will know the truth, and the truth will set you free" John 8:32).

4) CHOICES ARE SIGNIFICANT AND HAVE CONSEQUENCES. The consequences of our good/right/wise decisions lead to rewards and life; the consequences of our bad/wrong/sinful decisions lead to punishment and death.

5) WE ARE CALLED TO BE CHANGE-MAKERS WITH GOD. God is a missionary God, His Son is a missionary Messiah, His Spirit is a missionary Advocate, and His Word is a missionary Book.

ROOTS = BELIEFS

The roots to the tree are our basic beliefs, which must grow out of the truth of God's Word or our tree can't bear good fruit. All of our beliefs must be rooted in the Scripture.

Other elements of our basic root system include things like believing the truth about GOD'S NATURE (the essence of who He is: all powerful, all knowing, all present, etc.) and HIS CHARACTER (how He chooses to express His nature: He is loving, kind, just, holy, merciful, etc.) Of course, we could spend volumes and eternity describing these foundational roots, because there is no end to the vastness and wonderfulness of our great God! But these are some of the most basic things we must learn from the Word and teach to those we disciple, in order to develop deep roots that can nourish their lives and influence every decision.

All of our YWAM Discipleship Training Schools should spend a major amount of time teaching and wrestling with the root system of our basic beliefs. The curriculum defined by the International DTS Centre and approved by the YWAM Global Leadership Forum gives excellent guidelines to follow in building strong roots (www.ywamdtscentre.com).

When we truly know God ... when we learn how to hear His voice through time spent in relationship with Him ... when we understand that because He loves us, His will is always the highest and best for us, for others, for Himself and for the universe, we will spend far less time in the syndrome of "I should have ... could have ... would have ...." We are more settled in knowing that His will is always good and His grace is always sufficient.

TRUNK = VALUES

In Youth With A Mission, we place a strong emphasis on our "Foundational Values." I am the one who began the process of identifying and writing down these values so that we could pass them on to successive generations of YWAMers for continued fruitfulness. I have come to realize that the values on their own pre-suppose that everyone has the same worldview and foundational belief system, which they do not. That is why, in recent years, I've begun teaching the "Belief Tree" – because our values grow out of and clarify our underlying beliefs. Just as a tree doesn't begin with the trunk at ground level, our values are not the starting point. The starting point for producing fruit that remains is first the seed of Jesus planted in our lives, aligning our worldview with a Biblical Christian worldview, and then the root system revealed throughout the Bible: Who is God? Who is man? What is truth? etc. For example, Foundational Value #14 states: "YWAM is called to value each individual ...." Why? Because God is a personal God, who created mankind in His image, as personal beings, so that we could live together with Him in a relationship of love. We are to value what God values.

BRANCHES = DECISIONS

The limbs of the tree represent the principles by which we make decisions, whether personal or corporate. Again, our decisions must grow out of and reflect our values or they lack strength. Jill Garrett, who introduced the *Strengthsfinders* assessment tool to YWAM, uses the architectural definition of the word "integrity" to illustrate the need for consistency between our purpose, vision, beliefs, values, decisions and actions. All must be in line with each other and with the word of the Lord in order for the structure to be sound and have "integrity."

Have you ever been in a situation where a policy (i.e., a corporate decision) was implemented that just didn't "set right"? Usually, it is because it is not consistent with what we say we value. Our decisions and actions should be born out of our beliefs and values: they should be the seamless extension of them. When a practice is established, there should be a response in our spirits that says, "Well, of course! If we believe and value *this*, then the automatic fruit of our decisions should be *that*!"

Let me give you a really practical example: there was a situation once at a campus where I was the operations leader. While I was away on a trip one time an experienced older person was put in charge of the transportation department. When I returned home from my trip, I discovered that a new policy had been established regarding drivers of YWAM vehicles: no one under 25 years of age was allowed to drive the YWAM vans! I thought "oh, we must have changed insurance companies, and they have set this rigid requirement" so I set out to find the reason for this new rule, because it seemed very restrictive. When I asked, "Why do we have this new restriction? Has the government made a new rule? Or have we changed insurance companies?" I discovered that it was neither: the transportation manager was of the opinion that young people tended to be more careless and irresponsible than older drivers and decided to set the age limit higher!

God called us to be YOUTH With A Mission! Our sixth Foundational Values states: "YWAM is called to champion youth." We can't challenge young men and women to go into difficult and dangerous places, and possibly even lay down their lives for the Gospel, and then tell them we don't trust them to drive the vans! It would be okay to have a requirement for all potential drivers to pass a driver's test based on skills, but it is not okay to have an automatic judgment that "youth are irresponsible."

Think about it: if decisions have been enacted at your campus or in your school that do not reflect who God is, or what He has called us to value, then guess which things needs to change?! I am constantly in this evaluation process myself, and have faithful friends who challenge me with questions like: "Darlene, how does this or that decision reflect the justice of God and our call to be international?" God has called us as a Mission to a season of "re-alignment" – we need to be diligent to see that there is consistency between our beliefs, values, decisions and actions. This needs to be continuously evaluated.

We have made a "policy" – a corporate leadership decision – in the University of the Nations that we are required to have at least three hours of intercessory prayer per week in all of our courses. Why? If this is just a "rule" which is disconnected from our values and beliefs, then prayer can become a totally lifeless dead work. Buddhists pray. Hindus pray. Muslims pray five times a day! But they are not praying to the true God. Because of our root belief that God is both personal and infinite, we value prayer as the avenue of two-way communication with this God who hears and cares and has the power to act. Not only that, but He designed us to be co-creators with Him through prayer! He chooses to involve us in releasing His will "on earth as it is in heaven" through praying the things on His heart. It will transform our prayer lives when we really grasp this and make ourselves available to hear from God like we believe He wants to create with us in prayer!

FRUIT = ACTIONS

The fruit is the outward expression of the life of the tree. On an individual basis, it is our actions and behavior; on a corporate level, it is our programs and practices. In a healthy tree, the roots draw in life-giving nourishment that flows through the trunk and the branches resulting in the production of good fruit. That's what we want for our lives and our ministries: good fruit that remains.

The amazing thing about fruit is, it has seeds inside! The seeds carry the DNA – the essential genetic data that will reproduce future generations of healthy, fruitful trees. Every successive season, there is new fruit, and though each fruit is unique, it carries the same DNA and will reproduce the same kind of tree as the one that it came from. You've probably heard it asked, "You can count the number of seeds in an apple, but can you count the number of apples in a seed?"

Programs like the Discipleship Training School are "fruits" of our ministry tree that should reflect our beliefs, values and principles. Every DTS around the world can and should look different from the others – just as every apple is an apple but each one is unique, because the people God brings will be different and the needs will be different. We must continuously evaluate our methods and models as well, to be sure that they support the new life and growth. God wants to give a fresh infusion of His Spirit and creativity into each school, but they should all carry the DNA – the genetic code – of a DTS and of YWAM.

Oftentimes people look at a program such as the DTS and want to replicate it. But it doesn't work when it is disconnected from the YWAM "tree" from which it grew. Another ministry or a church may draw elements from a YWAM DTS or run a similar discipleship program which may be very effective. Though the basic Bible beliefs are similar, the values for every organization are different, and their programs should grow out of and reflect the unique characteristics of the things God has called them to embrace.

As mentioned earlier, "integrity" is when our worldview, beliefs, values, decisions and actions flow seamlessly, with no "disconnect." Our actions and behavior should clearly align with what we say we believe. When this isn't happening, there is a "break" in the flow.

Here is another personal story that illustrates this point so clearly: As is our custom, one night Loren and I were hosting a large group of YWAMers for a meal at our home. Afterward, a number of people offered to help me clean up. One young leader, holding an armload of aluminum soda cans, asked "Darlene, do you recycle?" I replied, "I believe in it, but I don't do it." When I heard the words come out of my mouth, I was so shocked that I gasped out loud. I had been teaching on the Belief Tree to that very group of people! I asked the helper, "Did you hear what I just said? I said that I *BELIEVE* it, but I don't *DO* it!" It's true that in Hawaii, recycling is not required by law, and they don't make it easy to accomplish, as recycle systems are not in place. But I went out the next day and bought recycle bins for aluminum cans, plastic bottles and glass and I have recycled from that day to this.

The Purpose of Pruning

In John 15 we read a key passage about the relationship between pruning and fruitfulness. Jesus says "'I am the true grapevine, and my Father is the gardener. He cuts off every branch of mine that doesn't produce fruit, and he prunes the branches that do bear fruit so they will produce even more.'" He also says in Matthew 7 "You will recognize them [false prophets] by their fruit …. A good tree produces good fruit and a bad tree produces bad fruit. So every tree that does not produce good fruit is chopped down and thrown into the fire. Yes, just as you can identify a tree by its fruit, so you can iden-tify people by their actions.'" Romans 11:16b reconfirms this seamless con-nection "… if the roots of the tree are holy, the branches will be, too."

So if a tree produces **no** fruit, God cuts off the branches; if a tree pro-duces **good** fruit, He prunes it to produce more fruitfulness; and if a tree produces **bad** fruit, He totally uproots it and destroys it, because it has grown out of false beliefs.

God's purpose for us is love and fruitfulness. He prunes us to produce **more** fruit and **better** fruit. If we realize that we have become unfruitful, a good question to ask may be "have I somehow gone astray from godly beliefs and values?"

My friend and co-worker, David Hamilton, has added another dimension to this Belief Tree teaching which will help you in using this as a very practical tool in your life:

WORLDVIEW = what is REAL

This is our un-thought-through presuppositions about reality. It's what we generally accept or believe from our environment or the way we were raised, without questioning.

BELIEFS = what is TRUE

You may ask, "But aren't what is real and what is true the same?" Yes, if there is integrity; but if there is not integrity, what seems real to us and what is actually true may be very different. (Remember the foundational truths of Christianity outlined above: there is absolute truth, and it is constant and knowable.)

For example, in Africa some tribal people are animistic, so what is REAL for them is that they believe spirits exist in different forms of nature – rocks, the sea, lions, etc. According to their worldview, if you get sick it's because someone has put a curse on you. When an animist becomes a Christian and believes that Jesus is the Son of God, they believe this is TRUE. When they become sick, they know Jesus can heal them because He is powerful. But if they pray to Jesus and don't get well, they often quickly revert to the reality that they have known, which is that sickness is caused by evil spirits. So they may go back to the witch doctor to remove the curse.

This syncretism (mixture of opposing belief systems) works against integ-rity. Every culture and every individual has issues of syncretism. Identifying and ridding ourselves of it occurs as we mature in integrity.

VALUES = what is GOOD

Isn't truth good? Yes, it should also be considered good. Why is this different? When you embrace something as good, it's something you do because you like it – you find it desirable or beneficial. There is some internal delight.

When you read through the 18 YWAM values, you might read one and think "I've got to achieve this" or "I need to work on this one ...." This is an indicator that you see this as a principle or truth that is right, but you have not yet learned to really love it. As long as it's something external that you have to live up to, rather than something internal that you delight in, then it has not yet become a personal value.

PRINCIPLE-BASED DECISIONS / POLICIES = what we think is RIGHT

Once you have embraced something true and attributed value to it, it will lead to right decisions and policies. Just living by the rules and doing what is right is not discipleship! What we want to see as a result of true discipleship is internal government! This is one of the most important things in the world – to be self-governed, have self-morality, and lead ourselves based on God's principles, not on external boundaries.

ACTIONS / PROGRAMS = what is WISE

If all these others things are aligned, our behavior/actions will be wise.

We need to learn to make decisions that bring harmony between what is real and true and right and good and wise. Only then are we are walking in integrity! How do we discover whether there is seamless integrity or disconnections? By asking questions...

There are two questions that will lead you to insights at every level of the Belief Tree:

1. "WHY?" This is a discovery question that leads us to foundations/ presuppositions.

Let's look again at the example Darlene shared about young people not being allowed to drive YWAM vehicles, and use the question "Why?" to lead us from the action back down to the pre- suppositional worldview.

ACTION: young people can't drive YWAM vans.

Why? Because of a faulty POLICY.

Why was the policy wrong? Because it did not reflect that we VALUE young people.

Why should we value young people?

Because our BELIEF about God, based on His Word, tells us that He values young people: Jeremiah, Mary, Timothy, David, Samuel, Daniel, Joseph ... all of the disciples. Our Biblical Christian worldview tells us that we are made in the image of God from birth, not just from the age of 25!

When you get down to the "belief" part, you should always have a "God said in His Word" upon which to base your belief.

It is so important to ask the WHY question. You cannot get understanding and make wise decisions without this. When people don't understand beliefs and values, they just copy a model, and the life soon goes out of it – it becomes dead works.

You can also do the opposite – move from the roots to the fruit by asking the question:

2. "SO WHAT?" This question leads us to understand implications/applications.

WORLDVIEW – we are made in image of creator God.

So what? We BELIEVE we can co-create with Him.

So what? We VALUE prayer as a good thing – it changes things!

So what? We make PRINCIPLE-BASED DECISIONS: I will give up whatever it takes to have time for prayer: sleep, food, social activities.

So what? My ACTIONS line up: I establish a lifestyle of prayer.

The reason a lot of Christians fail is because they go straight from understanding something to be TRUE to doing something because it is RIGHT. They skip the step of VALUE and it becoming GOOD and delightful. It's not hard for me to do what I embrace as good and delightful. But if I only try to do something because I know it is RIGHT, I will fail much more easily.

As you keep asking the Holy Spirit to examine your life and reveal any place where there is a lack of integrity, you can invite God to transform your mind and thinking so that you will grow in maturity and greater likeness to Christ!

SUMMARY:

We must know WHY we believe WHAT we believe. Our actions should be a reflection of our beliefs, values and principle-based decisions. We should be able to give an answer when asked, "Why do you do what you do, the way you do it?" It is an opportunity to share our beliefs, values and principles. And if we don't have an answer or we don't know why, it is an opportunity to seek answers and make sure that our actions and the fruit of our lives and ministries are a true reflection of Jesus.

I love the story of one family – a husband, wife and two teenage kids – who came to do a DTS at YWAM/UofN Kona and heard me teach on the Belief Tree. They were fairly new Christians and the husband was a very successful businessman. I'm sure he had sat through tens of courses on decision-making, but the Spirit of God had a profound impact on him and the whole family through understanding the Belief Tree. It gave them a simple yet practical framework for making decisions and evaluating whether their lives were in alignment with their beliefs. When they returned home after DTS, the family spent most of a two-week vacation to Ireland working on their family Belief Tree, defining their beliefs, values, principles for making decisions and actions. They drew it on large piece of poster board, and upon returning home, they hung it on the kitchen wall. It is there, in the busiest room of the house, that they gather to make family decisions, evaluate where they have come from and where they're going. It is there that they also have that occasional discussion regarding outward behavior that may or may not match what they say they believe – not only the children's behavior, but the parents have invited the children to hold them accountable to live what they say they believe. What a wonderful and simple yet profound tool for checking the "integrity" of our lives and ministries!

Scriptures for additional meditation/study:
Psalm 1:1-3; Colossians 2:6-7; Matthew 7:15-23; Matthew 13:1-9; Jeremiah 17:7-8; Isaiah 61:3,11; John 15:1-17; Colossians 2 & 3; Romans 11:16.

Appendix 3

YWAM'S Four Legacy Words

I found myself facing a dilemma in 2015. Loren was turning 80 at the end of June and I knew that YWAMers around the world would want to celebrate this milestone – but Loren would NOT! It's not that he was in denial about getting older, but he would not want to be the center of attention. He would much prefer to let the occasion slip by with just a family party and an ice cream cone!

Fortunately our good friend David Hamilton knows Loren's heart well, and he understood the dilemma. So he came up with a creative plan: in September of 2015, approximately 1,300 staff and leaders from 72 nations converged on Townsville, Australia for YWAM Together. As a birthday gift, at the end of the event, we honored Loren by reflecting on four key, directional words from the Lord that he brought to Youth With A Mission throughout our history. They came to be known as the "Four Legacy Words."

Each Legacy Word was presented to Loren in story form, recalling how God gave the word, in front of the whole congregation, complete with fanfare and related gifts. The time ended with a mammoth birthday cake, carried in on the shoulders of six Pacific Island "warriors." It was shaped like a Bible, representing the fourth legacy word, End Bible Poverty Now. The whole process was filled with joy and laughter, alongside awe-filled ponderings of the magnitude of the words God had given both to YWAM and to the body of Christ through Loren. Thus, he was able to fully enjoy and enter into his "party," focusing on Jesus and His words to us!

– Darlene Cunningham

LEGACY WORD #1:
The Vision of the Waves – 1956

YWAM'S FOUNDATIONAL COVENANT

It was June of 1956. Loren Cunningham was in the Bahamas with four other young men to evangelize and gather young people together using their musical gifts. On a Wednesday at 3 PM, a few days before his twenty-first birthday, he was kneeling by the bed in the simply furnished guest room of his missionary host. He was asking the Lord about the message he was to speak that evening. Then, as he looked up at the white walls, something unexpected happened. He Says,

> "Suddenly I was looking at a map of the world, only the map was alive and moving! I could see all the continents, and waves were crashing onto their shores. Each wave went onto a continent, then receded, then came up further until it covered the continent completely. The waves become young people – kids my age and even younger – covering all the continents of the globe. They were talking to people on street corners and outside bars. They were going from house to house and preaching the Gospel. They came from everywhere and went everywhere, caring for people. Then just as suddenly as it had come the scene was gone."

(Excerpt from *Is That Really You, God?* by Loren Cunningham with Janice Rogers, YWAM Publishing.)

God had spoken to Loren through this vision of the waves. This remarkable initiative by God to share His dream with Loren would lead to the launch of Youth With A Mission four years later. Within a generation millions of young people would have their lives touched by God because of this vision of the waves.

We are some of those young people. Our lives have been changed because of how God met Loren that day in the Bahamas. As we reflect back on that event, we realize that that moment had significant parallels to other moments throughout history; moments when God stepped in to share His heart and His purposes for the world. Indeed we have come to realize that this vision, this unexpected encounter, was a God-initiated, destiny-defining, foundational covenant that God gave Loren in order to birth a new missions movement.

What should that movement look like? What were the major elements of this covenantal vision?

First of all, it was about **youth**. This was both a concrete reality and it can also serve as a metaphor for something more. Concretely, if we ever move away from championing young people we have moved away from the call of God upon us as the YWAM tribe. Metaphorically, this is the language of missional deregulation and innovation. Young people were not considered candidates for missions in the mid-twentieth century. It was simply not something that was done when Loren saw this vision. And so it is today that this covenantal vision continues to call us to do what is not being done by others in the church. It calls us to lead out apostolically to birth fresh, entrepreneurial initiatives in the Spirit in order to accomplish Great Commission goals. It calls us to a lifestyle of viral pioneering, co-creating with God, doing and encouraging others to do new things in new ways.

Secondly, it was about **all** and **every**. The waves of young people covered every nation in all the continents. It is about being global, comprehensive, inclusive. If we ever lose sight of the alls and the everys we have lost sight of God's vision for us as a movement. This is not limited only to the geographic alls. It also includes every thematic all, as we move redemptively into all the spheres, all the languages, and all the other various categories of human life and experience. As we do so, this covenant compels us to growth. It is about recurring and ever-expanding waves. This speaks of multi-generational re-iterations of the vision that expand in fractal-like multiplication. Each wave builds on that which has gone before. Each one makes fresh impact in new ways, reaching heights not previously achieved. It's never static. It's always dynamic, focused on going where we are not.

LEGACY WORD #2:
The Seven Spheres of Influence – 1975

The legacy word about engaging with the seven influential spheres of society came through hearing God's voice, as this important story relates.

ROCKY MOUNTAIN REVELATION

The phone call was received by the ranger's station in the Colorado Rockies as the Cunninghams were enjoying a family vacation. Would Loren and Darlene join Bill and Vonette Bright – founders of Campus Crusade – for dinner later that week? Loren eagerly accepted the invitation, eager to share with his friend the fresh insight God had given him. He had been asking God for understanding on how to see a nation discipled and God had just spoken to him about seven influential spheres of society that shape the worldview, beliefs and values of a culture. This was a breakthrough insight! He thought, "If we could simply teach the principles and practices of God's kingdom in each of these seven arenas then we could see the transformation of our communities and nations ...."

As they met for dinner, Loren had this new understanding scrawled on a yellow sheet from a legal pad tucked inside his jacket. After shaking Bill's hand he was reaching for the paper in his pocket when Bill blurted out, "Loren, you won't believe what God has just shown me. If we are going to see our nations changed, we have to impact seven different spheres of society ...." Initially deflated that Bill had beat him to the punch, Loren was soon encouraged by the fact that God was confirming through his friend the word that he had received from God only a few days earlier.

Within a month after that encounter in the summer of 1975, Darlene heard Francis Schaeffer – founder of L'Abri – speaking on the radio. He too spoke of how we could see nations changed by shaping seven different areas of society with Biblical truth. God certainly had their attention. He was clearly saying something which had great implications for Great Commission strategies.

A couple of years later, based on this new understanding, the Cunninghams together with their dear friend, Howard Malmstadt, would launch the University of the Nations. It would be a new kind of Christian university, designed to be a multiplier for missions in a digital, globalized age, eventually equipping young men and women from over 200 different countries in the ways of God. The goal of this new kind of live-learn training? To bring transformational change to nations by intentionally applying kingdom principles in each of the seven spheres of influence!

THE SEVEN SPHERES OF INFLUENCE

Once you read the last chapter of a well-crafted mystery novel, all of the clues – which previously may have eluded you, the reader – fall into place, revealing an unmistakable pattern that leads to the solution of the mystery. It's all so obvious once the great detective explains the compelling evidence. Then when you re-read the novel, all that which was once obscure becomes amazingly clear. In a similar way, an understanding of the framework of the seven spheres of influence allows us to be able to re-read the text of the Scriptures and grasp essential, God-inspired concepts, which we might have easily glossed over without first being aware of this framework. But once we see the pattern, we see it not just here or there, but everywhere through Scripture. It becomes apparent to the student of the Word that God has been concerned with the discipling of nations throughout all of human history.

A MESSAGE FOR THIS GENERATION

The time is now ripe for this message. Even though several variations of the theme have emerged in recent years – some with 7, others with 8 or even 12 spheres – the foundational principle is the same: God created individuals (Genesis 1:26-27) and loves them, wanting to redeem them from brokenness and sin. In the same way God created nations (Acts 17:26-27) and loves them, and wants to bring kingdom transformation into every dimension of their societal interactions. So whether you call this reality a "sphere" a "mind-molder" or a "mountain" – it points to a God who cares for both individual and corporate humanity. This same God sent prophets of old to speak the word of God at times to individuals (a king, a general, a widow) and at times to corporate expressions of humanity (a tribe, a city, a nation). God has a heart for lost individuals and lost nations and invites us to collaborate with Him to bring a transformative impact of the kingdom of God into every area of life, both private and public.

These seven spheres exist in every society from the most primitive stone-age tribes to the most sophisticated megacities. They include the areas of **family, economy, government, religion, education, media, and celebration**. The seven spheres are to every society what the basic biological systems are to the human body – an intrinsic part of God's design, which give life when they are functioning in a healthy manner. Since God is the designer of these spheres, it would be good for us to dedicate effort to understand His purposes for each of them.

No part of the human experience is to be lived outside of the bounds of God's kingdom. We are to do all that we do *coram deo* – intentionally living our lives in the presence of God. This is because Jesus is and intends to be Lord of all dimensions of our life, both private and public. Therefore, let us pray that God will teach us how to rightly represent Him in all of these different arenas of society. May these new understandings help us all discover how we can faithfully walk in God's purposes for every societal sphere of influence.

LEGACY WORD #3:
The Christian Magna Carta – 1981

It was late in 1981 when YWAM leaders from around the world gathered in Kona, Hawaii, for the First International Strategy Conference. YWAM was 21 years old and there was a sense that we had "come of age." There was great anticipation for what the Lord would say and how He would lead us.

As the leaders gathered for their initial meeting they had a profound time of worship. When that time drew to a close, Loren said, "Our goal is not to pursue our own agenda, but to hear from God. Before we do anything else, let us each seek God alone. Ask Him what He wants to tell us and then we will come back and share that with one another." Everyone dispersed to listen to God individually. As soon as Loren was alone, he sensed God began to speak to him. He reports, "I wrote as fast as I could on what I understood to be the Christian Magna Carta."

Now, the original Magna Carta is a famous historical document composed in England in the year 1215. It is one of the first political documents that details basic human rights. In a similar way, the Christian Magna Carta details the Gospel rights that every human being has. It expresses all that which is implied in the Great Commission, as seen through the eyes of all those who should benefit from the Good News of the kingdom. What can those who do not yet know Jesus expect from Jesus' followers? The six points lead to a compelling, holistic answer that echoes both the actions and the words of Jesus, "Whatever you did for one of the least of these brothers and sisters of mine, you did for me" (Mat 25:40).

The Christian Magna Carta
Loren Cunningham – 1981

Everyone on earth has the right to:

1. Hear and understand the Gospel of Jesus Christ,

2. Have a Bible available in his/her own language,

3. Have a Christian fellowship available nearby, to be able to meet for fellowship regularly each week, and to have Biblical teaching and worship with others in the body of Christ,

4. Have a Biblical Christian education available for their children,

5. Have the basic necessities of life: food, water, clothing, shelter, and health care,

6. Lead a productive life of fulfillment spiritually, mentally, socially, emotionally, and physically.

We commit ourselves, by God's grace, to fulfill this covenant and to live for His glory.

Committed to by YWAM international leadership 1981.

LEGACY WORD #4:
End Bible Poverty – 1967

The fourth Legacy Word was passionately embraced in the early years of Youth With A Mission as young people went about sharing the Good News of Jesus. In 1967 Loren was leading one group of young people on an outreach. He tells us,

> "I was with a YWAM convoy traveling through Mexico to Central America. We had stopped in a dusty Mexican town to repair a flat tire. While some worked on that, the rest of us delivered a Gospel of John to every home, then held an open-air preaching service.
>
> After our meeting a woman in a faded red dress came up to me. My Spanish wasn't very good, but I understood her to say, 'There's no place in my town to get a Bible, and there aren't any in the towns around here. Do you have a Bible in my language?'
>
> I managed to find a Spanish Bible for her. She grasped it to her chest. '*¡Muchísimas gracias, señor!*'
>
> As we drove away, the woman's question continued to haunt me. 'Do you have a Bible in my language?' Then, a picture suddenly came before my eyes – I believe it was what the Bible calls a 'vision.' I saw a big truck – not a semi, but more like a large moving van. Painted on the side was, '*Sólo los deshonestos temen la verdad. Santa Biblia, gratis.*'
>
> I didn't know Spanish well enough to think in the language, so seeing these sentences was a complete surprise. I translated them slowly in my mind. They meant, 'Only the dishonest fear the truth. Free Bibles.' What an exciting thought! The phase 'Only the dishonest fear the truth' was completely new to me, and it rang in my mind. It was especially pertinent at the time, as communists were spreading their cause across Latin America.

As the vision continued, I saw young people standing in the back of the truck handing Bibles into eager hands as fast as they could."

(Excerpt from *The Book That Transforms Nations*, by Loren Cunningham, YWAM Publishing, pp 184-185.)

The vision starting to become reality as those young people distributed 50,000 New Testaments to university students in Mexico that summer. That encounter with the woman in the faded red dress eventually led to the launching of "Bibles for Mexico," which in turn birthed many Bible distribution projects in dozens of countries all around the world.

Then at the UofN Workshop in Singapore in 2003, Loren issued a compelling challenge to the Mission which he had received from the Lord. This was a time when YWAM recognized that there had been mission drift in our midst and we were intentionally realigning with our God-given DNA in order to see a new wave of apostolic initiatives around the world. Loren said, "I urge you to put a Bible in every home in the world by 2020. The Bible needs to be in their heart language and available in a means which they can easily understand." As Loren turned 85 years old in 2020, this cry of Loren's heart is like that of Caleb when he too was 85, "Give me this mountain" (Jos 14:12). This challenge to end Bible poverty gripped the hearts of many.

In late 2014, Loren, together with Darlene and several other YWAM leaders, visited key Orthodox, Catholic, Anglican and Evangelical leaders around the world, urging them to do all they could to help end Bible poverty. There was great unity of purpose around this theme among these influential leaders. As a result, "The Covenant to End Bible Poverty" was written, calling on Christians everywhere to pray, translate, publish, distribute, educate and motivate people for Bible engagement.

About the Author

Darlene Cunningham is the Co-founder, together with husband Loren, of Youth With A Mission, an ever-expanding global missions movement currently serving in more than 200 countries. She is also the International Vice-Chancellor of YWAM's University of the Nations. In the same way that Loren is the big-picture visionary, Darlene is the hands and heart of YWAM – the implementer of vision, and people developer.

When YWAM turned 25, Darlene began identifying, clarifying and teaching YWAM's Foundational Beliefs and Values, which fueled her passion to pass on the spiritual "DNA" of the mission to new generations. She has led scores of multi-lingual YWAM leadership training events on six continents, creating opportunity for those who did not have access due to geographic, linguistic or financial barriers. One of her greatest joys is discovering untapped leadership gifts in young men and women and helping them to reach their full potential in God.

Close friends describe Darlene as "Spirit natural" – totally non-religious, but always principled and godly. She is a lover of Jesus and will always, in every situation, point people to His great faithfulness.

Darlene and Loren live in Kona, Hawaii and are continuing their multi-generational missions legacy through daughter Karen, son David and his wife Judy, and three grandchildren.

About the Team

Dawn Gauslin...

... joined a YWAM "Summer of Service" outreach in Europe in 1972 and never turned back, now having served in training, mercy ministries and evangelism in more than 75 countries. With this kaleidoscope of exposure to the nations, leadership experience and a deep love for people of all cultures, Dawn moved to Kona in 1985 and began serving as an international assistant to YWAM Co-founder, Darlene Cunningham. She has been part of the "Values" process from the beginning, helping to distill concepts and find vocabulary to communicate YWAM's heartbeat. She has coordinated scores of leadership training events, working in team with Darlene and David Hamilton to help better equip and release more "next generation" missionary leaders. Dawn has a BA degree in Christian Ministries from YWAM's University of the Nations.

Sean Lambert...

... was born in Fridley, Minnesota, joining YWAM in 1979. He is the Executive Director of YWAM San Diego/Baja. He and his wife Janet pioneered *Mission Adventures* and *Homes of Hope,* two global programs of YWAM that have engaged more than 300,000 participants in 60 nations. Sean serves on the Board of Regents for the University of the Nations and on several international leadership teams within YWAM.

David Joel Hamilton...

... was born and raised in South America as the son of Methodist missionaries. He is a Bible scholar and lover of God's Word, and served as one of the senior content editors for the *Christian Growth Study Bible*. David co-authored a book with Loren Cunningham called *Why Not Women?* laying out the Biblical basis for women in missions, ministry and leadership. David headed a team to create the *SourceView Bible*, the first new format in 500 years for referencing the Bible. It re-emphasizes the dramatic narrative of the Scriptures, helping it to "come alive."

David serves as University of the Nations' Vice President for Strategic Innovation. He also serves on a number of leadership teams for partnerships between YWAM and other major 21st century missions organizations. David and his wife Christine reside in Kona, Hawaii.